MERCEDES-BENZ
W196

MICHAEL RIEDNER

MERCEDES-BENZ W196

Last of the Silver Arrows

Foulis

Haynes

®

"Sometimes I regret that I never asked for square wheels: I have a funny feeling they would have had a car fitted with them within 24 hours."

Stirling Moss on his time spent as a Mercedes-Benz works driver.

A **FOULIS** MOTORING BOOK

First published in 1986 in German by
Motorbuch-Verlag, Stuttgart as 'Mercedes-Benz
W 196 – Der Letzte Silberpfeil'
English language edition published 1990

© Motorbuch Verlag 1986
English language © Haynes Publishing Group 1990

Published by:
Haynes Publishing Group
Sparkford, Nr Yeovil
Somerset BA22 7JJ England

Haynes Publications Inc
861 Lawrence Drive, Newbury Park,
California 91320 USA

British Library Cataloguing in Publication Data
Reidner, Michael
  Mercedes - Benz W196.
  1. Cars, history
  I. Title
  629.2'222'09
  ISBN 0-85429-717-0

Library of Congress Catalog Card Number
  89-85911

Editor: Robin Read
Translator: Raymond Kaye
Layout: Mike King

Typeset in Times med roman 10/12 pt and printed in
England by J.H. Haynes & Co. Ltd

Contents

WITHDRAWAL

APPENDIX

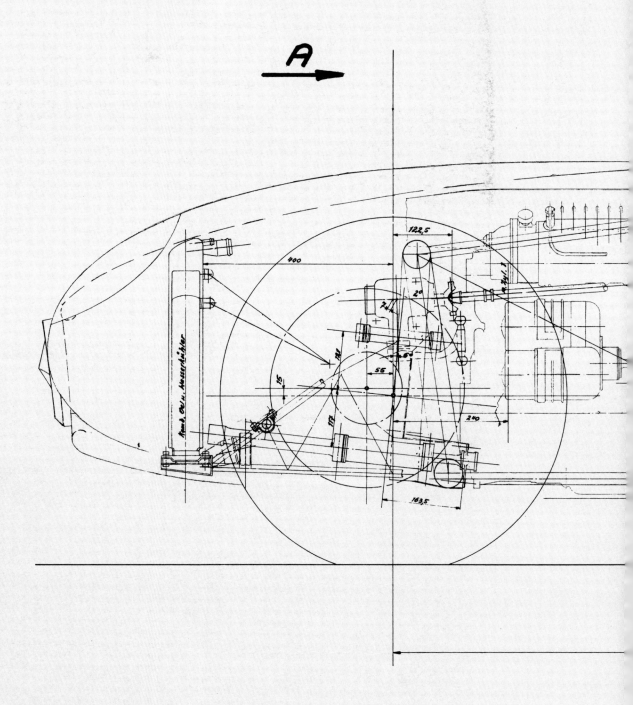

The technical drawings in the Gate Fold sections at the beginning and end of the book show the chassis layout, power unit and final drive unit including gearbox of the W 196 S (300SLR) Sports Racing Car. Drawings of this quality are not available for the Formula One car W 196 R. Both types differ only in detail; the principal mechanical elements being much the same. These drawings were obtained from the technical archives of Daimler-Benz AG.

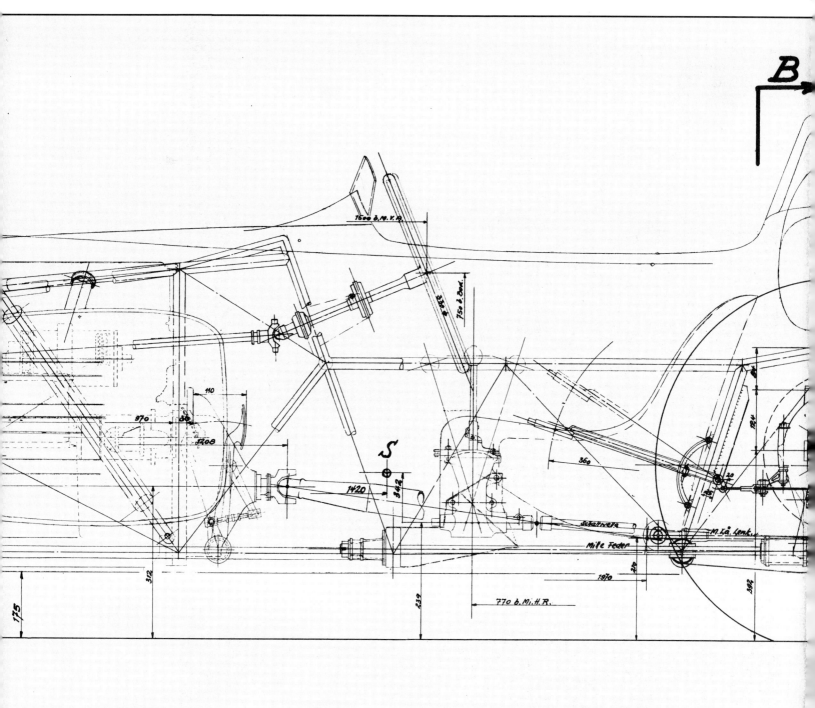

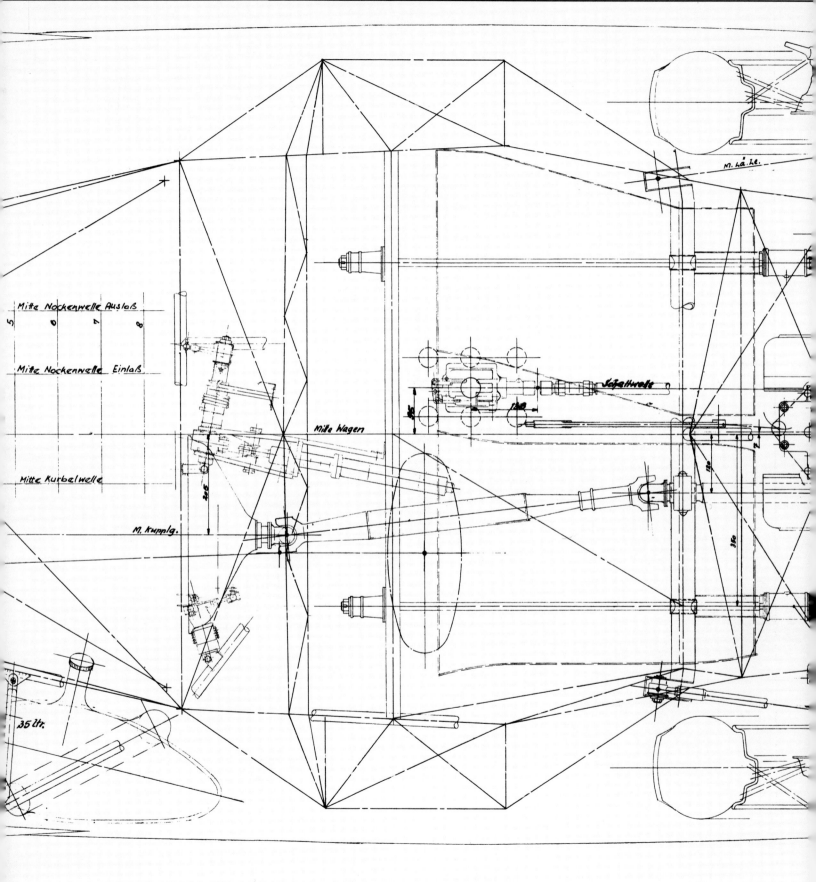

Mitte Nockenwelle Auslaß

Mitte Nockenwelle Einlaß

Mitte Kurbelwelle

M. Kupplg.

Mitte Wagen

Sattelwelle

M. Lä.Le.

35 ltr.

Größte Länge über Karosserie 5002

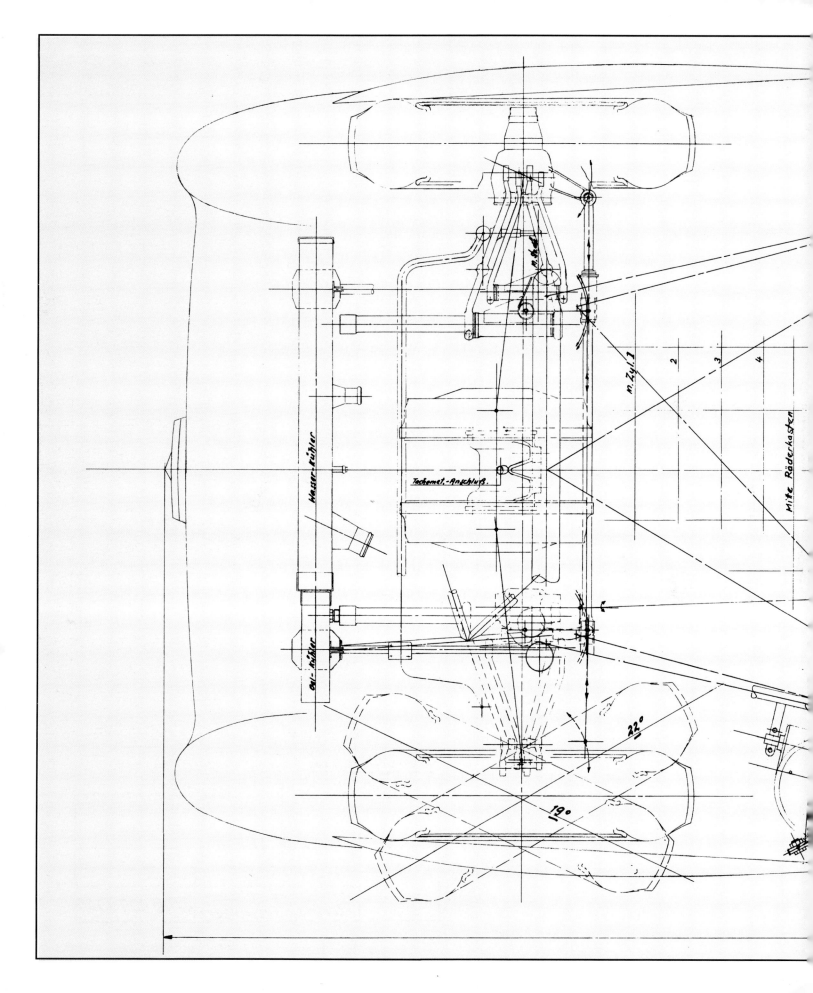

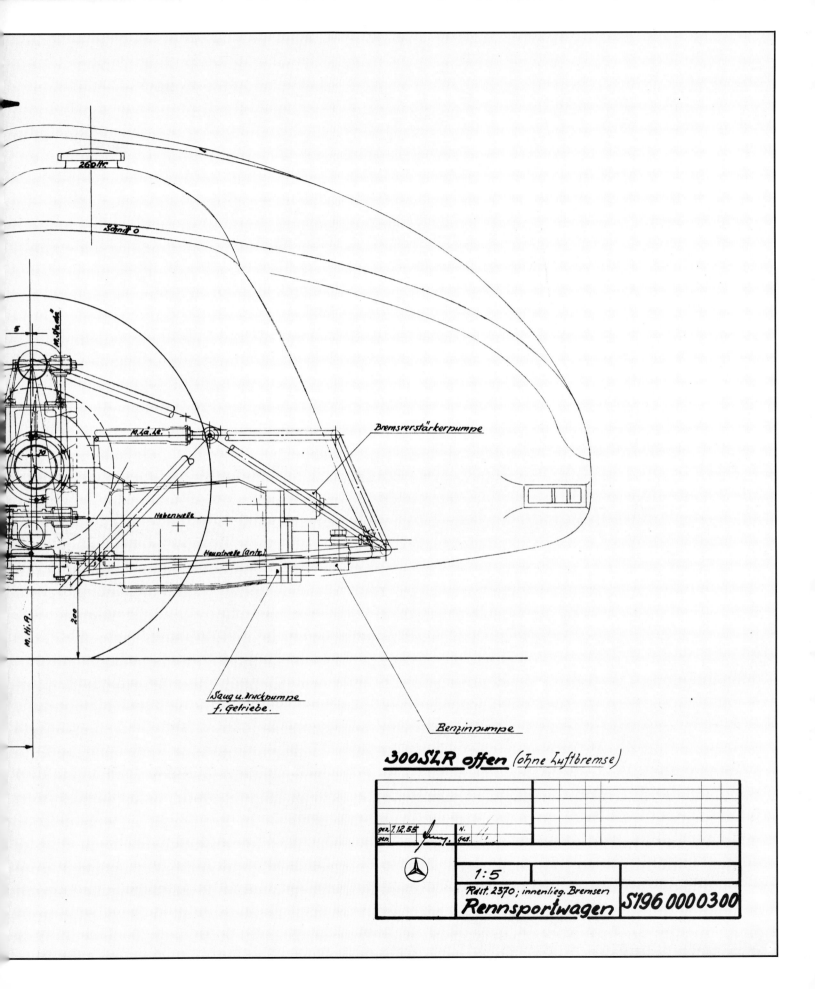

260 ltr.

Schnitt 0

Bremsverstärkerpumpe

M.la.le.

Nebenwelle

Hauptwelle (antr.)

Saug u. Druckpumpe
f. Getriebe.

Benzinpumpe

300 SLR offen (ohne Luftbremse)

gez. 7.12.55		N.			
gepr.		ges.			

1:5

Rdst. 2370; innenlieg. Bremsen
Rennsportwagen   S196 000 0300

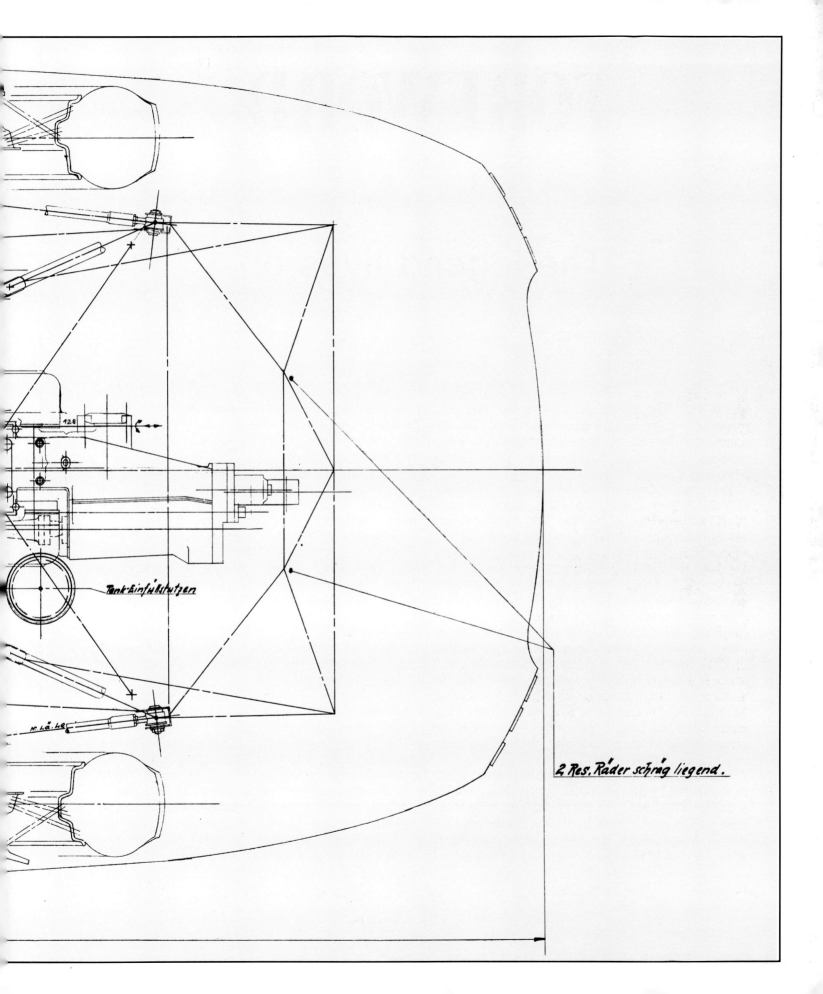

Tank-Einfüllstutzen

128

M. Lä. 40.

2 Res. Räder schräg liegend.

FOREWORD

The legend lives on

More than 30 years after the final race appearance of the W 196, Mercedes-Benz' last Grand Prix car, memories of its success remain fresh. So do the names of those who drove these last Silver Arrows to victories over their Italian rivals Ferrari and Maserati.

Everyone with an interest in motor sport knows that the Argentinian Juan Manuel Fangio won the World Championship five times. *El Chueco* ("Bandy legs" in Spanish) took two of his titles at the wheel of a Mercedes; that fact also sticks in the memory, if anything more than the other three which he took for Maserati, Alfa Romeo and Ferrari. There must be a reason for that.

It may be found in the legendary success of Mercedes racing cars before World War I and in the inter-war years. Victories in the French Grands Prix of 1908 and 1914, their return to the international arena in 1934 with the W 25, the first Silver Arrow, and the countless victories for Rudolf Caracciola, Manfred von Brauchitsch, Richard Seaman, Hermann Lang and Luigi Fagioli, remain so alive in the memories of so many that they might have been notched up only yesterday.

The Stuttgart firm's postwar achievements, which began in 1952 with the 300 SL sports-racing coupé, are of course closer to us today. Very many of those who used to sit in a sweat by their radio and root for the German cars are still alive, and go misty-eyed whenever the 1954 and 1955 cars are discussed.

Born in 1955, my first experience of the W 196 was a "Viking" model of one at the age of five or six. It was the streamlined version. As a child I believed that the streamlined and monoposto versions were two entirely different cars.

When in the spring of 1984 I was given the opportunity of becoming motor sport editor of the magazine *Motor Klassik,* I had one great ambition in mind: I wanted to drive the W 196 just once.

Of course at first this was just a dream, with little likelihood of coming true. But a surprise was in store in May 1985, at "Motor 100" at Silverstone, an event celebrating 100 years of the motor car. The W 196 was there, and so was the director of the Daimler-Benz Museum in Untertürkheim, Max-Gerrit von Pein.

Quite out of the blue he asked me over a cup of tea: "How would you like to drive the W 196 at the Nürburging one day?"

Such momentous words so casually uttered: von Pein had to wait longer than usual for a reply. I stood transfixed, mouth agape. Of course I would.

The appointment was in early summer. After a photo session there was a little spare time, and I drove alone in the W 196 for a full lap and a half of the Nordschleife, or North Loop. To this day it remains one of the most impressive experiences of my life.

A short time later, with the W 196 virus coursing in my veins, I was flicking through the book lists when it occurred to me that there was nothing about the last racing car from the Daimler-Benz stable – not even in Britain where there are books about everything that ever moved on four wheels. A call to von Pein confirmed my suspicions: "No, no book about the W 196 yet and, to my knowledge, no one working on such a project at the moment."

This time my reply was quicker in coming: "Well there is now." It used to be said that a true snob will write a book when there is something he wants to read. The truth of this was now about to be borne out – though with the firm conviction that the subject matter would be of interest to many others.

Days and days of work in the Daimler Museum archive ensued. Copies of race reports, technical data, biographies of drivers and management decisions piled up; suitable photos were looked for. And, yes, the whole lot needed writing up. Ever present was the nagging fear that someone else was working on exactly the same project; after all, the automobile was celebrating its 100th birthday.

The help I received from others was impressive. In February 1986 I spent three mornings with Rudolf Uhlenhaut, interrogating him on the W 196. Professor Hans Scherenberg expressed great interest and put in a lot of his own time: the many names at the back of the book are the fruits of his research, and he also proofread the important chapters on the engineering of the car. He alone was able to give me precise details of the costs of the 1954 and 1955 seasons. They ran to a total of 10 million marks in 1954 and in 1955, with both W 196 and 300 SLR competing, they topped 12.5 million. In 1955 salaries totalled 6.9 million, and materials cost 3 million. Mercedes-Benz' financial commitment to Formula 1

was enormous. In Stuttgart they are still dining out on their success: many believe that a Mercedes racing car built today would be just as great a success as the W 196 over 30 years ago and, indeed, the co-operation between Mercedes and the Swiss-based Sauber team now has this success in actual Group C racing.

Karl Kling and Hans Herrmann patiently answered my questions without noticing how quickly time passed, and how a planned two-hour session soon stretched to four or six.

In February 1986 I spent a whole day with Günther Engelen, a leading Mercedes expert from Mannheim. His photo albums and his private archive contained material that was very valuable in putting the book together. Half the illustrations came from this excellent source.

The staff at the Daimler-Benz AG Archive were always ready to listen to my constant requests for documents and photos. Rudolf Krebs, manager of the Merecedes-Benz technical archive in Untertürkheim, and Claus Peter Schulze were happy to locate and supply additional drawings.

There was no lack of moral support either. One day my colleague Hermann Ries placed a model of the W 196 on my desk with the words, "A reminder of what it is you are writing about." Encouragement also came from Frank Zähringer, at that time the *Motor Klassik* graphic artist; even before the first line was written he had drafted a cover design.

A wish to extend my heartfelt thanks to everyone who helped in the realization of this project. Without them it would not have been possible.

Michael Riedner

THE BACKGROUND

Benz racing car, 1899.

The ancestral line

Mercedes-Benz sporting history

The W 196, the Grand Prix car from Mercedes-Benz built to the new 2.5-litre formula for 1954, was the firm's first postwar machine in this category. It was not, however, the first to carry the three-pointed star, and still less the firm's first ever. The wheel of motoring history must be turned far back before it comes to rest at the first "racing car" built in Mannheim by Karl Benz.

It was 1899; the motor car was just 13 years old, a relative infant. Competitions had been part of the scene for a number of years. French manufacturers of motorized carriages in particular soon realized that victory over the competition in a 40- or 50-kilometre event had a positive effect on trade. Karl Benz saw no sense in deviating into such competition; his dream was that transport should become motorized instead of relying on the railways and horse-drawn vehicles of the day. Planning or participation in "races which bring no profit" (Karl Benz, 1901) was not contemplated.

His sons Eugen and Richard, however, were more receptive to the idea of competitions; and against their father's will they were able to see that a number of cars were built with specially increased power for city-to-city races. The first "racing car" to be built in the Benz factory in Mannheim had a *contra-motor* (the then current term for a horizontally opposed or boxer engine) delivering about 8PS. This twin-cylinder engine had an enormous capacity – 2280 cc. Drive was by belt, wheels were of wood, the rear wheels measuring over a metre in diameter. This car was driven to countless triumphs in events in Germany.

A year later, in 1901, the Benz chief mechanic Bender came away victorious from a race in Frankfurt, which he contested with a newly developed 4-cylinder engine. He averaged 48 km/h; Karl Benz considered a maximum of 50 km/h as respectable.

In 1894 a car powered by an engine of Gottlieb

Nice Race Week, 1901: Wilhelm Bauer at the wheel of the 35PS car.

Daimler's design notched up a number of victories, but the first specialist racing car was not built in Cannstatt until the turn of the century. The Austrian Emil Jellinek gave the initial impulse. He was in the diplomatic service and also represented a large French insurance company. He lived like a king on the Côte d'Azur and wanted to take part in the car races that had been held there for several years. He had no luck with his 6PS double-phaeton, so he wrote an urgent letter to Cannstatt, ordering a Daimler car capable of at least 40 km/h. And he did

not want just one – he ordered four there and then, to speed the work up. Daimler and Maybach built a car, but only to whet their customer's appetite. Jellinek however was well versed in engineering matters and knew that a 4-cylinder engine would be a better bet than the old twin suggested by the Cannstatt engineers. He ordered six cars (a huge number for the time), but insisted on a 4-cylinder engine, which was to follow the example of the French Panhards and be mounted at the front. Thus emerged the first "real" Daimler racing car, known

18

as the Phoenix. But in the Nice event the car was unable to rise from the ashes of the middle placings and the ambitious Jellinek was prompted to have another go. Impetuously he wrote to DMG (Daimler Motoren Gesellschaft) and ordered a car that would guarantee victory. It was as simple as that.

Gottlieb Daimler died on 6th March 1900 and never lived to see the Phoenix in its newest guise. A 28PS engine powered the car, a feature of which was a modern square radiator replacing the older rounded one. Sadly its driver was killed at the end of March: Wilhelm Bauer, a Daimler craftsman, died from the severe injuries he suffered when the car skidded into a wall during a hillclimb at La Turbie near Monaco.

The new Phoenix incorporated a variety of new features of automotive design: scroll clutch, engine mounted on the chassis members, a special light alloy crankcase, worm steering gear and external contracting brakes were to set new standards in design. With their maestro Wilhelm Werner at the wheel, Daimler practically cleaned up at the Nice Week in 1901, winning hillclimbs, circuit races and acceleration tests. Jellinek actually suffered as a result of this success: he was overwhelmed with orders.

This was the first step along the path of competition glory. In the following years, success came in leaps and bounds. Engine capacity and power outputs grew, races became more important

Cutaway drawing of the 1903 Gordon Bennett car.

Daimler Motoren Gesellschaft had its first fatality in motor sport to mourn. Recriminations flew back and forth between the company and Jellinek. The matter was resolved when Jellinek entered into a contract with the manufacturers giving him the sales rights for the German cars. Jellinek ordered the company to build a more powerful car, which at his special request was to be named the Daimler-Mercedes. Mercedes was the name of one of his daughters. To cap it all, Jellinek actually ordered 36 of the new cars. Such a thing was unprecedented.

and competition fiercer. More and more frequently, however, the Stuttgart cars came out on top. But there were also regrettable incidents. In 1903, Count Eliot Zborowski was killed at the La Turbie hillclimb, at almost exactly the same spot where Bauer came to grief in 1900. Then in 1903 Mercedes had their most successful year so far. A two-car team went to Ireland to contest the Gordon Bennett race. The American press baron James Gordon Bennett, owner of the *New York Herald,* had instituted his challenge cup in 1899. The first race took place in

France, after which the venue moved annually according to the victor's homeland. Entries were limited to three cars per nation, and individual components of the cars were strictly scrutinized to ensure that they were actually produced in those countries in whose name they were entered. On 2nd June 1903, the Belgian Camille Jenatzy triumphed in the arduous race at the wheel of à white 60PS Mercedes. This was the first really significant win for a German car in a big international race.

In 1904 Baron de Caters set a new outright speed record of 156.6km/h near the Belgian resort of Ostend. It was to remain Mercedes' only listing in the record books. In 1904 the Gordon Bennett Cup was lost after being won so convincingly the previous year. Jenatzy could manage only second place behind a French Richard-Brasier, in 1905 Mercedes cars were placed fifth, seventh and tenth, and the following year the race was not held.

Even so, these races had aroused interest in international racing and the comparisons between marques that they allowed; therefore the newly-announced Grand Prix de l'Automobile Club de France (ACF) was welcomed as an important event.

The French had realized from the outset that fairness could only be achieved by stipulating cylinder dimensions and weight of cars. Rules for the first race in 1908 limited cylinder bore to 155 mm and laid down a weight of 1100 kg. This still allowed unlimited capacity.

Disagreements with Wilhelm Lorenz, a member of the board of Daimler, had in the meantime led to the resignation of Wilhelm Maybach; Paul Daimler, son of the founder of the firm, took over his position as Chief Designer. Daimler's engine had a stroke of 180mm and a bore of 144.7mm, giving a capacity of 12,780cc. Its output was 135PS at 1400rpm. The car was driven in the 1908 French Grand Prix by the Mercedes test driver, Christian Lautenschlager, who took victory on the triangular course near Dieppe on 1st March; this win being comparable to the success in the 1903 Gordon Bennett Race. In subsequent years, big car manufacturers, including Daimler and Benz, agreed to stay out of international racing. The result was that Mercedes' next Grand Prix start was in 1914, again in the French Grand Prix, after the agreement had run out in 1912 (a measure that had in any case been frequently circumvented in the

The Grand Prix car of 1908.

20

The 1914 French Grand Prix was run over dusty roads.

intervening years by hefty backing for private entrants).

The French Grand Prix of 1914 is like no other in the annals of motor sport. To begin with, the organizing body decided its own interpretation of the rules. Then, in September 1913, the news was broken that for the first time there would be a capacity limit in conjunction with a maximum weight limit for the cars. Capacity was fixed at a maximum of 4.5 litres (a very low figure for the time) and maximum weight 1100 kg.

Preparations got under way in Stuttgart. Initially there was some complaining at the organisers' new set of rules because they were regarded as quite clearly favouring British and French firms, who had been developing smaller engines for some while; in the end though, the Mercedes team grasped the nettle.

On the basis of their aero-engine experience, the designers decided to build a power unit with individual steel cylinders, and welded water jackets.

Bore measured 93 mm and the stroke 165. The first engines broke crankshafts like toothpicks. This was a result of engine speeds of anything up to 3600 rpm, whereas previously maximum revs had been around the 2000 rpm mark. Eventually, the Austrian firm of Danner came to the rescue with a special type of steel. Special sparking plugs were also required to withstand high speeds; they were supplied by Eisemann, were specially insulated and had a platinum electrode. A single plug of this type cost 40 gold marks. The cost of a bread roll in 1914: two pfennigs.

In the spring of 1914 an engineer was sent to survey the course near Lyon. A week later he returned with detailed records of the length of the straights, radii of curves and the types of road surface. At Easter a meticulous test was carried out under the direction of Max Sailer, who was responsible for the supervision of Mercedes racing cars.

The Germans were well prepared for the race,

One of the successful Mercedes-Benz racers of 1914.

22

which took place on 4th July. Their rivals had not been quite so thorough in their build-up. Peugeot and Delage were the favourites. In the eyes of public and experts alike, Georges Boillot driving a Peugeot, who had won in both 1912 and 1913, was the man most likely to take the laurels on this occasion, too. At the time he was indisputably the world's number one driver and had just returned from Indianapolis, where a chassis failure had denied him certain victory.

Competitors went to the start line in groups of two, first away being Boillot in car number 5 and Sailer with the Mercedes number 12. Another four Mercedes started this race, driven by Christian Lautenschlager, Louis Wagner on loan from Fiat, Otto Salzer and the Belgian Mercedes importer, Théodore Pilette. The last-named had attempted to persuade Baurat Daimler to use the traditional chain-drive system. Sailer, however, pressed for a modern shaft transmission, which was given the nod by Paul Daimler.

The distance to be covered in the race was over 750 km, making almost excessive demands on the physical and psychological make-up of the participants. To the cheers of his compatriots, Boillot completed the first lap of 20 in just over 21 minutes. A little later, calm descended when Sailer was timed to be 18 seconds faster than the Peugeot.

Sailer continued to build on this until, with four laps complete, he led Boillot by exactly two minutes, and the Delage of Duray by almost three. Then on lap six, the French went crazy. Boillot was in the lead: the pace had been too hot for the Mercedes, which had suffered a big-end failure. By this time, however, Lautenschlager was in second place, Wagner in sixth and Salzer in eighth. Pilette was also out. Lap by lap the Germans advanced on Boillot's blue Peugeot as the battle went on. Lautenschlager, the mechanic, hurtled round after Boillot, the professional driver. The gap between the two came down until the breathless crowd discarded their stopwatches; the two men were separated by only a

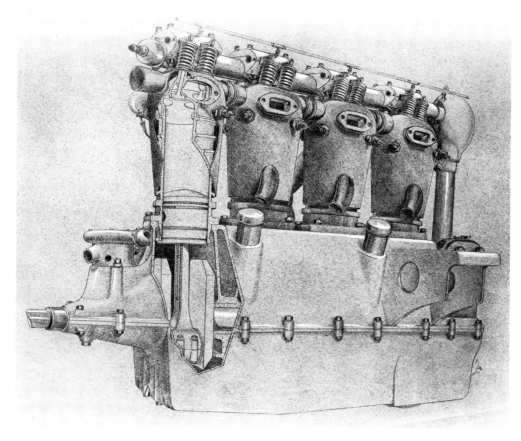

The engine that powered the 1914 cars to victory. Output: 115PS.

23

matter of seconds. Two laps before the end came the upset. Thousands cheered, Lautenschlager was leading. Into the final lap, he already had a lead of over a minute.

Boillot had yet to suffer the final blow; with his compatriots still hoping for a miracle, his rear axle broke. At the Rive de Gier, the dusty blue Peugeot came to a halt. Boillot crouched beside it, his grimy face streaked with tears.

It was left for Mercedes to celebrate the most famous victory in the short history of motor racing. Three of their cars took the first three places, Lautenschlager leading Louis Wagner and Otto Salzer home after more than seven hours' racing. A message came from the Kaiser: "May we convey our best wishes."

In the weeks and months that followed, politics played out a bloody leading role. The Austrian heir Archduke Franz Ferdinand had been murdered six days before the Grand Prix in Lyon, and in July the armies of Europe were mobilized. World War I raged. Boillot was killed at the controls of a biplane, and Mercedes' fabulous victory was forgotten; after 1918 Germany, beaten, had other worries.

It was much later that news reached Europe that the 1915 Indianapolis 500 had been won by Ralph de Palma at the wheel of one of the 1914 Mercedes cars. The cars were eight years old (and fitted with four-wheel brakes) when they won the Targa Florio in Sicily. Though Lautenschlager and Salzer contested the race in two works Mercedes, it was the Italian privateer Count Giulio Masetti who took the flag in his scarlet-painted car.

In the early and mid-1920s, the supercharger appeared on the company's racers. The Targa Florio of 1922 was the first race in which a supercharged car was tried. They were not so fast at that time (the aces sticking to conventional cars, which they reckoned gave them a better chance of victory) but Salzer still managed sixth place.

The wind of change was blowing through the Daimler company. At the end of 1922 Paul Daimler left his father's firm to work for Horch in Zwickau and his successor as design chief at Untertürkheim was Ferdinand Porsche. Among Porsche's retinue was Alfred Neubauer who was to make such a name for himself in ensuing years as race department chief and the driving force behind the firm's motor sport plans.

In May 1923 the firm contested the Indianapolis 500, and though the cars could do no better than eighth and eleventh places, they still beat the best of the Bugattis. Further battle honours were won in 1924 with a victory in the Targa Florio. Christian Werner was the winner, Lautenschlager took eleventh and Neubauer fifteenth place.

In the meantime a sensational new car had been produced by Benz in Mannheim which aimed at harmonizing aircraft building techniques with the demands of circuit racing. The *Tropfenwagen* ('teardrop car') was the first design to place the engine behind the driver. The 'fuselage' was very slim and resembled a cigar on wheels. Though the car did not win on its first outing at Monza, it was awarded a trophy for being the most sensational design at the meeting. Sadly, the car never contested another international race. In 1924, in the face of a worsening economic situation, Benz had reached an agreement with Daimler in Stuttgart for mutual cooperation, which led to a merger between the two firms two years later. To preclude undesirable mutual competition in racing, it was agreed that in future Daimler would take on the bulk of activities in the sporting arena. Also, Ferdinand Porsche was at work on the design of a new supercharged 8-cylinder engine.

The 2-litre racing car was Daimler's first 8-cylinder and the first design completed by Porsche for his new employers. When this all-out racer arrived at Monza (Christian Werner and Neubauer had built a transporter so that the car did not have to make the trip under its own power) it became apparent that it was still suffering from teething troubles. After a few laps, the cylinder heads, which Porsche had cast in bronze for better heat conductivity, had become porous and in a welter of smoke the car returned to the pits. Mercedes informed the organizers that taking part in the Italian Grand Prix was impossible in the circumstances and the race was simply postponed for six weeks until 19th October 1924.

By October, the Mercedes had been fitted with conventional steel cylinders with welded water jackets. The new cars were to be raced by Werner, Masetti, Neubauer and Count Louis Zborowski. In the race, where the only serious challenger was Alfa Romeo, Masetti retired with a fractured fuel pipe. Neubauer did not start because of a serious accident in practice, which left his car too badly damaged to be repaired in time and Zborowski was victim of a

The Benz 'teardrop' of 1922.

fatal accident on lap 44 when he lost control in the fast Lesmo curve and collided with a tree. Like his father 21 years previously, the young Zborowski lost his life at the wheel of a Mercedes racing car. Antonio Ascari was the winner of the race in his Alfa.

After Neubauer's practice accident and the death of Zborowski, the new Mercedes soon gained a bad reputation and was used only infrequently thereafter. The excellence of the engine design was undermined by the disastrous chassis, which would often cause the car to change direction abruptly to the surprise of its drivers. The reason lay in the car's very low centre of gravity, which Porsche had

The quirky chassis of the Monza car, dating from 1924.

arrived at by locating the fuel tank beneath the chassis frame. The result, however, was that the car's limits of adhesion were very fine, and if it crossed them it would go straight into a four-wheel skid, behaviour that only a very few drivers were able to cope with. Christian Werner proved that the 8-cylinder was basically sound when he modified the car slightly (relocating the fuel tank behind the driver, for instance) and won the hillclimb at Schauinsland near Freiburg in 1926. Rudolf Caracciola's first important win for Daimler-Benz (the merger became final on 29th June 1926) was in the 8-cylinder car at the Avus in Berlin in the first German Grand Prix.

The late 1920s and early 1930s were great times for the mighty supercharged Mercedes S, SS, SSK and SSKL. The most powerful version of the muscular 6-cylinder developed about 300PS, an incredible output for the time. Drivers like Rudolf Caracciola, Otto Merz and Hans Stuck notched up countless victories with these cars, including Caracciola's triumph at the inaugural race at the Nürburgring on 19th June 1927.

The true peak for the Mercedes race department was yet to come. The AIACR (Association Internationale des Automobiles Clubs Reconnus), a forerunner of the FIA (Fédération Internationale de l'Automobile) had worked out a new formula for the 1934 season, which later became known as the 750 Kilogram Formula. The regulations stipulated only a maximum weight for the cars, 750kg, other details such as capacity and supercharging being unrestricted. In March 1933, when Adolf Hitler had been Chancellor for two months and had raised hopes for the beleaguered German economy, Daimler-Benz announced their official return to motor sport. The SSK types had been raced unofficially and against the true wishes of the board. The Reich Chancellery in Berlin allocated funds, although Daimler-Benz and Auto-Union in Zwickau, where Ferdinand Porsche was now working, had to share the yearly 450,000 Reichsmark support. Daimler-Benz themselves had to stump up about 75 per cent of the budget, a small matter of 1 million Reichsmarks per year. It later transpired that the amount of money spent on the Mercedes racing programme in the 1930s was many times higher, and that State grants accounted for only about a tenth of the budget. The rest had to be provided by the firm itself.

In Stuttgart, Fritz Nallinger, Hans Nibel, Jakob Krauss and Max Sailer got down to work. The result was the W 25, a single-seater based on the Type 380 saloon. There was a full swing axle chassis with transmission in unit with the rear axle, and the car was powered by a supercharged straight eight, the first version of which developed over 350PS from a capacity of 3.4 litres. The first car to be completed was presented to the board in February 1934, but its first race outing was not until 3rd June that year, at the Eifelrennen on the Nürburgring. At the race, the white-painted cars were found to be 1 kg overweight. Neubauer then came up with the wonderful idea of removing all the white paint frcm the aluminium bodywork to achieve the desired weight reduction. The Silver Arrows were born!

The W 25 won its first race at the Nürburgring with Manfred von Brauchitsch at the wheel, but on the first occasion when they faced international competition in a Grand Prix, both Mercedes and Auto-Union, whose car was rear-engined like the Benz 'teardrop', were taught a lesson. At Montlhéry near Paris, Louis Chiron won in his Alfa Romeo. But then Mercedes' Italian driver Luigi Fagioli won the Pescara race, as well as the Grands Prix in Italy and Spain. Hans Stuck took the Europameister title, however, with the 16-cylinder Auto-Union.

The 1935 season was more successful. By now the engine of the W 25 had been enlarged to 3.9 litres and developed over 400 PS. The Silver Arrows took victory in eight important races, Rudolf Caracciola scoring six to secure the European crown. But the following year, Mercedes domination was a thing of the past. At Untertürkheim too much energy had been expended on the creation of a 12-cylinder engine, the Type D, which turned out to be a dud. The W 25 was no longer a match for the Auto-Union, and the team stayed away from four Grands Prix to make conscientious preparations for the 1937 season. With the new W 125 chassis, and a 5.6-litre engine producing initially nearly 600PS, Mercedes regained their superiority with Rudolf Caracciola taking the European Championship in 1937, the last year of the 750 Kilogram Formula.

Because the power of the 750 Kilogram Formula cars had risen enormously, the AIACR put limits on capacity for the 1938–40 seasons. Supercharged engines up to 3 litres and unsupercharged engines up to 4.5 litres were allowed. There were weight limit steps from 400 to 850 kg, depending on engine capacity. Mercedes built the W 154 with a 12-

551

German Grand Prix
1927 on the new
Nürburgring: Christian
Werner put up fastest
lap and came home
second.

Otto Merz, winner of
the 1927 German
Grand Prix.

27

The mighty Mercedes SSKS, powered by a 7.1-litre 300PS engine.

cylinder engine from which more than 460PS was extracted. The offset propeller shaft allowed a very low driver position, giving the car its sensational low-slung appearance. In the two years up to World War II, Mercedes-Benz walked off with race after race. Caracciola and Hermann Lang, who had made

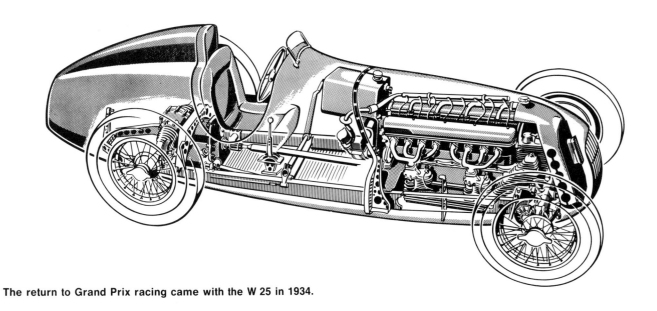

The return to Grand Prix racing came with the W 25 in 1934.

the leap from mechanic to Grand Prix pilot, took one European championship apiece.

In the midst of all this the W 165, a 1.5-litre car, contested a single race, the Tripoli Grand Prix of 1939 run to the current *Voiturette* formula, at the insistence of the Italians in whose colony Libya the race was held and who believed that the Germans would be unable to build a suitable car in time. For this car the Daimler engineers created an engine producing 160PS per litre. In the face of this mighty atom, the traditionally successful rival Alfa Romeo and Maserati *vetturete,* which had prompted such sweeping alterations of the rules for the Tripoli race, were totally powerless. By winning this race, Lang notched up a hat trick of victories in the prestigious North African event.

A gap of many years was to follow. Half of Europe was laid waste by war, and when they finally surrendered the Germans faced the task of rebuilding a devastated country. By the end of the 1940s there were already car and motorcycle events being held, even in Germany, but a company like Daimler-Benz had other concerns more pressing than motor sport.

Finally, in 1950 the wailing supercharged engines of the W 154 could be heard once again in the forests of the Eifel around the Nürburgring. Daimler-Benz planned to participate in the Argentine series in January 1951; the dust was blown off the pre-war cars and they were given a thorough going over. The company also planned to enter Indianapolis. But in Buenos Aires, the Mercedes line-up of Fangio, Lang and Kling suffered two defeats by the smaller and more nimble Ferrari of Gonzalez and this prompted the shelving of all further activities with the highly complex 12-cylinder.

W 25 engine: a 3.36-litre straight-eight developing 354PS.

29

Manfred von Brauchitsch (10) and Rudolf Caracciola round the Station Hairpin in the 1937 Monaco Grand Prix.

30

The cockpit of the
W 125 of 1937.

There were also plans to develop the 1.5-litre of 1939 for the newly created World Drivers' Championship but this project was also dropped when it was realized that the pre-war hardware, though a match for the Italian Alfas and Ferraris, would never be superior to them. It was 1952 before the racing team appeared in international competition at its old strength. The 300 SL was on the scene, a sports car developed from the 300 saloon, and was driven to famous endurance victories at Le Mans and in the Carrera Panamericana Mexico.

The success of these cars and their acknowledged value in marketing eventually persuaded the board of Daimler-Benz AG to approve the design of a completely new Grand Prix machine. From 1954 Mercedes wanted to contest the premier motor racing category. The W 196 was born.

30204

Between 1938 and 1939 the W 154 (here) and W 163 were virtually unbeatable.

Left Top: The plan view emphasizes the elongated shape of the W 154.

Left Bottom: The 3-litre engine of the W 154, which powered Caracciola and Lang to their European titles.

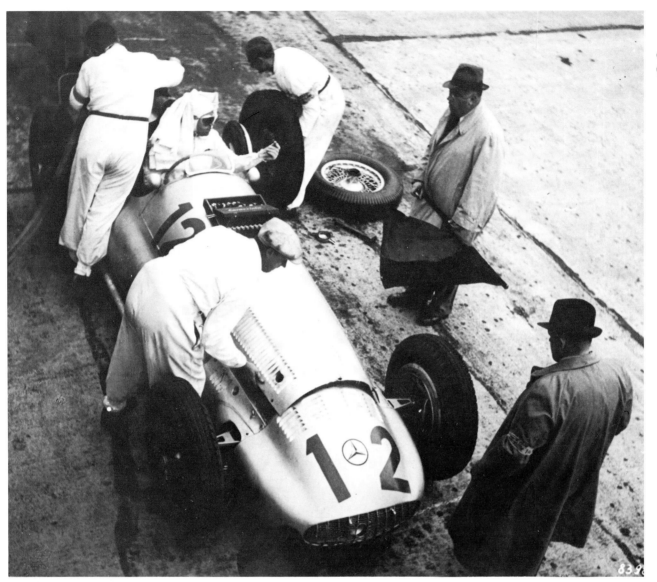

Caracciola in the pits
(1938 German GP).

Postwar outing: the
Mercedes on the grid
in Argentina in 1951.

The Mercedes works team at the German Grand Prix of 1938: from the left, von Brauchitsch, Neubauer, Seaman, Lang and Caracciola.

At Le Mans in 1952 the 300 SL coupés scored a one-two.

The world at large

Germany in the 1950s

At school it was always said that no attempt should be made at evaluating works of art, literature or architecture without reference to the era in which they came into being. Books bear the stamp of the social climate and movements of the age, paintings often reflect their times by their subdued or vibrant colouring, and are frequently critical caricatures or perceptive snapshots. Buildings represent the prevailing way of life (though they can often be diametrically opposed to the norm) or else document the self-imposed image of governments and regimes.

It is when times are particularly harsh that the best expressions of ironical and cynical humour are heard. ("The people are having it too easy – there are no good jokes any more ...") Satirical journals are never more popular than during times of oppressive government; restraints and the threat of reprisals promote dissent. How should the racing department of a large motor manufacturer be viewed in the context of the times in which it was formed? Is it inappropriate to look for similar parallels, and might the racing department be raised on an undeserved pedestal?

This is not intended to be a piece of social criticism on the discrepancy between capital-intensive participation in motor sport, and the pitiful existence and poverty of large sectors of the population during the 1950s. (Though any number of suitable titles for such a thesis spring to mind, for instance: "State of the art technology at the expense of the working classes".) Nitpicking of this nature is not to everyone's taste; it is more suitable as a subject for social science lecturers than authors of books on specific racing cars. The aim of this chapter is to give a brief outline of the political, social, cultural and sporting conditions in postwar Germany. It gives ("seek and ye shall find") a number of interesting dates on which the Mercedes entourage was away at races just when significant events were taking place on the political scene, or within a day or two of their occurrence. And this kind of synchronisation can be amusing.

On 4th July 1954, the West German national football team beat the hot favourites Hungary 3–2 in the World Cup Final in Switzerland. The self-esteem of many Germans was restored by this and they felt able to walk tall once again. They were no longer nobodies. Whatever criticism there may be of nationalism in sport (and its oft-berated function as a war substitute – the sociologists again), a kind of charge went through the nation, which in actual fact of course was a nation no longer (nor has it been since Partition and legal revision).

That same day, the two W 196s of Juan Manuel Fangio and Karl Kling won the French Grand Prix at Reims. This success against strong foreign opposition also boosted the Germans – supported by the jubilation of the French spectators at the Mercedes victory.

On 17th July 1954, when the Mercedes team was humiliated at Silverstone, Theodor Heuss was elected Federal President for a second term.

On 23rd October 1954, the Treaty of Paris was signed, an important act that established the sovereignty of the Federal Republic of Germany, and also its membership of NATO. The following day at Pedralbes, a suburb of Barcelona, the Spanish Grand Prix was held and again Mercedes tasted the bitterness of defeat.

Between the two races in Argentina on 16th and 30th January 1955, the Soviet Union declared the official cessation of hostilities with Germany; the Western Allies, the United States, Great Britain and France, had taken this step on 9th July 1951. And on the weekend when, at Monza, Daimler-Benz AG contested its last Formula 1 race (Fangio and Taruffi scoring another double), Adenauer the Federal Chancellor was in Moscow and secured the release of tens of thousands of German prisoners of war.

What was it really like in Germany in the early and mid-1950s? Practically everyone remembers to this day that the West German footballers were World Champions in 1954. But who knows that in 1953, a third of the inhabitants of the western part of Germany were dependent on social assistance, because they were unemployed, suffering special hardship, were war-disabled, or were refugees, war widows or orphans?

When the Board of Daimler-Benz AG voted to return to Grand Prix racng in 1952, the war had been over only seven years. In Germany the wounds were still fresh, many areas of the great conurbations still lay in ruins while elsewhere, reconstruction went ahead apace. Slowly but surely, the first signs of modest prosperity spread; refrigerators were the first consumer goods to seize the imagination of the housewife. After years of hunger, the need was not difficult to justify; eating was in – the Germans whose average weight a few years before had been several kilos lower than is normal, were suddenly overweight.

The building industry was booming. Blocks of housing, even whole new streets, went up in no time. By today's standards, the flats were ludicrously small. In their simplest form "social" flats, as the Germans termed them, consisted of no more than two rooms, bathroom and toilet being shared with other residents. But in the 1950s over three-and-a-half million new dwellings were built, a record so far unmatched in any other country in the world (but probably no other country had suffered such widespread and total destruction as Germany had during World War II).

Not only the building industry but also the furniture industry was working at full capacity. At first, the demand was for "utility" furniture: sofas had to double as beds by night and rooms were often multi-purpose because of restricted space. Gradually, with increasing prosperity, the demands of the paying customer became greater too. For many, solid wood wall-sized bookcases in the living room became pieces of furniture worth saving for, as did comfortably padded armchairs and coffee tables.

At the time of the currency reform in 1948, each resident of the western half of Germany (the Federal Republic was only founded one year later) benefited by all of 40 Deutsche Marks. In the ensuing years a number of people made rapid progress: Carl C.F. Borgward for instance, who established his motor empire in Bremen (which went bankrupt in 1961); also Max Grundig the radio manufacturer; and Helmut Horten the chain store magnate.

The state simplified the setting up of businesses. Ludwig Erhard the Minister of Economics preached the market economy – rewarding independent entrepreneurs with generous investment assistance. And under these arrangements only a fraction of profits was liable to tax. The *Wirtschaftswunder* was possible only on this basis: those prepared to take risks had to be rewarded, even if entrepreneurial motivation was comparatively low in a country with so much ground to make up.

In August 1955, the year when Juan Manuel Fangio won the Formula 1 World Championship again with his Mercedes, the millionth Volkswagen Beetle rolled off the Wolfsburg production line. Cars became more and more the object of German desires. Besides this, the motor industry was also a great contributor to the balance of imports and exports – almost 50% of Volkswagen production was destined for overseas markets. Within Germany, the cheaper types of four-wheeled transport were favoured to begin with. The Beetle cost nearly 4000 DM; on the other hand the products of Borgward (Lloyd) and Hans Glas (Goggomobil) were a good deal cheaper, the small Goggo costing only 2800 DM for instance.

Cars from Mercedes were beyond the reach of the bulk of the population. These star-spangled vehicles were often driven by those who had secured themselves a slice of the West German craze for eating – the master butchers. This is still reflected in the image that some Mercedes models have today: if a 180D ever turns up at a vintage rally, someone is bound to make a comment about a *Metzger auto* (*Butcher-waggon*).

Germany was taking to the air again too. Lufthansa went back into business at the end of 1955 with a small twin-engined Convair and a proud crew of pilots and stewardesses. In the years that followed these became the dream occupations of many youngsters.

The cinema became a magical attraction. Romy Schneider as Sissi moved the whole nation and James Dean became the idol of the younger generation. There was no shortage of scandal either: with nude scenes in *One Summer of Happiness* and *The Sinner*, Ulla Jacobsson and Hildegard Neff ensured a wave of outrage. Musically, a shake-up was on the way too: rock'n'roll engulfed Europe and juke boxes pumped out Elvis and Bill Haley. Dancing was all the rage, women going for petticoats and stiletto heels.

Over all of this hung the shadow of renewed war. Practically no one seriously believed that peace would endure as long in Europe as the 20 years it had lasted between the two World Wars. The Korean War was raging at the beginning of the 1950s; then in 1953 came protests in the German Democratic Republic, which were put down violently. Algeria had been fighting for independence from France since 1954 and in October 1956 the Hungarian rising was crushed by Soviet troops – the 1950s were characterized by the fear of losing all that had been newly rebuilt.

This, then, is the background against which Mercedes once more engaged. Whether it was football or motor racing, the masses were sport crazy. Sport offered an opportunity to forget a dismal existence, and if German sportsmen or German marques were contesting victory, enthusiasm overflowed and knew no bounds.

THE MEN

**Dr Fritz Könecke,
Chairman of the Board
of Daimler-Benz AG,
1953 – 60.**

40

The Chairman

Dr Fritz Könecke

For the opposition, things were a little easier. Enzo Ferrari built his cars as and when required, raising the money for this mode of working by selling wickedly expensive sports cars; because of their name and their exotic sporting character, these rapidly became valuable collector's items that increased steadily in value.

With his relatively small team, Ferrari could guarantee spontaneous reaction to the demands of race development. Thus at Modena it was nothing out of the ordinary for him to have two or three different racing cars or engines under development at a given time. Ferrari always liked to have more than a couple of irons in the fire. Although he found himself in a disastrous financial position in the mid-1950s, everything eventually turned out well when Fiat stepped in in the middle of 1955.

The Orsi family, represented by Commendatore Adolfo Orsi and his son Omer, who headed a machine-tool empire in Modena, had found an expensive hobby through their acquisition of the Maserati company. The Orsis were also able to react speedily to changes in regulations, the flow of money to the team (at least in 1954-5) being determined more or less by the simple pleasure they took from their involvement. By contrast with Ferrari, where decisions needed no hammering out, at Maserati there were always two at the table discussing projects.

At Gordini there was yet a third situation.

Amédée Gordini was a hopeless case – from the financial point of view. With almost suicidal commitment, he pursued his goal of representing France in international motor sport. He suffered from constant lack of funding: no sooner had he scraped together a few francs than they would disappear into racing car development.

In constant hope of the great breakthrough – or the great benefactor – Gordini worked away on his blue racers. But decisions always came promptly, for the engineer from Paris always felt above all responsible to himself.

In Britain there was a long tradition of small racing teams consisting of ambitious, eccentric individuals often pronounced crazy by outsiders. ERA, Connaught, BRM, Lotus – these were all the product mainly of a single mind. Known on the Continent slightly disdainfully as "hobbyists", the British were to begin to enjoy great success at the end of the 1950s.

So how did it happen that one of the largest of all German businesses, Daimler-Benz AG, came to announce its return to motor racing? And this time, not with the supercharged car dating from 1939 that had contested the two Argentinian races in 1951, but with a totally new design. The decision could be reached only after lengthy discussions among those most highly placed in the hierarchy. In 1953 its members were as follows: Dr Fritz Könecke as chairman, Dr Otto Hoppe, Otto Jakob, Karl C.

Müller, Dr Fritz Nallinger and five other deputies.

The name of Nallinger is one that catches the eye. He had been one of the supporters of Daimler-Benz pre-war racing campaigns, an engineer who constantly sought competition in sport. Might he therefore have argued the chairman around to his position?

The affair cannot really be simplified in this way. To pinpoint the motivation for the return of Mercedes to racing, particularly Formula 1, it is necessary to cast the mind back 30 years.

In its formative years the Federal Republic still had to struggle with the legacy of the war which had been lost by the Third Reich. The economy looked healthy in many respects. Sales of private cars soared (at the end of 1954 production stood at 670,000 cars, about 40 per cent higher than in 1953); but at Daimler-Benz the Board was still thinking of how luxury saloon car sales could be increased.

Dr Fritz Könecke, born in Hanover in 1899, was a member of the board of Continental Tyres there before the war, and moved to Stuttgart in 1952 when the supervisory committee of Daimler-Benz AG appointed him to the Board. Könecke was a far-sighted leader who always took account of public relations in his deliberations.

At the beginning of the 1950s in the magazine *Aussenpolitik* he wrote, "In common with any other nation, our future lies in whether we want to stand together, whether damage to part of us becomes a concern for the whole, whether our thoughts and acts encompass all of society, whether we are prepared to place the good of all above private advantage – even in important questions. The world struggle against the ideology of Eastern Europe cannot be won with refrigerators, cars, radiograms and movies."

Könecke naturally wanted to see more and more German cars exported, especially the products of Mercedes-Benz, but he was mindful of the important fact that if this was associated with high quality, then the image of the Federal Republic would be enhanced abroad.

These two considerations were combined in the decision to re-enter racing. In the spring of 1953 the Board of Daimler-Benz AG in Stuttgart-Untertürkheim voted in favour of contesting the Formula 1 World Championship. Sports car racing was suspended in preparation for the new project.

Last but not least, the great success of the Mercedes 300 SL in 1952 played some part in the Board's decision. In the Mille Miglia, in Bern, at the Nürburgring and especially on the Carrera Panamericana Mexico, the car had scored victories and taken point-scoring places in the hands of Karl Kling, Hermann Lang and others.

Karl Kling, victor in the Carrera, was even voted Sportsman of the Year in 1952; motor sport enjoyed great popularity and in the minds of many, memories of the great days of the Silver Arrows had returned.

Dr Fritz Könecke saw his ideas largely confirmed in the press, now that the momentous decision was making headlines. But journalists on a number of papers were of the opinion that withdrawal from sports car racing was not necessarily a good move, because those German drivers who were to represent Mercedes in Formula 1 in 1954 would be denied the chance of sizing up their opponents. Elsewhere, however, there was unanimous endorsement of the firm's ambition. The Federal Republic awaited the new car from Untertürkheim with excitement.

Two years later, with a roll of honour listing two Formula 1 World Championships, the World Sports Car Championship and the European Touring Car Championship, Mercedes had taken every important title in motor racing. Such overwhelming success left no room for improvement.

The decision to withdraw from racing at the end of 1955 had, in the case of the Grand Prix team, been taken at the beginning of 1955 and had nothing to do with the accident at Le Mans, despite claims to the contrary repeated to this day.

Thus *Stern*, no 48, 1986, p. 102: "But after the catastrophe at Le Mans which claimed 80 victims, the Stuttgart firm withdrew its cars."

It is entirely wrong to make such connections as these and they bear witness only to a lack of research on the part of the writer. At Stuttgart there was naturally great shock at the Le Mans accident – but it had next to no impact on the decision to withdraw from racing. Mercedes had the unique opportunity of bowing out on a high note (not without winning further races in the 1955 season), just as Juan Manuel Fangio did three years later after taking his fifth World title.

Sales of Mercedes-Benz products had soared throughout the world and the marque's image had reached a new high point. The Board's intention had been converted into reality – after all, economic considerations had played a considerable part in the decision taken in 1953. At Untertürkheim racing was seen as an efficient means to an end, but never an end in itself.

But all the highly qualified staff, the best engineers and mechanics were now required on the shopfloor, where production of road cars had to be stepped up. The exit from the sporting scene had been planned for a long time but perhaps its rapidity was a little surprising; even so, the reasons were simple enough. Even the two top drivers saw the motivation for their employers' action. "They are bowing out on a high note," said Stirling Moss. "Any sportsman with any sense would wish to do the same."

The decision taken by Dr Fritz Könecke, who had raised the curtain on Daimler-Benz's racing campaign, showed an entrepreneur's foresight, and the words of his New Year's address to his staff in 1956 – "We have not only retained our market position, we have improved it! Our export turnover compared with 1954 has risen by about 40 per cent" – surely reflected the contribution made by the firm's participation in international motor racing.

Daimler-Benz had breathed life into racing and given it renewed vigour but, for a concern of its size, there were other more important areas of activity. When for instance Porsche represents West Germany on the racetracks of the world these days, then that is quite natural. As a manufactureer of quality sports cars Porsche can bolster its image among sporting drivers the world over: just as Ferrari has done in the past and continues to do today.

Similarly, Renault's withdrawal from Formula 1 in 1985 after eight years on the Grand Prix trail was understandable bearing in mind the firm's real brief, and especially with the unions putting a coherent case. A company the size of Renault – like Daimler-Benz – has other concerns besides motor racing. Though welcome if it serves to boost a firm's image, it is not of the first order of importance.

Dr Fritz Könecke, a noted pragmatist, had realized this 30 years before and acted accordingly. Using the platform of international motor sport to improve sales of his private and commercial vehicles, he simultaneously promoted other products of the Federal Republic, in keeping with his world view.

In August 1954 in an interview with the motoring journalist Rainer Günzler, Könecke said, "Bearing in mind the great national and international interest in motor racing events and the strength of foreign competition, a successful racing team can influence the overseas image of the victorious marque to a huge extent. This promotes the reputation of all German quality products abroad and thus aids Germany's overall export economy."

Könecke, whose unmistakable trademark was his pair of black framed glasses, received widespread recognition outside his own firm. He was a member of the Presidium of the Organization of West German Industry, the Confederation of West German Employers' Associations and the Motor Industry Organization. He was Chairman of the Board of Daimler-Benz in Stuttgart until 1960. He died in 1979.

Rudolf Uhlenhaut during testing at Monza in 1954.

The Helmsman

Rudolf Uhlenhaut, 1906 – 1989

In the hectic high-speed world of motor racing, Rudolf Uhlenhaut was an exception to every rule. He built the Silver Arrows for Mercedes-Benz, which were so dominant between 1937 and 1939. After World War II he was co-author of the sequel to that success when he brought his genius to bear on the design of a raceworthy sports racer based on mass produced technology. Then with the W 196 he set new standards for two full seasons in 1954 and 1955, giving the team's Italian rivals a hard time.

Uhlenhaut was born on 15th July 1906 in London, where his father was a director of the Deutsche Bank. The young Rudolf spent his first few years in that city, which at the time was still the hub of a mighty empire. Uhlenhaut was brought up bilingually, a fact that later led to many contacts among the British specialist press (George Monkhouse, Laurence Pomeroy) and to the high esteem in which the German engineer was held in Great Britain.

His upbringing continued in Brussels, and then in Bremen once his family had moved to that great North German centre of commerce. His interest in technical matters began at an early age. He wanted to know how machines worked and to delve into their innermost workings. His early choice of career was as a designer of steam engines.

His university course was thus decided: mechanical engineering. The choice of university itself was made on the basis of private and sporting considerations. Uhlenhaut's passion for skiing was at least the equal of his interest in steam engines. In 1926, therefore, Munich was the only possible choice. At weekends he could enjoy himself on the slopes with his friends. "We mostly went to Bayrisch-Eisenstein." he says, remembering his student days. "It only cost 2.50 marks – whereas it cost 4.50 at Garmisch, and we couldn't afford that very often. Still I never missed Saturday lectures in favour of skiing. I took my studies seriously."

He left university in 1931 having switched allegiance from heavy and unfashionable steam engines to the automobile. During his student days, Uhlenhaut used to hurtle around Munich on a 250cc DKW motorcycle, an unreliable machine that spent more time in the yard than on the road. At that time, of course, he could not have afforded a car – how could he have known that in the whole of his life he would never possess a car of his own?

With some help from the Deutsche Bank (his father died at the end of the 1920s) Uhlenhaut managed to secure a job at Mercedes-Benz in Stuttgart at a time of economic depression. On his arrival, he was not put to work just anywhere, but in that engineer's paradise, the experimental department. The value of his labours was estimated at only half that of a skilled worker: 60 pfennings an hour. When Uhlenhaut arrived Fritz Nallinger was already head of the experimental department.

Uhlenhaut's first tasks were on carburettor development and the development (not the design) of the 170 V. Team spirit was the hallmark of Daimler-Benz even then, at least in the experimental department. Solo performers were deemed undesirable. The head of design, Max Wagner, often made suggestions, but they would only be transformed into reality if they appeared genuinely reasonable.

In mid-1936, a time when motor racing was so important both as a marketing weapon and as propaganda, the firm's sporting fortunes were at an all-time low; the Chairman of the day, Dr Kissel, put responsibility for racing car development on Uhlenhaut's shoulders. Other engineers, like Otto Winkelmann who had come to Stuttgart with Röhr, had no desire to get their fingers burnt designing racing cars, and declined the offer with thanks. The lot thus fell to Uhlenhaut, who shirked none of the responsibility that came with the job.

To begin with, the new chief himself got behind the wheel of the W 25 and drove mile after mile around the Nordschleife at the Nürburgring. "I wanted to see for myself what was wrong and what needed improvement on the car. The best way to do that was by driving the car myself. Of course I had to learn. It was not simply a question of sitting in the car and going quickly. It was hard work."

Hard work that also had its moments of drama. Once, on the long straight (Döttinger Höhe) a rear wheel came adrift and Uhlenhaut calmly allowed the car to roll to a halt. On another occasion, the clutch exploded and practically sliced the car in two; the engineer coolly dealt with this too. After several thousand kilometres he knew what would need to be different on the new car in comparison with the old. (In Uhlenhaut's words, "Adhesion was bad, suspension was bad, steering was bad.") The chassis frame, for instance, was much too flexible and had to be reinforced because it was acting as part of the suspension (as a result of the hard damper adjustment favoured by the drivers). The winter months of 1936-7 were busy ones for the racing department.

Success soon became tangible: the W 125, which carried Mercedes hopes in 1937, dominated the opposition – Rudolf Caracciola became European Champion.

For the new 3-litre formula Uhlenhaut built the W 154 (for 1939 the W 163), a car which, against the trend of the day, was built very low. Caracciola and Lang played cat and mouse with their opponents in these cars, taking the title in 1938 and 1939. For the race in Tripoli in 1939 Mercedes built the W 165, a 1.5-litre car which according to Uhlenhaut was equipped with "the best racing engine ever built". Then came World War II.

After the war the former racing engineer ran a small haulage business, which soon was unable to keep up with the increasing demand for transport capacity. With his truck fuelled by methane gas, Uhlenhaut was mainly engaged in bringing back to Munich furniture that its citizens had evacuated to Lower Bavaria during the war. Around this time he was also approached by a British team who wanted him to build them a chassis. In later years Uhlenhaut chuckled, "Happily it was never built."

In 1948 he returned to Untertürkheim and Mercedes-Benz, at first working on the development of private cars. By 1950 there was reason to begin thinking again in terms of racing. Race chief Alfred Neubauer was foremost among those pressing the management for the revival of Mercedes' dormant racing potential.

The pre-war W 163 took to the circuits in Argentina in 1951, but the foray was unsuccessful. Even so, Uhlenhaut soon found an opportunity to enter sports car racing with production-derived machinery; the 300 SL that chalked up so many victories in 1952 was based around the motor of the 300 saloon. The top echelons of management felt encouraged by this and wanted to take part in

Formula 1; Uhlenhaut would once again design a Grand Prix car.

The W 196 became one of the most successful of all postwar racing cars, crammed full of prophetic technicalities. Uhlenhaut remained true to his pre-war beliefs. In 1954-5 he was the only engineer who was able to drive his creations on the track, thus bringing personal knowledge to bear on his own designs. To this day, there has been no other engineer like him. Present-day Grand Prix designers like Gordon Murray, Patrick Head and John Barnard know how to build a fast car, but they cannot drive them and must therefore rely on what their drivers tell them, which is frequently expressed in layman's terms, making interpretation difficult for the engineer.

In Mercedes' two years of Grand Prix involvement, Uhlenhaut often posted unheard-of times in practice or testing, commanding the respect of his drivers. As a Grand Prix driver, Uhlenhaut could probably have achieved as much as he did as an engineer. On one occasion in the summer of 1955, in identical conditions in the same car, he drove round the Nordschleife $3^1/2$ seconds faster than the great Juan Manuel Fangio after lunch at the Sporthotel; Uhlenhaut "didn't really feel too good after having so much to eat".

After the team's withdrawal from the sport in 1955, Uhlenhaut once again devoted his efforts to the development of production cars, which, if we are to believe him, gave him far more pleasure than building racing cars. In his years as head of research up to his retirement in 1972, the outstanding product of this department with its several hundred staff was without doubt the rotary-engined C 111. In this mobile test bed were crystallized many design ideas from the early 1970s that were destined to be taken up again years later. The rear axle of the C 111, for instance, was the precursor of today's four-wheel steering technology. In retirement, Rudolf Uhlenhaut lived with his wife in a villa on the edge of Stuttgart, although in residence there only for six months of the year. The rest of the time he spent skiing in Davos, Switzerland, or during summer months, on a yacht based at Malta.

On 8 May 1989, this most gifted of all automobile development engineers died.

The Team

The people around the W 196

It is stating the obvious to say that if a driver emerges victorious from a race, the general opinion is that the triumph was made possible by his great personal efforts alone. If he is forced to retire or has to visit the pits during the race with mechanical trouble, then it is "Oh well, the machinery has failed again."

The driver is thus usually more favourably placed at least in the eyes of the world outside. Team managers and mechanics alike realize, however, that certain failures can also be attributed to harsh treatment dealt out by the driver. Any number of drivers have been forced to leave a team for this reason though the fans, deprived of real inside knowledge, were unable or unwilling to grasp the facts of the matter.

But motor racing is like that; personalities give it life. The driver is always the hero. Frequently (and unjustly) other responsible members of the team fade into the background. They and their many colleagues are the ones who make success possible in the first place. Designers, mechanics, panel beaters, timekeepers, the team manager, tyre experts and the oil company specialists who mix the fuel cocktails. In a firm the size of Daimler-Benz there are any number of others beside – those on the Board, the men who test the reliability of power units on the test bed for days on end, the special staff who survey each and every circuit and do the calculations, producing from them charts giving drivers exact gear change points, the likely engine revs at given points on the track and the probable lap times. There are technicians dealing with fuel injection systems, first introduced into racing by Mercedes, then the countless draughtsmen who translate concepts drawn broadly with the stroke of an engineer's pen into precise workshop drawings. Then there are also the manager's secretaries going mad over their boss's endless alterations to team travel plans.

Fritz Nallinger on the Austro-Hungarian evaluation trial in 1923 . . .

This chapter aims to introduce a few of these people, and at the end of the book there is a list of over 100 who worked on the Daimler-Benz W 196 racing programme between 1952 and 1955. Thirty years after the event it is of course difficult to find out the names of individual mechanics and metalworkers, for an outsider at least. Without the detailed assistance of Professor Hans Scherenberg the author would never have been able to compile such a complete list of names. But even now, a number of those who worked on the W 196 will find their names omitted. They must excuse the author if, after his best efforts, he has not included them.

Enough of the preamble. We have already heard about the Chairman of the Board, Dr Fritz Könecke. The next rung down the ladder was

occupied by Dr Ing Fritz Nallinger. Born on 6th August 1898, he served as a pilot during World War I and afterwards studied engineering design at the Karlsruhe Technical College. Having passed his diploma examinations in October 1922, he then joined Benz & Cie in Mannheim.

In 1924 Nallinger was one of the first to move a short way up the river Neckar to Untertürkheim as the merger of Daimler and Benz got under way. In 1932 he was given power of attorney and in 1935 he was appointed technical director. This was the period of the company's involvement in Grand Prix racing and this excited Nallinger, himself an enthusiastic participant in reliability trials in the 1920s. From 1940 Nallinger was a deputy member of the Board of Daimler-Benz AG, becoming a full member in December 1941. Nallinger was in development and worked closely with Hans Scherenberg and Rudolf Uhlenhaut after 1952. The three could often be seen together at the Grands Prix in 1954 and 1955. Whenever Alfred Neubauer, the corpulent team manager, hogged the limelight on the circuits, to the accompaniment of dozens of clicking shutters, the Daimler PR chief Arthur Keser would shout his famous line, "Don't just photograph bellies, what about heads?"

Nallinger remained at Daimler-Benz until 1965, when he retired at the age of 67. He died on 4th June 1984.

Professor Dr Ing Hans Scherenberg was born on 28th October 1910 in Dresden and studied at the Stuttgart Technical College and the Karlsruhe Technical College between 1930 and 1935. Joining Daimler-Benz in Stuttgart in the summer of 1935, his first task was the testing of the world's first diesel-engined passenger car, the 260 D, after which he was employed in research. At the end of the 1930s, Scherenberg's chief areas of work were on increasing power output, and the possibility of using fuel injection systems in aero engines. Daimler-Benz built the engine for the Messerschmitt Me 109 fighter.

After the war, Scherenberg was dismissed from Daimler-Benz under Allied Control Council legislation and worked for the Schnürle engineering consultancy. Scherenberg's responsibilities with this firm included the small-car manufacturer Gutbrod and the development of 2-stroke engines. In 1948

. . . and overall winner of the 1924 Alpine run in a Benz 16/50 sports car.

Scherenberg joined Gutbrod as technical director, taking with him his assistant of many years' standing, Karlheinz Göschel, who had become a specialist in fuel injection. With Göschel, Scherenberg designed the injection system for the Gutbrod-Superior in conjunction with Bosch. In 1951 the first fuel-injected private cars were produced.

Nallinger in the 1960s.

Nallinger behind a cannon on the ramparts of the Palace in Monaco in 1955: who is he aiming at?

The big four: Uhlenhaut, Nallinger, Scherenberg and Kraus.

In 1952 Scherenberg rejoined Daimler-Benz, his contract containing a clause stating that he was to concentrate on the introduction of fuel injection on Mercedes-Benz vehicles. Karlheinz Göschel followed him to Untertürkheim and later also worked on the W 196. His injection system on the last of the Silver Arrows was to cause the opposition some headaches in future. After Rudolf Uhlenhaut left in 1972, Göschel succeeded him as chief of research.

In December 1955 (after the company had withdrawn from the sporting arena) Scherenberg was appointed a deputy member of the Board of Daimler-Benz, and ten years later took over the seat vacated by Fritz Nallinger as development representative. He was responsible for development and styling of the new S-Class (280 S up to 450 SEL), developed the 3.5-, 4.5- and 6.9-litre 8-cylinders, worked on experimental safety cars and collaborated closely with Rudolf Uhlenhaut on the C 111. Scherenberg retired in 1977, but even today visits his office at Untertürkheim several times a week. His

Professor Dr Hans Scherenberg today.

advice and critical faculties are as much in demand as ever.

Scherenberg's special contribution was the establishment of a *Rechnungsabteilung,* a staff to do the calculations, and the setting up of test facilities. At the beginning of the 1950s he saw the possibility of calculating the demands that were likely to be put on engines before they were built. Characteristics of a

54

variety of engine concepts for the W 196 (12-, 6- and 8-cylinder) were set out in advance by the *Rechnungsabteilung* under Karl Wilhelm Müller, Dr Kurt Enke and Dr Otto Lang. On the basis of their results, the designers went for a straight-eight with central power take-off.

This staff also produced precise circuit diagrams for each track on which the W 196 was to race. This allowed correct choice of gear ratios while the car was still under preparation in the workshop. Drivers received an exact picture of the circuit and the data was so accurate that on certain tracks, it deviated only one or two per cent from true road speeds and engine speeds (with the exception of Reims in 1954).

In the racing workshop the engineer Walter Kosteletzky supervised the building of the cars to the drawings and saw that they underwent thorough overhaul in between races, ensuring that all new features were incorporated as soon as possible. The sheet metal specialist was Walter Schüller, Hans Meyer was responsible for test facilities and Hans Michalski for the running of them. Trouble-free servicing was also ensured by Wolfgang Faber and Julius Gassmann, who kept precisely to deadlines for engine and chassis modifications.

The design department naturally had many members who had a hand in the W 196. Ludwig Kraus should be mentioned here as one who did a great deal of work on the engine, and so should Hans Gassmann, who had the inspired idea of the desmodromic valve system. Manfred Lorscheid and Josef Gnambs also worked alongside Kraus and Gassmann. Ludwig Kraus lives in Munich; Manfred Lorscheid died in 1985.

The great organizer and team manager Alfred Neubauer has his own chapter but while referring to him mention should be made of his assistants Alexander von Korff and the pre-war driver Hans Geier, who both worked as timekeepers (a valuable service also provided by Karl Kling's wife), and Neubauer's two secretaries Gertrud Heinze and Erna Reclam.

It would not be possible to mention every mechanic by name here; as already pointed out, they are listed at the back of the book. One thing is certain: without the diligent efforts of the "Boys in Blue" the W 196 would not have been such a sight as it was on the racetracks of the world. Even a Fangio would have been unable to win two World titles for Mercedes without them. And every driver who was honoured enough to drive the car could rely totally on the machinery at his disposal.

Only one mechanic will be singled out here: Hermann Eger, Fangio's personal mechanic. This small energetic man always ensured a good atmosphere. He stayed with the team from start to finish and knew "his" cars back to front. His greatest feat was co-driving with Hans Herrmann in the 300 SLR in the 1955 Mille Miglia. If it had not been for the unfortunate episode with the lost fuel cap, victory would probably have gone to Herrmann/Eger instead of Moss/Jenkinson. Eger at all events showed his stamina. During practice the speed and many curves forced him to request Herrmann to make frequent stops to give him an opportunity to discharge the contents of his stomach. In the race itself he held out manfully without a single break. Hermann Eger died in the summer of 1985.

It is a sad fact that in the 30 years that have passed since the W 196 last took to the track in anger, the number surviving of those who were actively involved has fallen steadily. Most have retired, many have died and the number who witnessed those days has grown ever fewer.

The Fat Man

Alfred Neubauer, 1891-1980

He was much more than a race manager. He was an institution. His voice boomed like thunder, his criticism was feared, his talent for organization proverbial and his appearance theatrical. He was a colourful character, known affectionately around the racetracks of the world as "The Fat Man", an epithet earned for him by his monumental physical build. He personally contributed much to the myth and legend surrounding the great years of the Daimler-Benz Silver Arrows. For many, Alfred Neubauer was the Daimler Racing Division personified, the human expression of a perfectly organized racing apparatus.

Neubauer was born on 29th March 1891 in Neutitschein (or Nový Jičîn, today part of Czechoslovakia). He was technically minded from an early age, and as a child he would issue racing forecasts from the entry lists of all the big races which appeared in the papers. "But in those days they didn't obey my instructions," he would quip.

After his basic education he moved to college because he aimed to join the Cadet College at Traiskirchen. During service in the Austrian Imperial Army, however, it soon became clear that Neubauer, who with his looks must have been quite a hit with the ladies at the time, was not really suited to a serious military career. When asked, "What should you do on first taking up a new position with your battery?" he replied in his straightforward manner, "Take cover."

A further event highlights his state of mind, which was as receptive to technical matters as it was unsuited to military necessities. On manoeuvres Neubauer, by now a lieutenant, was instructed to fetch new orders from his commander on horseback as a matter of urgency. After a few kilometres the fresh-faced lieutenant stumbled on an abandoned artillery tractor. After a brief inspection Neubauer diagnosed a faulty clutch and very soon, up to his elbows in grease, he was underneath the vehicle. By evening, after several hours' concentrated work, the tractor was fixed and Neubauer set off on his way a happy man – not to his commander who was waiting in a rage for his appearance, but back to the men of his battery who had been awaiting their lieutenant's return all day.

This deviation from such basic principles of military discipline as orders and obedience had its consequences of course. Neubauer was severely reprimanded by his colonel (though escaping lightly). At the same time, however, his superiors remained mindful of his technical abilities. When a short while later officers were being sought for the Austrian army's motorized artillery, Neubauer was among those chosen to undergo training at Austro-Daimler in the operation and servicing of the new equipment. When at Austro-Daimler, Neubauer met for the first time the engineer Ferdinand Porsche, who had designed the tractors for the heavy mortars.

During World War I Neubauer was in charge of the motor pools of two mortar batteries and later, at Austro-Daimler, was responsible for the transfer of new equipment to the front. With the war over and lost, Neubauer remained at the firm, keeping in close touch with Ferdinand Porsche. Shortly after that, Porsche was engaged by Count Alexander Kolowrat to develop a small car with 1.1-litre engine, christened the Sascha. A racing model of the Sascha was tried out on the 1922 Targa Florio with Alfred Neubauer at the wheel. They were a great success, coming home in second place behind the Mercedes of Count Masetti (one of the three winning French Grand Prix cars from 1914).

Neubauer at the wheel of his 2-litre 1924 Targa Florio car.

Around this time, Paul Daimler split with his father's firm in Untertürkheim. Ferdinand Porsche succeeded him and brought Neubauer along in his retinue. Porsche's hobbyhorse at the time was super-charging, a technique perfected by Paul Daimler. Porsche could see the opportunities that supercharging would open to racing cars and went into action. In the 1924 Targa Florio, the super-charged Mercedes gave an impressive display of technical superiority. Christian Werner, that Titan among racing drivers reputed to be able to lift oak tables with an outstretched arm, was the victor in this race, Neubauer coming home third, as though in confirmation.

But in 1926, the year when Daimler of Untertürkheim and Benz of Mannheim merged into Daimler-Benz AG, Neubauer hung up his driving gloves and devoted his efforts to race management.

Neubauer's golden age came in 1934, when Daimler-Benz and Auto-Union combined to carry the German flag into battle against their foreign Grand Prix rivals. Now at last Neubauer could work just as it suited him. In the most thorough detail, he planned and organized preparation, transport and the races themselves.

In 1934 Neubauer even "invented" the Silver Arrow. The white-painted Mercedes cars built to the 750 Kilogram Formula were weighed before practice for the Eifelrennen and proved to be 1 kg overweight. As everyone racked their brains for an answer, Neubauer arrived at the inspired solution of removing the paint from the cars. This done, the gleaming metallic racers were just within the weight limit. The Silver Arrow was born!

Neubauer was Rudolf Caracciola's greatest fan. He discovered him, and during the era of the Mercedes SS and SSK cars the relationship that grew up between them was almost one of father and son. In years to come, this would lead to all sorts of difficulties within the Mercedes team, with its line-up that included Hermann Lang, Manfred von Brauchitsch, Dick Seaman and Luigi Fagioli, men who were usually hardly any slower than Caracciola and often even faster. Anyone who wanted to beat him would have to disregard Neubauer's orchestration of the event, and that was not to be recommended.

The respect of the gentleman racing driver for his manager before World War II is best illustrated by an episode at the 1938 German Grand Prix held at

The Mercedes racing manager in the 1930s.

the Nürburgring (it also highlights the relaxed British sense of humour). At this race, Manfred von Brauchitsch was leading from Richard (Dick) Seaman. When von Brauchitsch pitted to change tyres and refuel, Seaman followed him in with the same procedure in mind. Neubauer had kept a close eye on Seaman's rapid progress, but on this occasion wanted von Brauchitsch to win and therefore ordered the speedy Briton to hold station behind his team mate.

But suddenly fire broke out in the German's car, a particularly nasty situation because the flames from the special fuel were practically invisible. Neubauer acted quickly to haul von Brauchitsch out of the car and extinguishers were rapidly brought to bear, blanketing it in foam. Then Neubauer almost had a heart attack: Seaman, whose car had long been ready to rejoin the race, was standing calmly by his

Neubauer with his favourite driver, Rudolf Caracciola.

pit. Neubauer immediately ran over and asked him what was up. Seaman merely replied that he, Neubauer, had after all forbidden him to overtake von Brauchitsch, who was now at a standstill in front of him. Neubauer could hardly believe his ears. He tried all his powers of persuasion on Seaman and eventually managed to talk him back into the fray. Seaman took the chequered flag for Mercedes. And he showed Neubauer, the anti-militarist, that even his instructions should not always be interpreted to the letter.

One driver even left Mercedes in a dispute over Neubauer's behaviour. The Italian Luigi Fagioli felt particularly disadvantaged with respect to Caracciola and when instructed to let the German win in one race, even though it was quite obvious – to the spectators too – that Fagioli was the faster of the two, the fuming Italian brought his car into the pits and walked away, not only leaving the track but the team as well. The dazed Neubauer is said to have stood around for a while clutching his "Hold position" board.

Neubauer's real gift was the tactical planning of a Grand Prix. Because they were run over several hundred kilometres, the cars had to make planned stops to refuel. Correct timing of stops often decided a race. Neubauer would also take tyre wear into account in determining whether a slower pace would conserve them to the point where a stop for new ones could be avoided and time saved. His advance planning often gave Mercedes a tactical advantage over the opposition.

World War II then interrupted international racing. Fighting raged in North Africa and France and on the Eastern Front. With the war lost, everybody's primary concerns lay elsewhere than in racing. Alfred Neubauer's too: on 15th November 1946 he was dismissed from Daimler-Benz without notice.

This is a little-known aspect of Neubauer's career, probably because the dismissal was reversed a few days later, reducing the whole affair to a minor incident. No matter, on 14th November Neubauer was summoned by the Military Government of the American Occupying Power to Room 404, Olgastrasse 24, in Stuttgart.

He was supposed to bring a large questionnaire with him. As was his wont, he arrived late, and without the questionnaire. By some devious channel, the Commissioner had got wind that Neubauer had criticized the treatment of German prisoners of war in American camps. Besides this, it was said that he had stated that the Daimler management had

Neubauer at his favourite occupation (apart from eating): giving pit signals.

60

appointed Nazis. These claims must naturally have made a bad impression on the Americans.

A member of the personnel department had done the dirty – the company's image had to be unsullied and no exception could be made for Neubauer. But he had reckoned without the man himself. Three days after his dismissal Neubauer arrived armed for the decisive battle. In a nine-page argument the former race manager denied all claims against him, and exploited the opportunity to list in detail his humane record during the course of World War II. Between 1944 and 1945 Neubauer had worked on Daimler-Benz's Special Commission for Vehicle Repair in Vienna, and whenever the young staff

were called up for service in the Waffen SS or the Organisation Todt, he protected them by saying that they were indispensable, and that without them satisfactory repair of vehicles could not be continued.

After Neubauer had been heard out there was mention of his 23 years with Daimler-Benz. A man with the cunning of Neubauer would not miss an opportunity like this. "In keeping with Mercedes-Benz company policy, I also had a hand in employing famous international drivers from Britain, France, Switzerland and Italy. The highest national sporting authorities and also German racing drivers often called for my removal. Under

Even the most hardworking must take a rest sometimes.

62

Neubauer with his drivers at Monza in 1954. Left to right: Lang, Neubauer, Fangio, Kling and Herrmann.

my direction, Seaman the Englishman won the German Grand Prix in the war year 1938.'' How lucky that von Brauchitsch had been foiled by the fire that year and his team mate had gone on to win! Neubauer's usual infallible accuracy had not totally deserted him when he described 1938 as a war year, either. But that was his way: certain tricks were permissible when they served a higher purpose.

The Fat Man was in any case soon fully rehabilitated, even though he was able to maintain no more than a shadowy presence in the offices at Untertürkheim until 1950. But after that, it was plain sailing. First, in 1951, there was the Argentinian Expedition (as Neubauer called the foreign sorties with the racing department) and in the following year, long-distance racing with the Mercedes 300 SL coupés.

In a cover story devoted to Neubauer in 1954 the magazine *Der Spiegel* wrote, ''At this time, the Neubauer machine was unleashed and ran at peak

Meeting General Perón in Buenos Aires in January 1955.

revs, even though a short while before he had loitered like a sort of mythical museum piece somewhere on the second floor of the administration block."

And the magazine continued, "Then one day they dusted off their race manager and installed him in a two-roomed suite. Daimler-Benz had decided to build a new Grand Prix car, despite the ban on supercharging: 2.5-litre normally aspirated, according to the new rules."

Neubauer's talent for organization was able to blossom once more, especially in the 1955 season when Mercedes graced sports car racing with the 300 SLR as well as Grand Prix events. But he felt more restricted than in pre-war days. Pit stops, at least for refuelling, had become almost superfluous.

The new cars did not use so much as their predecessors, and even the tyres could withstand 500 km of torture. Neubauer's "prime" function, therefore, was as an orchestrator, deploying mechanics, booking hotels, agreeing timetables for practice and racing with the department, and similar tasks. But of course, Neubauer could still be seen as of old, sitting or standing in the Mercedes pit, showing off his mighty stomach. And he would still have his two famous stopwatches dangling at his chest, though even then, many of the team knew perfectly well that he was unable to operate them correctly. The role of timekeeper was played far better by Karl Kling's wife than by the corpulent racing manager.

Race engineer Uhlenhaut had been in charge in

Suffering in the heat at the British Grand Prix in 1955.

the pits for some time now. All matters concerning the cars or tactical lap times agreed before the race were down to him. Uhlenhaut and Neubauer complemented one another perfectly – and Uhlenhaut would often play a mediating role when the ship hit stormy weather.

Just before the Mille Miglia in 1955 there was one such occurrence. Hans Herrmann, who was fond of overdoing things a bit and liked to stay out late, once again returned to the hotel after the time stipulated by Neubauer. The manager knew the youngster well enough and for this reason (probably thinking he could keep control of his escapades better) preferred to have his room next door to Herrmann's; but this time things had gone too far. When Herrmann had still not returned by midnight, the manager ordered the hotelier to wait up personally for Herrmann's return and then wake him up.

When Herrmann finally returned at about two

a.m. he could hardly believe his eyes: the hotelier was playing porter, and at that time of the morning. After being told what was afoot, he still did not take things seriously, "I crept upstairs into my room, and got undressed. Suddenly the door burst open and Neubauer stood there in the middle of the room in a vast nightshirt covering his belly, took a deep breath and then screamed blue murder for about five minutes."

"You have endangered the expedition," bellowed Neubauer, "You'll be out of the team on your ear." And anyone who had remained asleep through all this drama was woken personally by Neubauer. The hotel was like a madhouse. Doors slammed, men shouted, Neubauer played Rumpelstiltskin, and Herrmann had no idea whether to laugh or cry. Eventually Uhlenhaut calmed things down, telling Neubauer he was right and giving Herrmann a talking to, and then the matter was laid to rest.

Everyone who knew him realized that in Neubauer, the world had lost a great actor. In his company, things were never dull, whether he was telling dirty stories, undeterred by female company, or reading with pleasure from the menu: Neubauer was a true one-off, his character a mixture of steamroller and mother hen.

When Mercedes decided to withdraw from racing, the news reached Neubauer during the Targa Florio

Neubauer was always at his most boisterous in female company.

66

when the team secured the World Sports Car Championship. At 64 years old, Neubauer was naturally less than ecstatic. By the time the official farewell party had come around though, he had regained his sense of humour. From a trouser pocket he hauled out a giant handkerchief and poured out floods of crocodile tears.

Three years later, Neubauer took well-earned retirement, though he remained active at Daimler-Benz for a few years more. He was to write the history of Mercedes racing exploits, which remained unfinished. Practically every week he would receive visitors from all over the world, all of whom wanted first-hand accounts of the great days of the Silver Arrows; few of them went away disappointed. Neubauer died in his 90th year on the night of 21st August 1980.

Among his papers there was a poem characteristically entitled *Das Leben – ein Rennen* ('Life – a Race'). A poem (loosely translated) to close this chapter on the most famous racing manager ever:

Life's a race no doubt about it,
If you make a flying start,
Get the gearbox working smoothly,
You'll be quickly off the mark!

Flat out straights and hairpin corners,
Right turn, left turn, slow – now fast,
So you fly, a champion driver,
Round the Nürburgring of life.

Never mind if brakes are failing,
Never mind the worn out shocks,
Many men have tasted victory,
When the needle's off the clock.

Keep your eyes fixed on the finish,
Let this be your only aim,
Man, it's just as good as winning,
When you've been round sixty times.

Alfred Neubauer

THE DRIVERS

The Maestro

Juan Manuel Fangio, born 1911

Whenever racing enthusiasts, be they professionals or fans, dispute various drivers' claims to greatness in the 40 years of the World Championship of Drivers, there is one name that is accepted without argument: Juan Manuel Fangio. He is usually placed first, more highly rated even than the aces of more recent history, such as Clark, Moss, Stewart, Lauda, Piquet and Prost. For many, Fangio is still the greatest even today.

Between 1951 and 1957 the Argentinian was World Champion five times, driving for Alfa Romeo, Mercedes-Benz, Ferrari and Maserati. Fangio won 25 Grands Prix, and drove for a number of manufacturers in sports car racing – although, especially towards the end of his career, he was no longer too keen on such events.

Fangio's father Loretto was an Italian by birth. Around the turn of the century the Fangio family left the small town of Castiglione in the Abruzzi and emigrated to Argentina to make a new start. On 24th June 1911, the feast of San Juan, Juan Manuel was born, the fourth child of six. According to his mother Erminia, Juan was a frail child, but was quick to learn at school. Because of his particular interest in things technical, his teacher tried to secure him a scholarship to study at Technical College in Buenos Aires. Juan, however, preferred life in the provincial town of Balcarce where the locals supported themselves almost exclusively on potato farming.

In that town of 40,000 there was a repair shop that refurbished American Fords and Chevrolets. As a 12-year-old, Juan learned a little about cars from the foreman, Capetini. When Capetini left Balcarce, Juan's father got his son a job in the workshop owned by Señor Viggiano. Quite soon, Fangio junior was a skilled mechanic who was so obsessed with the subject that he tinkered with engines in a shed on his parents' land – not only did he want to repair them, he also wanted to know what made them tick.

At 18 he suffered severe inflammation of the lungs and was confined to bed for two months in the care of his mother. Three years later he was called up for national service, joining the cadet school at Campo de Mayo near Buenos Aires. His technical gifts soon paid off as he became the commanding officer's driver. As anyone who was ever in the armed services knows, that is hardly the most strenuous of jobs.

Shortly after finishing his service, Fangio set up his own workshop back in Balcarce and soon took part in his first race. The similarities with European style motor racing were slight, but competition was as fierce as could be. The strange vehicles lining up for the start on the dusty Argentinian pampas were ancient American cars stripped to bare essentials, but with engines robust enough to withstand the torture. Fangio usually had the best machinery.

Soon he realized that the old Ford chassis that

had been thrashed for so long would be no good for serious events in future, so he built his own 2-seater. Two years passed before the Ford-powered "Fangio Special" was ready for action. In his first race Fangio came in third – the winner was the famous Carlos Arzani in a 3.8-litre Alfa Romeo, though Fangio had outdragged him at the start and led the race for a short time.

Further success soon came Fangio's way and he became a renowned figure in Balcarce, where collections were even taken up to enable him to buy a new Chevrolet to contest the murderous Gran Premio Internacional del Norte. The event covered a 10,000 km route throughout the South American continent, from Buenos Aires to Lima and back. In order to win, a driver had to be absolute master of his machinery – and also be able to push himself to the limit of endurance.

Fangio had the necessary toughness. Of all participants, he alone aimed to drive solo; all other cars carried a pair of drivers who would share the workload. At the halfway mark in Lima Fangio was leading in his 1940 Chevrolet. His photo made the front pages of the dailies and he was famous all over South America, the people rooting for him all the way.

After a total of over 109 hours at the wheel, Fangio crossed the finish line in Buenos Aires with the rest of the field in his wake. He was made a freeman of Balcarce. In Europe, World War II was being fought and its effects spread even as far as Argentina. Because South America was a supplier of raw materials, especially rubber, industry there was running at full blast. For the time being, Argentinian motor clubs were unable to stage race meetings and Fangio's career, which had only just begun, was interrupted.

Argentina also saw change on the political landscape at the end of the war in Europe and the Far East, when General Perón came to power. He was a great sports fan and motor racing was his special interest, a fact that was to have a decisive effect on Fangio's fortunes. With state assistance, the Argentine Automobile Club set up its own racing stable, bringing in a number of European cars, true single-seaters like the 1.5-litre supercharged Maserati 4CLT and the nimble Simca-Gordini.

This was the car driven by Fangio at Rosario in 1948. Also on the grid were the European aces

Jean-Pierre Wimille, Giuseppe Farina, Achille Varzi and Luigi Villoresi. In the early stages a ferocious struggle developed between the two Simca-Gordini drivers – Wimille, in the eyes of many the world's finest, and Fangio. But just as the newcomer seemed set to deliver the death blow, his car packed up. Even so, Fangio in his first single-seater race had shown that he could compete on equal terms with the world's élite.

In the summer of 1948 the South American arrived in Europe for the first time and, in the Gordini, contested a race at Reims that was the curtain raiser to the French Grand Prix. Here, too, his machinery failed him. On his return to Argentina he took part in a long-distance event from Buenos Aires to Caracas in a Chevrolet and it was during this race that he had his first serious accident. He went off the road on a curve and the car rolled over. Fangio was rescued without serious injury, but it was too late to save his co-driver. It was Fangio's first personal experience of the darker side of motor sport. Throughout the winter, he wrestled with the agony of self-doubt. The time had come to decide whether to give up motor racing or continue regardless.

By the time of the first big event of 1949 in Argentina, Juan Manuel Fangio was on the grid again: motor racing was too much in his blood. The European stars had made the journey to Palermo Park in Buenos Aires to measure themselves against the South Americans again. Wimille, Villoresi and Farina were there and so was a new face, the young Italian Alberto Ascari who, like Fangio, was driving the Maserati 4CLT. The race was overshadowed by the death of Wimille. In final practice he rolled his blue Gordini several times and died of serious internal injuries. France's greatest driver was no more.

Ascari took the winner's laurels and Fangio was fourth. It was the first time that these two extraordinary drivers met on the track: in future their duels would transfix crowds all over the world.

On 27th February 1949 Fangio scored his first win over the Europeans who were stricken with mechanical problems. As a result of this success the Argentine Automobile Club decided to send Fangio and Benedicto Campos to Europe that spring. In their Maseratis they were to fly the Argentine flag at European events.

Fangio got straight down to business. He won on

Fangio with Karl Kling.

his second appearance in Europe at the San Remo Grand Prix on the Ospedaletti circuit. In second place was Prince Birabongse of Siam, followed by "Toulo" de Graffenried. Fangio won again at Pau and at Roussillon, but these were small events of lesser importance. Fangio was pleased at his success but wanted to take on the European stars in a Grand Prix. The place was Spa-Francorchamps, the event the Belgian Grand Prix, but not before Fangio had won at Marseille in the 90PS Simca-Gordini against the 4.5-litre Lago-Talbot of Etancelin, with more than twice the power, and Nuvolari in a Maserati.

Then came the race that Fangio had waited for on the super-fast Spa circuit in the Ardennes. His chief rival was Dr Farina, who also drove a 1.5-litre

Maserati, but the scrap lasted less than a lap: Fangio was forced to retire with a damaged piston.

In the Monza Grand Prix, run to Formula 2 regulations, Fangio was victorious again. The first two laps were led by Hans Stuck driving the silver AFM (Alex von Falkenhausen, Munich), but thereafter Fangio, Ascari and Felice Bonetto fought it out. Fangio won again at Albi ahead of Prince Bira, but in national Grands Prix he was out of luck. Back home, however, he received a great fanfare on his return after the European campaign.

In 1950 the Drivers' World Championship was held for the first time. Supercharged engines up to 1.5 litres and normally aspirated engines up to 4.5 litres were allowed. The Alfa Romeo company, which had developed its pre-war Type 158 (a straight-eight now producing 334PS) was planning to compete for the title, held over six European rounds and the Indianapolis 500. Race chief at Alfa, Giovanni Battista Guidotti, who had won the 1930 Mille Miglia in record time with Tazio Nuvolari, chose Farina, Fangio and Fagioli (who had driven for Mercedes on a few occasions before the war): the three "Fs".

At San Remo, Fangio won his first race with the Alfetta, as Alfa Romeo's Formula 1 car was known. The Italians carried him shoulder high. In the Mille Miglia, the renowned sports car race, Fangio took fourth place with a 2.5-litre Alfa. Ahead of him were drivers who were all far better acquainted with the route than he.

In the British Grand Prix at Silverstone, Fangio's race ended in retirement, but in Monaco he received the trophy from Prince Rainier. In Switzerland he retired again, but he won at Spa. Victory and defeat came turn and turn about. At Reims he broke his sequence, winning twice in a row for the first time. Because his closest rival Farina could manage only seventh place, Fangio overtook him in the title race. After two more victories, neither of them World Championship rounds, Monza was the scene of the shoot-out, in the Italian Grand Prix. The Championship was settled in favour of Farina, who won the race. Fangio had to retire when first his car, and then that of Bonetto which he had taken over, went out with engine failures. Fangio's runner-up position in the Championship was in any case a great achievement.

For the following season, 1951, Ferrari had produced a new engine. With his engineer Aurelio Lampredi, Enzo Ferrari had built a 4.5-litre 12-cylinder. Ferrari made life difficult for the Alfettas that had grown so accustomed to success. Whereas 1950 was the year of rivalry between fellow Alfa drivers, the main battle in 1951 was between Ferrari and Alfa.

But before the World Championship got under way, two races were held in Buenos Aires in Argentina. On the grid were three Mercedes. Three of the pre-war supercharged Type 154s had been sent and Neubauer had engaged Fangio and the two Germans, Hermann Lang and Karl Kling, to do the driving. But the Mercedes were not up to it. Both races were won by Fangio's fellow Argentinian, Froilan Gonzalez, known as "Puma" because of his gait and his diminutive stature. Fangio came third in the first race and retired in the second. He felt that he was himself to blame in some measure: when a few months earlier he had been asked to lay out the course to his liking, he had assumed that he would be driving one of the agile, lightweight Ferraris, the same car that Gonzalez finally drove. The Mercedes by contrast were too cumbersome for the twisty course. Nevertheless, the first contact with the Germans had been made.

In 1951 Fangio was World Champion for the first time. He had used all his powers to beat the Ferraris. Even so, time had run out for the supercharged Alfas. At the end of that successful season, Alfa withdrew from Formula 1, dealing the category a death blow. Come 1952, the Ferraris were the only cars with a chance of winning and so most organizers were wary of financial failure should spectator interest be dulled by the prospect of a tedious series of races. In 1952, nearly all organizers therefore ran their events for the smaller Formula 2 cars. Thus the almighty Ferraris themselves were out of the race.

In Formula 2, where 2-litre unsupercharged engines were eligible, opposition to Ferrari came from a wide variety of stables: Maserati, OSCA, Connaught, HWM, Alta, Veritas Meteor, AFM. Fangio's choice for the World Championship rounds was a Maserati, and for those races that were still run under Formula 1 regulations (above all in France and Britain) he would drive the 1.5-litre BRM. This British design featured a supercharged 16-cylinder engine whose most notable characteristic was the shattering scream it produced.

After testing with the BRM, Fangio drove overnight to Monza to race the Maserati. Fangio was not fully race fit after the long journey and, going into the Lesmo curve for the first time, his car careered off the track. He was fortunate that he only broke a bone in his neck in this accident, which could easily have cost him his life. With his neck encased in plaster, the World Champion's season was over.

Practically a whole year passed before Fangio next took part in a European event. In the Mille Miglia, he drove the Alfa Romeo *Disco Volante*, "The Flying Saucer", so called because of its unusual shape. At halfway-house in Rome, Fangio's team mate Karl Kling was in the lead but retired shortly afterwards. Fangio seemed to be set for

Fangio with Stirling Moss after their one-two in the Eifelrennen in 1955.

victory but then a trackrod broke, leaving the left front wheel virtually uncontrollable. Wherever the Alfa showed up the thousands of spectators could hardly bear to watch. They had seen virtually everything in that crazy race, but even this was new to them. Fangio crossed the line in Brescia having held on to second place, the last remaining Alfa driver in the race.

His injury sustained the year before and the months spent in the plaster cast still caused Fangio some discomfort. His movements were stiff and he had to turn the whole of his body if he wanted to look round. Still, he took advantage of every chance to race, driving both Maserati and Gordini. By the time the Grand Prix season came around, he was almost back to his old form.

By this time, however, the Ferrari Formula 2 cars were also vastly superior to their rivals. Ascari, Farina, Gonzalez and Hawthorn divided the spoils, and Fangio could only take points-scoring positions behind the scarlet racers from Maranello. Only at Monza, where the Ferraris are so often on form, did Fangio gain the upper hand in an extraordinary tussle with Farina, Ascari and Marimon. The race was only decided on the last corner of the last lap.

At the end of 1953 Fangio won the Carrera Panamericana Mexico in a Lancia, but victory was far from sweet for the Lancia team: Felice Bonetto was killed while in a dominant leading position. Wanting to go even faster on the dangerous road, he hit a gully which sent the Lancia sports car out of control, killing him instantly.

Although Maserati knew that Fangio would be driving the new Mercedes Grand Prix car as soon as it was ready, the team from Bologna put a works car at his disposal for the first two races of the 1954 season. The new Formula 1 was now in force, allowing engines with a maximum 2.5-litre capacity unsupercharged (or 750cc supercharged). Accepting Maserati's generous offer gratefully, he took maximum points with the 250F in Argentina and also at Spa. Thus Fangio already had a healthy points advantage when he moved to Stuttgart.

The following year and a half was a story of the absolute dominance of a single driver and a single car. The W 196 from Daimler-Benz and Juan Manuel Fangio formed an invincible union. Of the twelve Grands Prix that Fangio contested as a Mercedes driver in 1954 and 1955, he won eight. Both years he was undisputed World Champion. Neubauer, his manager, said of him: "Fangio knew how to use his car "economically". That is to say, he would not just set about the opposition regardless and view a Grand Prix as a simple matter of driving. Rather he had the ability to develop an understanding of tactics, the capabilities of his machine and his driving skills, and to adapt this whole to the requirements of a given moment."

In both years he saw dreadful accidents. In practice for the Grand Prix of Europe in 1954 at the Nürburgring, his young friend Onofre Marimon was killed, the man whose father he had competed against in his first long-distance event. In May his great rival Alberto Ascari was killed in testing at Monza, and he was on the spot at Le Mans when the worst accident in motor racing history occurred. More and more, thoughts turned to a point in the near future when he would hang up his helmet for good. Fangio – "el Chueco" – had signed for Enzo Ferrari for 1956 and that year drove the Lancia

D 50, which had often been a match for the Mercedes W 196 in the past two years because of its roadholding characteristics. In the aftermath of the death of his great driver Ascari, Dr Gianni Lancia pulled out of racing and, with state support, Ferrari had taken over the complete race department and improved the cars. Fangio took his fourth World title in this car, driving it to victories in Argentina, Britain and Germany. But life at Ferrari was not to his liking, with team squabbles often upsetting his concentration. In 1957 he returned to Maserati to drive the 250F.

He scored four victories at the wheel of this superb racing car and his final Grand Prix triumph was also his greatest. The 46-year-old Argentinian drove the race of his life at the German Grand Prix at the Nürburgring. Because the Maserati's fuel consumption was higher than its opponents, Fangio had to stop to refuel. The Ferrari drivers Hawthorn and Collins took advantage of the stop, which cost him almost a minute, and hurtled on towards the chequered flag. The final act of this drama is one of the greatest in the history of motor racing. Fangio carved second after second from the old lap record as he chased the two cars from Maranello, themselves lapping well under the previous year's mark.

Within six laps Fangio had made up the deficit and posted fastest lap at an incredible 9 minutes 17.4 seconds, almost ten seconds faster than the old record. Two laps before the end he overtook Collins at the end of the home straight, and Hawthorn shortly afterwards. This victory, celebrated wildly by the fans, secured Fangio his fifth World Championship.

At Reims, scene of his first race on European soil almost a decade earlier, Juan Manuel Fangio drove his last Grand Prix in 1958. Maserati had brought the 250F with a new 12-cylinder engine to France. The car was too new to win in Fangio's hands and he had to be happy with fourth place. After the race he announced his irreversible decision to retire from motor racing, reinforced by the death of yet another driver, the young Italian, Luigi Musso.

Fangio was a critic of the progress being made and the ever-increasing speeds he was forced to drive at. He had nothing else to prove, either to himself or the world, and the death of so many of his fellow drivers had affected him deeply.

He continued to run his Mercedes dealership in Buenos Aires, a business that still belongs to him.

74

Now and again he would show up at Grands Prix, especially during the 1970s when his fellow Argentinian Carlos Reutemann was on the World Championship trail. Whenever he appears on the motor racing scene voices are hushed and all eyes turn to him. He remains a living symbol of the sport. Sometimes he even drives an Alfetta, his winning car from 1951, in the odd historic event: as at Laguna Seca in 1985, when he drove it so fast that he executed an elegant spin. The Yanks went crazy.

There is debate as to the actual number of heart attacks he has suffered, but whether three or five, Fangio is fine. On 24th June 1989 he celebrated his 78th birthday.

A racing driver's still life: Fangio's helmet and driving gloves alongside the handbag belonging to his wife, Andrea.

The Englishman

Stirling Moss, born 1929

"Sometimes I regret that I never asked for square wheels: I have a funny feeling they would have had a car fitted with them within 24 hours."

This quote is attributed to Stirling Moss, probably the fastest Grand Prix driver of the 1950s and early 1960s. By "they" he means the Mercedes team. It was an exemplary summing up of the relationship between management and driver and much better than any amount of description or explanation. For Moss, a new signing to Untertürkheim for the 1955 season, a dream had come true. And the way in which his wishes were fulfilled was something entirely new to him.

On his first outing in Argentina in February 1955 he told Rudolf Uhlenhaut, the team engineer, that the brake pedal pressure seemed too high. Uhlenhaut drove around Buenos Aires until, in a Chrysler repair shop, he found a vacuum servo that fitted the W 196. When Moss climbed aboard the next day, it had been installed. As the season progressed an *Ate*-brake servo became standard equipment on all W 196s.

Another similar example springs to mind: Moss told Uhlenhaut of his preference for a three-spoked steering wheel. By the time of the next test session the four-spoked wheel, fitted to all Mercedes since the 1930s, had been swapped for one that accorded with the English driver's wishes.

In his one season at Daimler-Benz, Moss reached full maturity as a driver; one reason may have been his position as team mate to Juan Manuel Fangio, at that time the world's best driver by a significant margin. In their race-long duels at Spa and Zandvoort in 1955 the young Briton (he was only 25 years old) finally came of age. In the two years of Mercedes Grand Prix involvement it was the dream of every driver to take the wheel of one of the Silver Arrows. Daimler-Benz could pick and choose: the company had three or four cars available for each race, guaranteeing (if that is possible in motor racing) a shot at the World title, and could choose from about 30 drivers. What, then, prompted Alfred Neubauer and Rudolf Uhlenhaut to go for Moss?

At 25, Moss (born on 17th September 1929) was already an incredibly accomplished racing driver. He could sit in any car and immediately go fast, even if the seating position was a shade out, the steering was slightly too heavy or the dampers fading a little. He spared no unnecessary thought for external factors and regarded it as his job to perform to the maximum in every car. Jochen Rindt and Ronnie Peterson were two drivers who were similar to Moss in this respect.

Provided you believe in the theory of such characteristics being inbred, then motor racing was in Stirling Moss's blood from the start. His father Alfred Moss, a dentist, went to the USA for a year to study, where he introduced himself to Louis Chevrolet with the (none too accurate) claim that he was one of Europe's best-known racing drivers. Immediately the New World proved its reputation as the land of opportunity: Moss was given a works drive at Indianapolis, survived the race and took a midfield position in the final classification, a noteworthy performance in the eyes of the Americans in this very specialized form of racing.

At the age of 15 Stirling announced that his career would follow his father's example – as racing driver rather than as dentist. He had already bought an Austin Seven which he had stripped of mudguards, doors and boot lid in order to go faster. His requirements soon outgrew the capabilities of the open 2-seater and after dalliance with an MG, he plumped for a BMW 328 – with the generous assistance of his father of course. With this car he competed in trials events. When his son showed signs of great ability, Alfred Moss decided to smooth his path to a career in motor racing.

The late 1940s was the golden age of a new category in British racing, for 500cc Formula 3 cars. As a nursery formula, the cars gave drivers the opportunity to gain single-seater experience for modest financial outlay. The cars, mainly built by Cooper and Kieft, were powered by Norton or JAP motorcycle engines.

After he had gained initial experience with the tiny racer in 1948, his father had a new engine installed in the Cooper chassis, a JAP V-twin of 1000cc capacity. With this new unit behind him, Stirling set a new record for unsupercharged cars at the Shelsley Walsh hillclimb. For the first time, he raised eyebrows among the professionals. That April he lined up for his first foreign race at Lake Garda, coming third behind Villoresi and Tadini, both of them driving 2-litre Ferraris . . .

His success soon brought results: in 1950 he got his first works contract, as team mate to Lance Macklin in the HWM team under the aegis of John Heath. The 2-litre Alta-powered Formula 2 cars also competed against Formula 1 cars, the Alfa Romeo Tipo 158/159, for instance. And in his HWM, Moss drove a masterly race over 320 kilometres to finish third at Bari behind Fangio and Farina (a driver he idolized for his calmness and composure at the wheel) in their Alfas, trailing them by only about two minutes: his car had less than half the power of the Alfas.

In 1952 Moss drove the ERA G-Type in Grands Prix in Belgium, Holland and Britain, but the car was unable to emulate the feats of its pre-war 1.5-litre supercharged brother. Moss also started two Grands Prix at the wheel of a Connaught, with no result. His next attempt at establishing a Grand Prix presence was with the Cooper-Alta, but again with this car Moss had to acknowledge that he had little chance against his Italian opponents, Ferrari and Maserati. Moss finally had to admit that patriotism (Hawthorn had become a works driver for Ferrari in 1953) would get him no further in racing.

His search for help led him to the door of Mercedes race manager, Alfred Neubauer, of whom he asked advice. At the end of 1953 Moss was probably already toying with the dream of being signed for the new Stuttgart works team. Neubauer advised the 24-year-old Moss to gain some more experience with a modern Formula 1 car.

That meant one thing and one thing only: Moss had to buy a Maserati 250F. The coffers were emptied to stump up the cash for the car from Modena, a small matter of 75,000 marks (by way of comparison, a Mercedes 190 SL cost 12,000 marks in 1955). At the rain-soaked British Grand Prix at Silverstone Moss showed his mettle in the green car. He held second place between the doughty Ferrari pair Gonzalez and Hawthorn, until nine laps before the end when his rear axle failed. He had led all the works Maseratis, however, and when Onofre Marimon was killed at the Nürburgring, Maserati signed up Moss and absorbed his private 250F into the

Stirling Moss before his first test session in the W 196 at Hockenheim at the end of 1954.

factory team.

At the Italian Grand Prix at Monza in September, Moss dominated proceedings. Driving for the works team his car was red this time, although its nose was painted British racing green at Moss's request. But again he retired and Fangio inherited victory in his Mercedes W 196.

Neubauer, however, had been watching his progress keenly. The Mercedes team manager knew that Moss should have won but for a cruel mechanical failure. Even Fangio had been powerless against Moss and from that point onwards, it was clear to Neubauer who would be bolstering his team's strength in 1955.

At the end of 1954 Moss drove the W 196 for the first time in testing at Hockenheim. After a few laps on a wet track he was faster than Karl Kling had been before. He was enthusiastic about the engine but in his opinion, the chassis would need some sorting before the start of the season. Great was the stir in Germany when he signed for Mercedes. Some newspapers carried reports of his salary for 1955, claiming 60,000 DM, a hefty sum for those days.

Although Moss deferred to Fangio's status as team No. 1 in Grands Prix, he showed that in the 300 SLR sports racer he could be quicker than the Argentinian. He won the Mille Miglia with Denis Jenkinson beside him "in the hot-seat" and also the Targa Florio with Peter Collins, the last race for this product of the Daimler-Benz stable. Like his team mates he was sad to see the exit of Mercedes from the sporting arena. Deep down he had counted on becoming World Champion in 1956 – in the Silver Arrow.

That was a title he would never take. In 1955 he came second to Fangio and in the years that followed he would fail time and again, just as Fangio had succeeded. In 1958, the year when Fangio announced his retirement and Moss at last had a chance, his fellow Briton Mike Hawthorn snatched the title in the last race of the season, the Moroccan

Grand Prix at Casablanca. The final position was Hawthorn 42 points, Moss 41.

In 1959, 1960 and 1961 in BRM, Cooper and Lotus cars (most of them entered by Rob Walker) he took third position every year. Besides this he drove some impressive sports car races. His victories in the Nürburgring 1000km events in the Aston Martin DBR1 and the Maserati "Birdcage" are among the great races of all time. He even won the odd race in the bulbous Formula 2 Porsche 718.

At Easter 1962, however, Stirling Moss's racing

Moss and Denis Jenkinson on their way to victory in the Mille Miglia in May 1955.

career came to an abrupt end. In a non-championship Formula 1 race at Goodwood, Moss went off the track in his Rob Walker Lotus and hit an embankment. He suffered eye injuries from his splintered goggles and also several fractured bones. When he climbed aboard a car for the first time some months later to see if he could still drive competitively, he came in after a few laps. His reflexes were not what they had been and Moss did the only correct thing in such a harrowing situation: he announced his retirement from active sport.

Today, Moss remains one of Britain's most popular sportsmen. He never misses an important race. In 1980 he was gripped by race fever again, and contested the British Saloon Car Championship in an Audi. The comeback did not meet with the approval of all his fans. They preferred to remember Moss as the driver who could beat anyone on any circuit at any time, and not as the also-ran in an amateur field.

Neubauer and Moss after the famous victory.

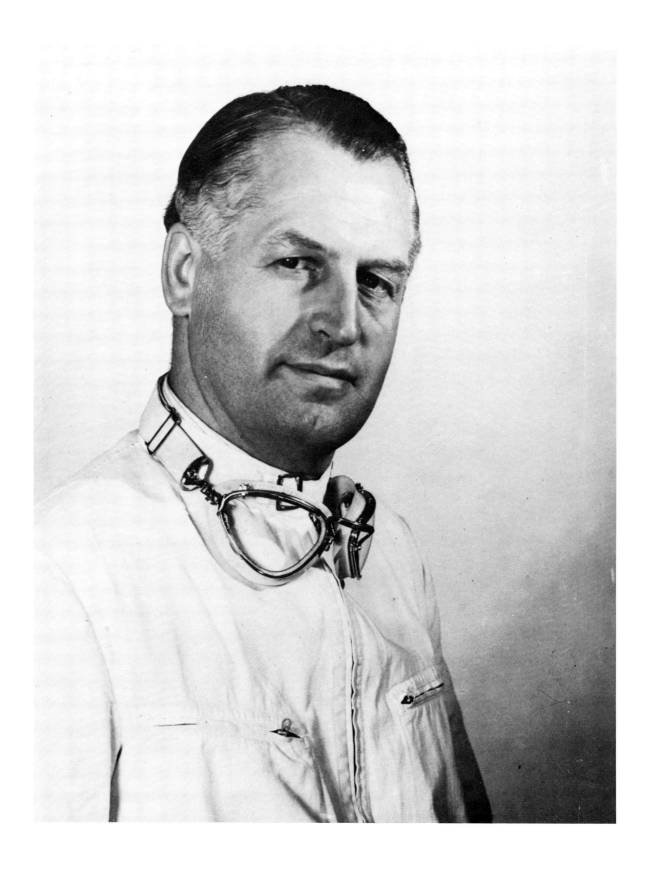

Karl The Unlucky

Karl Kling, born 1910

Kling was one of the first to know about the plans for Daimler-Benz to return to Grand Prix racing. He had been an employee of the company since 1936 and had scored some outstanding wins with the 300 SL; in 1952 he had even been voted Sportsman of the Year.

Karl Kling was a fixture when it came to Mercedes Grand Prix planning. He could bring his invaluable technical understanding to bear in testing; and when it came to racing, he showed that he ranked among the very best in the world during the 1950s. All he lacked was that final pinch of luck that would make him a true "great"; and besides that, he was often the one chosen to try out new features which would then let him down in the heat of battle. Kling was unfortunate in being too much of an engineer – Daimler-Benz always had Fangio, and later Moss, planned as race winners.

Karl Kling was born on 16th September 1910 in Giessen, a central German university town where,

during the 1980s, the all-too-short Grand Prix career of Stefan Bellof began.

Kling was interested in cars and motorcycles from an early age and served an apprenticeship with his local Mercedes-Benz dealership, Neils & Kraft. At that time he could be seen hurtling around the place on his motorcycles.

Among them was a 350 JAP-engined machine, which had a habit of dropping its valves. He also rode a Neander with pressed-steel frame and a Zündapp. Later he even progressed to an Imperia Ulster with a radial valve Rudge Python engine, and a two-stroke four (split) cylinder Puch. His enthusiasm was dampened, however, by the high cost of his passion and his trips to races on the Feldberg in the Taunus, or to the trials at Wartburg, became less and less frequent.

In 1936 Kling secured a job with Mercedes-Benz in Stuttgart as a customer service engineer. The sporting inclinations of the 26-year-old newcomer were soon noted and before long he was drafted into the Mercedes works team for the big trials held at the end of the 1930s. Those cross-country events were very similar to today's stage rallies. Names like the Rallye Polski, Internationale Winterfahrt, Ostpreussenfahrt and the trials in the Jura may be compared to events like the Thousand Lakes Rally, the Metz Winter Rally and the San Remo Rally of the modern era. Kling's mount on those events, lasting up to six days, would be either a 2-litre 4-cylinder or a 2.3-litre 6-cylinder car.

Numerous successes followed and so in the autumn of 1939 he was invited to a test session planned at Monza for the Mercedes Grand Prix cars to race in spring of the following year. The high-flown plans met a sudden end with the outbreak of World War II; and so it seemed had Karl Kling's Grand Prix career, before it had even begun.

After the war Kling worked on ex-Wehrmacht Mercedes at Untertürkheim. With his brother Hans, who had worked on engine research for Daimler-Benz since the mid-1930s, Kling put the first production line back into operation. His first postwar transport was a DKW 250 motorcycle and later he rebuilt a badly dilapidated BMW 328. He drove the BMW in the Bavaria-Rennen in Munich in 1946 and later also the Karlsruhe Dreieck-Rennen (Triangle Races), where he met Ernst Loof the former motorcycle ace. The meeting was to determine the course of the two men's lives for the next few years. Loof's dream was to build sports and racing cars in Germany, a country that was gradually undergoing reconstruction, and Kling was behind him both in word and deed: he started by procuring urgently needed materials like welding rods, hacksaw blades and tubing for the building of chassis.

When Loof had put together his first sports car he christened it the Veritas and the time had come for Kling to prove his talents as a racing driver. He passed the test in fine style and took the German Sports Car Championship in 1948 and 1949. Loof then built a Formula 2 car, the Meteor, but Kling's efforts with the single-seater were hampered by its lack of reliability and successes were few and far between. One such was on the twisty Solitude circuit near Stuttgart, and another was on the Grenzlandring where he won at an average speed of 203 km/h, the fastest race of the 1950 season

anywhere in Germany.

Kling was still employed at Daimler-Benz while driving for Veritas, using his year's holiday allowance for a prolonged session of work on the new car, the Meteor III with streamlined bodywork; his idealism would soon pay off.

Daimler-Benz race plans for 1951 included two races in Argentina and even the Indianapolis 500. The pre-war Type W 163 with their 3-litre supercharged engines were dusted off and put back into race trim; Alfred Neubauer nominated the local man Juan Manuel Fangio, the old hero Hermann Lang and Karl Kling as drivers. In Argentina the Mercedes proved to be rather long in the tooth, and were no match for Gonzalez's Ferrari. In his first single-seater race for Mercedes Kling had, however, taken sixth place and a week later, in the Premio Eva Maria Perón, he even took second place as best Mercedes driver. The immediate future held no prospect for him as a driver, however: after the Argentinian fiasco, the journey to Indianapolis was abandoned.

In the 1952 season Kling was nevertheless on the works driving strength in sports car racing with the newly developed 300 SL. In the famous Mille Miglia race he managed second place. The pre-war German racing idol Rudolf Caracciola, now aged 51, finished fourth in the 978 mile race. In 1931 he had been the first non-Italian to win the event.

A few weeks later Kling scored his first postwar victory for Mercedes. In the Bern Grand Prix at the Bremgarten circuit on the outskirts of the Swiss capital, Kling crossed the line first ahead of his team mates Hermann Lang and Fritz Riess. This race was Caracciola's last. To begin with he baulked his team mate Kling for lap after lap, and when Kling finally managed to muscle past him he tried to slipstream him. Two laps later Caracciola went off on a curve and was rushed to hospital with severe injuries.

These two races also paid off financially for Kling. Second place in the Mille Miglia earned precisely 10,654.10 DM (including 3200 DM start money from Daimler-Benz) and at the Bern event he netted 3700 DM – both sizeable amounts for the time.

In the classic Le Mans 24 Hours race he retired from first position, handing the prestigious victory to Lang, and at the Nürburgring he was also powerless against "Hermännle" (Little Hermann); his finest hour was yet to come.

After 18 hours 51 minutes and 19 seconds (to be

84

Kling with Fangio.

precise) on the afternoon of 23rd November 1952 he took the flag in Ciudad Juárez in the third Carrera Panamericana Mexico. "I really only won because I didn't take on new tyres at the service stops," remembers Kling, "I sorted through Lang's and Riess' used tyres, picked out the best and then carried on with no need to worry about the tread flying off like the others suffered."

This South American victory created quite a stir back home, with the result that on 20th December 1952 the German sporting press voted him Sportsman of the Year, several hundred votes ahead of the ice dancers Ria and Paul Falk from Düsseldorf and the young boxer, Edgar Basel.

When the official announcement of Daimler-Benz's return to Grand Prix racing was made in

Spring 1953, spelling the end of sports car racing activities, Alfa Romeo began its attempt to acquire Lang and Kling. Rodolfo Hruschka wrote to Alfred Neubauer on 26th March 1953, "I have been asked to inquire whether it might be possible – and more particularly whether you yourself would agree to this – for members of your team to drive other cars this year. Should your reply be positive, then the question would arise whether one or other of your drivers, e.g. Lang or Kling, could drive for Alfa in 3-litre sports cars racing."

As team manager, Neubauer had no objection to the idea; it was in his interest that his drivers should remain at peak form for the task ahead, and this they could only do by driving other cars. Kling, together with Fangio, therefore drove sports cars for

Alfa Romeo. Kling in a *Disco Volante* retired from the Mille Miglia and was down to compete in the Nürburgring 1000 km event.

On Saturday 13th July 1953 the Alfa Romeo people were at the Nordschleife on the Nürburgring for testing in preparation for the race that was to be held at the end of August. Test driver Consalvo Sanesi was there, as was Kling. After Sanesi had driven several laps and set a best time of 10 minutes 53 seconds, Kling took over the wheel of the red car. Three laps later he achieved a best time of 10 minutes 13 seconds. He stopped at the pits and then returned to the circuit, but on his second lap he left the road on the downhill stretch at Wehrseifen. He crashed through the parapet of a bridge, rolled twice and luckily came to rest right side up and managed to climb from the wreckage without assistance – which in any case would have been too long in coming. He crawled into the shade of a tree and then lapsed into unconsciousness.

In his statement the surgeon from Adenau, Dr A. Aymanns, wrote that Kling "suffered severe crushing to the ribcage with several broken ribs on the right, damage to both knee joints and the right shoulder joint, and flesh wounds on the lower and upper right arm." He also suffered serious traumatic shock. Kling's 1953 season was at an end.

After his convalescence Kling often spent time in the engine research department at Untertürkheim, observing progress on the experimental single cylinders for the Grand Prix engine. In the new year, with the complete 8-cylinder unit installed in the chassis, he was given the opportunity of trying out the car at the factory, driving past the factory gate, behind the research building and past the boiler house. In the spring, in wintry conditions, the team went testing at the nearby Solitude circuit and then later on the autobahn at Leonberg, which was closed for the occasion. Karl Kling covered hundreds of kilometres in the W 196 in testing. Hockenheim was another track where they tested regularly and here, as elsewhere, the engine was run in carburetted form as the fuel injection system was still giving problems.

Finally the big day came at Reims, where Kling was narrowly beaten by Fangio; at Silverstone he was sidelined with engine failure; and at the Nürburgring, where victory was on the cards, a delay in the pits saw him relegated to fourth. At last he was able to win at the Avus in the Grand Prix of Berlin, ahead of Fangio and Hans Herrmann.

For the 1955 season, Neubauer had secured the services of Stirling Moss, which meant that Kling's place in the team was as number three. He made his mark on the sports car scene, however, setting a furious pace in the 300 SLR on the Mille Miglia, until a wheel change in Rome cost him seven minutes. Four kilometres later he went off the road, suffering injuries once more. The winner in a new record time was Stirling Moss – the third non-Italian to win the event and, as in 1931, the car was a Mercedes.

Kling missed the 1955 Monaco Grand Prix and on his return, Moss was established as the definite number two. The German was further thwarted by

The state of this tyre is a graphic indication of the tortuous conditions on the Carrera Panamericana.

Kling on the 1955 Mille Miglia shortly before he dropped out.

mechanical troubles during the remainder of the season and when Mercedes announced its withdrawal, it meant the end of the line for Karl Kling too. Daimler-Benz did not want him to drive for another manufacturer.

When Alfred Neubauer retired in 1958 (though he remained on the staff as historian and archivist) Kling was nominated as his successor in the racing department, now responsible for private entrants. This was the era of Mercedes participation in long-distance rallying – thus Kling had come full circle. In a 190 Diesel he won the 1959 Algiers-Cape Rally and two years later ended his career with victory on the Algiers-Central Africa Rally.

Kling worked for Daimler-Benz until 1968, when he retired at the age of 58. "That had always been my wish, to retire at a relatively early age," he says today, settling back comfortably in his armchair. He remained contracted to the company as an adviser until 1975, and there was no shortage of demand for his opinions. His judgement is still valued – even by potential customers seeking advice on the choice of car from the wide range of Mercedes models.

As a racing driver, Kling had the misfortune of seeing his employers withdraw from motor racing too soon; what he might otherwise have achieved can only be guessed at.

The Youngster

Hans Herrmann, born 1928

Hans Herrmann was in bed when the call came from Mercedes racing manager Alfred Neubauer; he turned over and let the phone ring. He was not normally up and about at eleven in the morning, but when the ringing persisted he decided to answer anyway, for better or worse.

"Herrmann."

"This is Neubauer, I wonder if you would like to come to a test session at the Nürburgring . . . Hallo, are you still there?"

Hans Herrmann, 25 years old had suddenly lost the power of speech. Only two years before, this pastrycook had taken part in his first motor sport event, the Hessische Winterfahrt. The 15 kilometres from Frankfurt to Bad Soden alone took him an hour, then thinking he could make up time in the later stages, he forged ahead. This time, however, he was further penalized for arriving under the bogey time. He was driving a 1.3-litre Porsche, bought with generous assistance from his mother.

Straight after that came the Deutschland Rallye, where he won his class. Erwin Bauer, an experienced driver, gave invaluable help from the co-driver's seat. Herrmann therefore puts the victory more down to Bauer than to his own skill at the wheel. Even so, he won all the hillclimbs, which was a good sign.

In 1952 the trail led him to the Nürburgring for the Rheinland event. Like the other Porsche drivers, Herrmann had a 1.5-litre engine in the tail and this powered him to fastest time in practice on a circuit he had never driven on before. To cap it all he won the race, beating well-known drivers such as Richard von Frankenberg and Helmut Polensky.

With von Frankenberg he took part in the Lyon-Charbonnières Rally in 1953, coming fifth overall. The success made him set his sights higher and he entered his Porsche for the Mille Miglia. His friends had doubts about his sanity but Herrmann had to try.

His choice of co-driver was Bauer once again, but his place among the starters was almost jeopardized by bureaucratic blunders. Not until the very last moment did the necessary licence arrive from Germany. Herrmann drove a fantastic race over the unknown route, though Bauer soon put away his "prayer book": the masses of spectators changed the shape of each bend to such an extent that the notes so carefully prepared for the race were no longer accurate. When the two Germans reached the finish in Brescia after nearly 13 hours' driving, they had won their class.

The result of this success was a summons from Porsche to drive a works car in the Le Mans 24 Hours. Once again Herrmann was a class winner, this time sharing with Helm Glöckler from Frankfurt. With only a few races under his belt, the young Swabian already ranked among Germany's racing élite, and he confirmed this position by taking the German Sports Racing title.

And now the call had come from the fat man, Neubauer. Herrmann's heart was in his mouth. What did he say? A third driver for the coming season? Incredible.

Five drivers were called up for the session in the Eifel. The Belgian journalist Paul Frère, Fritz Riess from Nuremberg, Günther Bechem the Borgward driver, Hans Klenk from Stuttgart and Hans Herrmann.

No times would be taken that first day, it was said, to give the drivers a chance to get to know the cars, Mercedes 300 SL coupés. The crafty Neubauer had his stopwatch out though. Frère was quickest, as expected. Herrmann was biding his time, getting to know the car; after all he had only ever driven the rear-engined Porsche before. The 300 SL was front-engined and also far heavier than his Porsche.

On day two, Herrmann's big moment arrived. He pulled out all the stops and drove the fastest lap, and the following day he confirmed the feat. During testing, Hans Klenk had a serious accident on the Aremberg section and was taken to hospital.

Herrmann, however, had done it. Two and a half years after his first competition he was to drive for Daimler-Benz on the firm's return to Grand Prix racing, as third driver alongside Juan Manuel Fangio and Karl Kling.

When a firm offer later came from Maserati for 1954, he informed Neubauer, who soon settled the matter. Provided he waited until the W 196 was ready and drove no races in the meantime he would be well rewarded.

In testing at Solitude in 1954, on the winding, hilly track near Stuttgart, Herrmann drove even faster than chief test driver Kling, whom Herrmann had seen in 1949 driving the Veritas at Hockenheim. It was in that same farming village near Heidelberg that Hans Herrmann had his first serious accident on 12th May 1954.

During testing with the streamlined version of the W 196, the mechanics had repositioned a pair of new oil hoses. To save time they had been routed through the cockpit instead of the engine compartment. This was soon to have its consequences. When Herrmann took over from Kling he screamed up to the Friedhof (Cemetery) bend at about 240 km/h, where he lifted off a little. When he tried to brake for the Stadt bend (about where the fire station is sited today) horror lay in wait. One of the new oil hoses was leaking and hot oil was pouring all over Herrmann's right foot and the pedals. His foot slipped off the brake pedal repeatedly as he tried to stop and he had no other choice than to continue along a track towards the town centre, still travelling at 160-180 km/h.

He had Kling to thank that he was not decapitated at the entrance to the track. On a tour of inspection of the course, he had noticed that the points where the farm tracks met the circuit were closed off by wire to warn passers-by that the circuit was in use. "If someone goes off here, he'll be shorter by a head," said Kling, who had the wire removed straight away.

At the other end, the track led on to the main street; Herrmann knew that he only had to take the right-hander and then he could come safely to rest. As he prepared to take the corner he had to make a split-second change of plan. Two girls were approaching on their bicycles from the right and he had no choice but to attempt to guide the car into a narrow side turning, but he was travelling too fast.

As Herrmann recalls today, "That's when I thought to myself, it's all over, you're a goner." With a mighty thump the W 196 hit the corner of a house, throwing the driver from the cockpit. Stunned for a moment, Herrmann then tried to move and, incredibly, everything was working – he could even stand up. Opposite him he saw a door, entered it, went up three steps and there found himself in someone's living room with a sofa waiting invitingly. He lay down, and then fell unconscious.

He awoke to see the faces of Neubauer, Uhlenhaut and Kling bending over him. "It was like in a film, and I could see things only as a blur," he remembers. Kling put him in his car and drove him to Stuttgart where he was X-rayed.

To begin with, the doctors took no notice of his badly burned foot which caused the patient to faint time and again. They wanted the X-ray of his chest. Eventually they treated the wounded foot, which was burned to the bone. The scalding oil had done horrific damage.

The treatment was finished by the time of the first race appearance of the W 196 at Reims, where Herrmann was named as the No. 3 Mercedes driver. He lined up on the grid with a slight disadvantage because his engine had not been run in yet, whereas Fangio's and Kling's had already clocked a few kilometres and had proved their reliability.

Despite a fine performance in the race, during which he took fastest lap and then managed to avoid Gonzalez's spinning Ferrari, he had to retire at the pits with engine failure.

At the next race at Silverstone he was nominated as reserve driver: the new bodies had not been finished in time. In truth Daimler-Benz did not want to compete in this event, but because the organizers insisted the firm should stick to its word, the team made the trip with only two cars, driven by the Nos. 1 and 2, Fangio and Kling.

At the Grand Prix of Europe at the Nürburgring, Herrmann drove the streamlined car again (Fangio, Kling and Lang taking to the track with the open-wheelers for the first time). In practice he put up a great showing, but in the race he was sidelined before the halfway point with a faulty fuel injection pump.

Herrmann's big day was to come in Bern where he took third place behind Fangio and Gonzalez in his Ferrari. The victory ceremony appeared on the front pages all over Germany the next day, little Hans standing meekly alongside his two opponents. This was quickly followed by a fourth place at Monza and third at the Grand Prix of Berlin, an event that did not count towards the World Championship.

All three Mercedes drivers took the same prize money at this event, and when Herrmann also won the sports car race, he suddenly had more than 25,000 DM in his bulging wallet. He asked Neubauer, who was flying back to West Germany, to look after the money, but the latter replied, "I can't take the responsibility. If the plane crashes your money will go up in smoke." Herrmann was forced to undergo a lengthy procedure at the border – the Soviet customs officers must have regarded him as a most loathsome capitalist.

Curtain raisers to the 1955 season were the races in Argentina. The infernal heat caused both Herrmann and Kling, as well as the newcomer to the team, Stirling Moss, to drive the race in relays; Herrmann finished fourth. The only drivers to go the full distance without relief were Fangio and Mières.

On 1st May Herrmann and Fangio's mechanic Hermann Eger competed in the Mille Miglia. Going at a blistering pace, the Germans were among the leaders at the halfway mark in Rome, and when their team mate Kling retired later, Herrmann and Eger were in the best position to profit and win the race. Shortly after, there was a bang and the fuel cap flew off, from which point fuel sloshed into the car and over its occupants whenever they rounded a curve. A single spark and the Mercedes 300 SLR would have made a meteoric exit. The crew stuck it out for another 100 kilometres but then had to acknowledge that enough was enough, and sadly parked their silver car by the side of the road.

"When I think about it today," says Herrmann with a tinge of regret at the missed opportunity, "Moss drove the last 160 km virtually without brakes and we would have beaten him easily." It was, however, the Englishman who won in a new record time with Denis Jenkinson in the co-driver's seat.

Then 19th May 1955 came round, and Karl Kling's seat for the Monaco Grand Prix was vacant as he was still recovering from his Mille Miglia injuries: Herrmann was therefore called for duty. To add some spice to the first day of practice, the Thursday before the event itself, the organizers had decided to make the first three places on the grid dependent on the results of that day's session.

Although Herrmann, who had never raced in Monaco, had no hope whatsoever of a place on the front row of the grid, Neubauer ordered him to go flat out. Lack of local knowledge on the one hand, and his attempts at posting a good time on the other, added up to disaster. On the uphill burst to the Casino square Herrmann's W 196 swerved to the right, careering over the kerb and smashing into the concrete parapet. He suffered a broken pelvis and, worse, a broken vertebra. It was only by the greatest good fortune that he escaped being paralysed.

Herrmann was taken to hospital in Nice and a few days later, in a special aircraft chartered by Mercedes, was transferred to Munich where he spent the next few weeks learning to walk again. He was greatly assisted by his excellent constitution, built up by long forest walks and intensive boxing training under the watchful eye of Robert Theurer, coach at the Stuttgart Prag boxing club.

His season was over, however, even despite Neubauer's invitation to take part in the Targa Florio in mid-October, Mercedes' last race. After practice, Herrmann was of the opinion that he would be of no use in the race and he had to contend with a good deal of animosity from Neubauer. The manager believed that Herrmann was too afraid to go flat out any more, but the real reason lay elsewhere. "It took an eternity for the instructions from my brain to reach my right foot. There was always a delay of about a second. That is to say, between my brain saying 'now you must brake' and the corresponding reaction in my foot there was a delay. Obviously it was impossible to drive fast like that, it was very unsettling because I couldn't tell whether the reaction would suddenly return, or worse, if it would be delayed even longer."

On Mercedes' withdrawal from motor sport Herrmann's high-flying career was brought back down to earth. Whereas Neubauer had said a few months before that he wanted to see his youngest driver win the World title, the object of his praise now had no car at his disposal. The next few years saw a couple of outings with Maseratis and Stirling Moss's private BRM at the Avus in 1959. The photo by Julius Weitmann ("I was quite convinced you were dead") showing the disintegrating car flying through the air above Hans Herrmann, who is somersaulting across the track, is one of the most famous motor racing photos ever taken. For Herrmann that moment when he realized he was approaching the narrow South Turn on the high-speed track without any brakes was the second occasion on which he thought his number was up.

"A very curious feeling. I got to the corner, and only when I realized that the brakes had failed did I notice the spectators. The accident at Le Mans in 1955 immediately flashed through my mind – and only then did I think, 'You're a dead man. You've had it.' But there was no panic, I was just like someone watching himself in a film." Herrmann's unbelievable luck held: the impact with the straw bales marking the course threw the BRM skywards, flinging the driver clear, the battered car coming to rest after turning a few cartwheels without harming a single spectator. Herrmann himself suffered deep abrasions on both arms and one leg, but considering the scale of the accident, the injuries were almost laughable.

In the early 1960s Herrmann drove Porsche's bulbous Formula 2 cars and enjoyed increasing success in sports car racing. On the arrival of Huschke von Hanstein at Zuffenhausen as racing manager, personal differences caused Herrmann to leave Porsche and he switched to Carlo Abarth's Turin-based team. His three-year stint there made him into a first-class test driver who was able to communicate the precise nature of the car's behaviour to his technicians. The experience paid off when Herrmann returned to Porsche a few years later: in collaboration with Peter Falk and Herbert Linge, Hans Herrmann did most of the test driving at Weissach.

Le Mans in June 1970 was the scene of Hans Herrmann's greatest achievement as a racing driver. Sharing a red and white Porsche 917 entered by Porsche Austria with "Dickie" Attwood he won the 24-Hour classic. After the triumph, the former pastrycook announced his retirement from the sport, a sport he held dear, but which over the years had claimed the lives of so many of his friends: Wolfgang von Trips, Tommy Spychiger, Jean Behra, Hans Laine, Piers Courage, Bruce McLaren and Joakim Bonnier (his partner in the victorious Porsche on the Targa Florio in 1960).

He still drove the odd test session with the 917 at the Porsche track at Weissach at the special request of manager Peter Falk, but his racing days were over. Six months after victory at Le Mans he set up his own car accessory firm in Maichingen, his home town. The first product was the Snow Grip, a device to get stranded cars out of trouble. Further additions were a towing bar, engine heaters, snow chains and special exterior mirrors. Another favourite was the anti-theft device for Mercedes-Benz cars which immobilized the gear change and was marketed by all Daimler-Benz concessions at home and abroad.

Hans Herrmann managed the step from racing

Herrmann in the streamlined W 196 in practice at the Nürburgring for the Grand Prix of Europe.

driver to independent entrepreneur without serious problems. In his office the trophies for the Le Mans 24 Hours and the Daytona 24 Hours are on display, however. The rest of his mementos are in the cellar of his house a few hundred metres away: umpteen photos, trophies and memories. He still enjoys telling tales of his great days as a racing driver, but sentimentality never creeps into his accounts. Hans Herrmann does not live in the past but stands with both feet very firmly in the present.

The Thinker

Piero Taruffi, 1906 – 1989

Piero Taruffi was born in 1906, the same year as another great driver, Giuseppe Farina, winner of the first Formula 1 World Championship in 1950. Taruffi and Farina were similar characters, calm, sometimes pensive and always complete masters of themselves and their machines. Taruffi never won the World title but he scored many successes that were celebrated by his fellow Italians. His greatest achievement was his victory in the 1957 Mille Miglia at the age of 50. It was the final race to be held over the Brescia-Rome-Brescia course, because in that year the Spanish Marquis de Portago and his American co-driver perished in an accident after a tyre failure. Wolfgang von Trips, one of the world's leading drivers at the time, was often asked after the race if he, the Ferrari number 2, had let the older Taruffi win. The reply was always the same and, if witnesses are to be believed, came without the slightest hint of irony. Von Trips's statement must stand, "That day, Piero Taruffi was simply unbeata-ble. Of course I wanted to win but he was faster."

After this race Taruffi, whose white hair and permanently tanned face always stood out in the pack, announced the end of his 30-year career as a racing driver. He had made the promise to his young wife Isabella before the race and that day, the whole of Italy celebrated the man's feat. He managed to fulfil every sportsman's dream: to bow out at the climax of his career.

He entered his first event at the age of 17, driving a 4-seater Fiat 501S in the Rome-Viterbo race where he won his class. From that point on Taruffi was an enthusiastic competitor, testing his skills against other drivers on virtually every weekend throughout the season. At the end of the 1950s the writer Richard von Frankenberg was working on Taruffi's biography and had asked for a list of his triumphs. He had not counted on what followed. A list running to several pages landed on his desk, and it catalogued only those occasions on which Taruffi had mounted the victory podium as first, second or third placed driver. In his article in *Motor Revue*, von Frankenberg, snowed under with data, wrote, "I took the trouble of compiling a classified list, and what a job that was. He won 79 races and drove to 38 world records and 26 class records during his career. He was Italian champion on three occasions (in 1947 in 1.5-litre single-seaters, Formula 2 in 1949 and unrestricted sports cars in 1954). Besides that he came fifth in the Drivers' World Championship in 1951, and third in 1952."

This would seem to give the impression that Taruffi did nothing but race, but this is not true. He studied engine design, and after posting excellent exam results was soon taken on by the Italian motorcycle manufacturers Rondine as designer and rider. The motorcycle connection was no coincidence. During his student days Taruffi took part in many races riding AJS, Guzzi and Norton machines. His rivals at that time (the end of the 1920s) included Achille Varzi and Tazio Nuvolari. In the early 1930s the Roman-born Taruffi combined his activities, one weekend in the saddle of his Norton 500, the next at the wheel of his Alfa Romeo 1750. He was a member of Scuderia Ferrari, the Alfa Romeo works team.

By acquiring his services when they later took over the Rondine project, Gilera had pulled off a real coup because Taruffi immediately set about polishing up the firm's image by his sporting exploits. He developed a supercharged 500 that was to bring the outright world speed record for motorcycles to Italy. The battle for this honour was at full pitch during the 1930s, BMW and Ernst Henne laying long-term claim to the record, with the British making their mark later on. In April 1937 Eric Fernihough did 273.24 km/h on a supercharged 1000cc JAP-engined Brough Superior.

By now the new Gilera in its streamlined fairing was ready. On 21st October 1937, 11 days after his 31st birthday, Piero Taruffi climbed on the machine and, on the autostrada near Bergamo, made his assault on the world record. At 274.171 km/h his speed was very nearly 1 km/h faster than Fernihough's – the world record was in Italian hands. But only briefly: 38 days later Henne pushed the mark beyond 279 km/h, but Taruffi had shown the capabilities of the Italian motorcycle industry.

Taruffi played tennis as relaxation (in the early 1930s he was even one of Rome's top players), and was fascinated by the other "white" sport, skiing.

He took part in the big Alpine races, the Parsenn Derby at Davos, and competitions in Sestrière in Italy and Chamonix in France, in the days before the World Cup.

During his time at Gilera he raced cars on a number of occasions "on the side, just for fun". He drove an ERA in South Africa and took second place on the Targa Florio behind Villoresi. After World War II he joined Cisitalia as technical director of the sports department and, of course, drove the firm's 1100 cc sports and racing cars. Other drivers to race Cisitalias in the late 1940s were Count Lurani, Alberto Ascari and the rapid Frenchman, Jean-Pierre Wimille.

His successes at the wheel of these cars did not go unnoticed by the top Italian racing teams. In 1950 Taruffi lined up for Alfa Romeo in the Grand Prix des Nations in Geneva. Driving the famous Tipo 158 Alfetta he came third behind Juan Manuel Fangio and Emmanuel (Toulo) de Graffenried. He was engaged by Enzo Ferrari for the 1951 season. With the heavy 4.5-litre car, and again in Switzerland, but this time at Bern, Taruffi put in another impressive performance: he drove a thoughtful and controlled race in the pouring rain, skilfully drifting the Ferrari through the slippery bends to take second place about a minute behind the victor Fangio, but ahead of Farina the reigning World Champion.

Switzerland was also the scene of Taruffi's only Grand Prix win. At the Bremgarten circuit near Bern, in the opening race of the 1952 World Championship, the Swiss Grand Prix, Taruffi drove to victory in his 2-litre Ferrari. At the season's end he had amassed 22 points to come third in the World Championship behind his team mates Alberto Ascari (36 points) and Giuseppe Farina (25).

His greatest love was still long-distance racing in the big sports cars. When it came to endurance and consistency of performance over many hours, Piero Taruffi was among the very best. Lancia secured his services and in the 3.3-litre cars from Turin he won both the 1954 Targa Florio and the Giro Sicilia.

He continued to work as an engineer and designed an attractive twin-fuselaged car which he dubbed the Tarf. He built two versions of this "catamaran": the smaller was powered by a 500 cc Gilera motorcycle engine and the larger by a supercharged 1750cc 4CLT Maserati. Taruffi broke world records with both cars, both the standing kilometre and the hour record (at Montlhéry).

The winner of the 1957 Mille Miglia, Piero Taruffi.

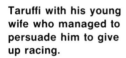

Taruffi with his young wife who managed to persuade him to give up racing.

In 1955 he drove two races for the Daimler-Benz works team after Hans Herrmann's Monaco accident, which had left the fourth Mercedes seat vacant. Taruffi was chosen for his thoughtful and reliable reputation. Thus he was the ideal complement to the genius of Fangio, the press-on style of Moss and the speed of Kling. His first appearance for the Stuttgart team was a low-key one: he finished fourth in the British Grand Prix at Aintree behind his three colleagues. At Monza, however, in his home Grand Prix, the last round of the 1955 championship he drove a fantastic race, duelling for many laps with eventual winner Fangio and coming home second. Next to his victory in Bern in 1952 this was his greatest single-seater performance. Between 1950 and 1956 he contested 18 Grands Prix, but his greatest triumph of all as a driver was still to come on the 1957 Mille Miglia.

With these racing successes, Taruffi had also proved a theory of his own: it was his view that success as a driver was not necessarily a matter of innate ability and the right temperament, but that scientific precision and the calculation of chances had just as important a part to play. He was too much of an engineer to ignore the theoretical aspects of the racing profession. His book, *The Technique of Motor Racing* is numbered among the classics of motor racing writing. And many who later took the wheel of a racing car (or at least dreamed of doing so) have read this book closely, absorbing its wealth of explanatory drawings on the correct choice of cornering line. Of all the drivers of his time, Taruffi was the greatest thinker, one who could coolly and clearly weigh up the capabilities of his car, but could also communicate invaluable information on his car's behaviour to the mechanics, rather like the later "human computer" Niki Lauda. But when the chips were down he could also go flat out: in such situations his Roman temperament would come to the surface.

Taruffi lived in Rome, until his death. His daughter wants to emulate her father's achievements and is currently shaping a career as a racing driver.

97

The Pre-war Idol

Hermann Lang, 1909 – 1988

Of the so-called pre-war Titans, Lang was the only one to drive a Mercedes Grand Prix car after World War II. It was 15 years after his astounding European Championship campaign of 1939 that he drove the Mercedes W 196. Though he drove only a single race he was at the wheel for testing on the Nordschleife at the Nürburgring and at Reims (before the new car's first actual race outing), as well as in practice for the Italian Grand Prix in 1954 and the Grand Prix of Berlin that same year. Thereafter, Lang's name disappeared from the line-up for the big races and a long career was over. "Hermännle" would drive no more.

His rise to the peak of his profession in the mid-1930s had something of the fairy tale about it. It was for this very reason that this calm Swabian soon came to be more popular than the big guns of the day, Rudolf Caracciola and Manfred von Brauchitsch: he had made the jump from racing mechanic to European Champion, proving that

anyone who believed in his own ability and pursued his goal energetically could reach the pinnacle of the sport.

Under the supervision of Merkle, chief mechanic at the Stuttgart Standard dealership, Lang served an apprenticeship as a motorcycle mechanic. He soon developed such a passion for motorcycles that in 1927, with his brother Albert, he took the step of buying a race-prepared machine. They paid 1000 marks for the privilege, a small fortune in those days, half the money coming out of their own pocket and the rest in the form of a loan. The result was a sensation: Lang won his first race on his new machine at the Solitude circuit near Stuttgart. His brother was enthusiastic, though his mother had her doubts. But now he was past the point of no return.

Lang contested his next race on an Ardie and was about to join Standard's works team – Merkle had been a great supporter. Around this time he met the love of his life, Lydia, who at first pretended to be unimpressed by the cocky motorcyclist but later found the dark-haired young man's charm irresistible.

Between 1929 and 1931 he raced almost exclusively in sidecar events, scoring victory after victory. In 1931 he took the German Sidecar Hillclimb Championship. By now, and against the wishes of his mother, he had decided to pursue a career in motor sport. His brother Albert was killed in a motorcycle accident in 1928 when he hit a horsedrawn vehicle in Stuttgart and two years later his third brother, Karl, lost his life when he went out of control on a wet track. To cap it all Hermann was seriously injured in an accident at a race in the Pfälzer Wald, a huge pile-up in which two other riders were killed. Both his mother and Lydia tried to persuade him to give up racing – the 1931 Championship did little to change the opinion of his mother and his bride.

The Depression then played a fateful hand in Lang's life: when Standard was forced to withdraw from racing he was fired. For Lang, racing was a thing of the past, but so was a steady job and he was on the dole. After six months he found a new job, becoming driver of a diesel locomotive. Speed did not come into it but at least he was earning. His daily route to work took him past the Daimler-Benz factory. After weeks of casting envious glances in the direction of the works, he decided to write a speculative application for the job of mechanic. He received a negative reply. His application had not been dealt with by the personnel department which appointed factory workers, but by Alfred Neubauer himself in the racing department. His reason for rejecting Lang, who had of course enclosed a reference from Standard praising his abilities as a race rider, was that Daimler-Benz had no use for racing drivers at the moment.

Through personal contacts Lang eventually secured a job at the factory in 1933; he ended up in the experimental department where work was going full steam ahead in preparation for the return of Mercedes to Grand Prix racing in 1934. Lang succeeded in progressing to the racing department itself, as a mechanic rather than a driver. Soon he was a *capo*, in charge of a team of three service mechanics.

While returning by train to Stuttgart from testing in Monza in the spring of 1934 with his supervisor Kraus and five colleagues, Kraus overheard Lang talking about his motorcycle racing in the late 1920s, and even remembered seeing him win a race at Solitude.

The apparently inconsequential discussion between Lang and Kraus (not the Ludwig Kraus who later worked on the design of the W 196 engine in the mid-1950s) had its repercussions: a few weeks later Kraus informed the mechanic Lang that he was going to put his name forward as understudy in the racing department. Lang could now see light at the end of the tunnel. However, he had to wait a whole season before he was invited to test drive a car, during which time he and his team were responsible for the preparation of the Italian Luigi Fagioli's supercharged W 25.

In the spring of 1935 at Monza the new car was to be tested, as were the abilities of a group of three junior drivers. Hermann Lang had arrived at last; also taking part were Karl Soenius, a motorcycle racer from Cologne, and the sports car driver "Bobby" Kohlrausch from Eisenach. Of the three, Lang proved to be the most "complete" driver, Neubauer being particularly impressed with his start and cornering technique. From then on, Lang was given a junior position in the Mercedes racing team.

At the age of 26 he drove his first race for Mercedes, in the Eifelrennen at the Nürburgring. Lang came fifth although he had been third until shortly before the end when, on the wet track on the Pflanzgarten section, he spun wildly and ended up in a ditch. He was able to carry on but the excursion had wider consequences: he detested wet conditions for ever after.

At the German Grand Prix he drove again but retired after only a few laps. At the Swiss Grand Prix he took sixth place after his fellow junior Hans Geier had survived a serious practice accident, though it spelled the end of the young driver's career before it had properly begun. He would often be seen in the Mercedes pits in the 1950s serving as a dedicated timekeeper.

It was 1936 before Lang drove his next Grand Prix. On this occasion, however, the German Grand Prix, he was allowed to drive the most up-to-date car like the "Greats," von Brauchitsch and Caracciola, instead of making do with the previous year's machinery. His practice time put him a sensational fourth on the grid and in the race itself he trailed the leader, Bernd Rosemeyer, until the Auto-Union driver had to retire. Now he was leading a car race

Hermann Lang (right) with Rudolf Caracciola pictured in Livorno in 1937.

for the first time, but bad luck was in store: making a rapid gear change he banged his right hand so hard against the cockpit wall that he broke his little finger. He drove on regardless until instructed to bring the car in and hand over to Caracciola, who had retired his car. On his return from the doctor, who put a splint on the injured finger, he took over Manfred von Brauchitsch's car and finished the race despite being in terrible pain. Though he did not finish among the leaders, the crowd cheered him as though he had been a victor.

In December 1936 he married Lydia and was also contracted as a senior driver. This put him on equal terms with those drivers he had revered. At Tripoli, in the first race of the 1937 season, Lang celebrated his first victory on four wheels. Consciously playing a waiting game, he had observed Caracciola,

Rosemeyer and Stuck ahead of him and how their battle had taken its inevitable toll of their tyres. As if to underline his victory in Africa he immediately won the race on the Avus in Berlin, where the Mercedes appeared with streamlined bodywork allowing a top speed of 380 km/h on the long straights. In practice Lang was given an almighty fright when, flat out in the Mercedes, the front of the car suddenly came unstuck. Calmly, Lang lifted off until his car-turned-aircraft touched down again on the tarmac.

No further victories came his way in 1937, though he had a bad accident on the Masaryk circuit near Brno in Czechoslovakia. His Mercedes lost grip when it hit a patch of sand thrown up by a skidding car in front of him, and he hit a solid chunk of granite that acted as a springboard. The car turned somersault over the spectator-filled ditch by the track and then came to rest. Though Lang escaped with a minor head injury, two spectators who had been standing in a prohibited area were dead and twelve others injured. As so often after such an accident, some of those affected tried to put the blame on the driver, but in court Lang was acquitted.

At the end of January 1938, while out shopping in Stuttgart, Lang heard of the death of Bernd Rosemeyer, a man he had always got on well with. Like Lang, Rosemeyer had been a motorcycle racer and at the end of 1937 had even tried to bring his Swabian rival into the Auto-Union team alongside him. In a record attempt on the motorway near Darmstadt, Bernd Rosemeyer died when his car disintegrated.

Lang's racing season began three months later than it had the previous year. In 1938 the name on the Tripoli trophy was again Hermann Lang, Mercedes-Benz, though not in one of the 750 Kilogram Formula (which ran out at the end of 1937) cars but with a machine of the new 3-litre formula which restricted supercharged engines to a maximum of 3000cc.

He was increasingly a challenger to Caracciola and von Brauchitsch and, in 1938, won the Coppa Ciano at Livorno in Italy. Rudolf Caracciola won the European title that year. At the end of the season, however, Lang was considerably happier than in 1937 as he had a number of second and third places to point to.

Hermann Lang's year of triumph was 1939. Other drivers often seemed like mere extras compared with him, whose name appeared among the winners time and again: Pau Grand Prix in April; Tripoli Grand Prix (for the third time in a row, this time with the 1.5-litre W165, built in record time) and the International Eifelrennen in May; the Vienna Höhenstrassenrennen and Belgian Grand Prix in June, German Hillclimb Grand Prix at Schauinsland near Freiburg and the Swiss Grand Prix at Bern in August. Lang won all these races and the European Championship too, a title comparable only to today's Formula 1 World Championship. At the age of 30, the former motorcycle mechanic had climbed

Lang's 1938 mount – the W 154.

102

Driving the 300 SL Spider to victory in the Eifelrennen at the Nürburgring in 1952.

to the very top rung of the ladder.

Vom Rennmechaniker zum Europameister ('From Race Mechanic to European Champion') was the title of a book published by Knorr & Wirth in Munich in 1943. The launch date, right in the middle of World War II, may be regarded as symbolic: the war had interrupted a racing career at its very peak, and when it was over, devastated Germany had more important things on the agenda to think about than motor sport. When Lang then attempted to revive his career of his own accord, using his savings to buy a Veritas Meteor, the car proved to be fundamentally unreliable. The result of the two races in Buenos Aires with the pre-war W163 supercharged cars in 1951 was far below the expectations of Mercedes. A year later, the pre-war idol Lang was in the Mercedes team driving the 300 SL in the big

endurance events. Lang's team mates were Karl Kling, Fritz Riess and Rudolf Caracciola, and Lang proved that he was still a race winner. He won at the Nürburgring and in the Le Mans 24 Hours, came second in Bern (behind Kling) and won the Carerra Panamericana Mexico.

These successes were the good-natured Lang's reply to the lies that had been spread about his postwar drinking habits – it was said that he was more fond of carousing than keeping himself in good physical shape. His reflexes at the wheel were perfect as ever, he was quick – usually more so than younger men – and he could bring his car home. Why did he not enjoy a second Grand Prix career?

The answer must be that Hermann Lang was unlucky, and time was not on his side (in 1954 he was already 45 years of age). He was unlucky at the

Lang decked in laurels after the 1952 Eifelrennen.

Nürburgring in his first – and as it turned out, only – Grand Prix after the war. Before dropping out he was holding third place after spending many laps behind Fangio. The spectators cheered his progress but suddenly, his drive came to an end. At Flugplatz his car went off the track, and that is not good for a driver's image. Later it transpired that the engine had seized just as he was rounding the bend, leaving Lang without a hope of controlling the car. But the (untrue) story did the rounds that the European Champion of 1939 had "thrown it away" on the bend.

At Monza, Lang was allowed to take the wheel of the W 196 again. In practice he had to prove himself against the team's newcomer, Hans Herrmann. The duel was resolved in favour of the younger driver,

Herrmann lapping a second faster than Lang. At the Avus he was down as reserve driver again but Neubauer preferred Herrmann on this occasion too. This spelled the end for Lang as a driver. He was realistic enough to see that he had no future as a pilot – he had too little support in the race department. He regarded the fact that he was never given sufficient opportunity to practise (driving seven practice laps at Monza and five at the Avus) as further proof that his racing days were over. Among racing fans and journalists alike there were many who condemned Daimler-Benz for denying Lang a real chance. But they, too, were unable to change the course of events.

Hermann Lang remained faithful to the "Old Firm" until he retired to enjoy his old age with his wife Lydia. Both sons have followed in their father's footsteps as employees of Daimler-Benz, though not as racing drivers. Hermann Lang himself often drove Mercedes at public events. He died in 1988.

At Monza in 1954, Lang tried in vain to secure a place on the grid.

The Reserve

André Simon

André Simon is still alive, or so it is believed. Today he is over 60 years old, living in Savoie, the French department that borders on Switzerland, by Lake Geneva. It is said that he lives the life of a recluse, alone and neglected by friends, an embittered man bemoaning his fate.

For 15 years Simon would appear in the big international races, in Grands Prix and in sports car racing, driving for Gordini, Maserati, Ferrari, Mercedes and Cobra. He was denied true success; a man who was always in financial difficulty, he felt himself to be at a disadvantage; who was often so very fast but could still not achieve the success that he expected of himself.

His international career began at the wheel of a little Gordini. Amédée Gordini was based in Paris; and on the outskirts of Paris, Simon ran a small filling station and workshop at a place called La Varenne. At the end of the 1940s the paths of these two racing fanatics crossed. Gordini gave the dark-haired Simon a seat in his works team for the 1950 season, perhaps hoping to find in him a replacement for Jean-Pierre Wimille who had died the previous year in an accident in Buenos Aires. Simon was joined by fellow Frenchmen Maurice Trintignant and Robert Manzon in Formula 2, and in sports car racing Aldo Gordini, son of Amédée, also came into the team. At Le Mans Aldo shared a 1.5-litre Gordini with Simon.

In 1951 he continued driving for Gordini and also drove at Le Mans, this time with Manzon, but their race came to an end after just over three hours with crankshaft failure. On 1st July 1951 Simon took part in his first Grand Prix at Reims, but was forced out with engine trouble again. In the German Grand Prix at the Nürburgring, a circuit unknown to him, he drove superbly in practice, faster even than his team mate Manzon, but after 12 laps out of 20 he was out – engine failure. In September at Monza in the Italian Grand Prix he put up ninth best time in practice, fastest of the Gordinis and faster than many more powerful cars. At last he finished a race: he took sixth behind Ascari, Gonzalez, Bonetto/ Farina, Villoresi and Taruffi. All but Bonetto and Farina (Alfa Romeo) were driving 4.5-litre Ferraris.

Simon's performance had impressed Enzo Ferrari who brought the Frenchman into his team for a number of races in 1952, when the Drivers' World Championship was run to Formula 2 regulations. In his late 20s, Simon seemed to have made it to the racing big time. In the Swiss Grand Prix, on 18th May 1952, after an hour's racing he was holding second place, only seven seconds behind Taruffi in the leading Ferrari. Shortly afterwards, however, he had to hand over his car to the team No. 1 "Nino" Farina, who had gone off the track. In the hands of the off-form Farina, Simon's car suffered a similar fate. Simon was rightly dismayed at this lost opportunity to finish in a top position.

His Le Mans mount was a 4-litre Ferrari, and he was leading the field after an hour. A lengthy pit stop saw him slip back to eighth, although he remained on the same lap as the leaders. During the night more stops were necessary and the car fell further and further behind, but on Sunday, Simon managed to pull back second after second until at 4 pm he crossed the line fifth, the best-placed Frenchman along with Vincent, his co-driver. But his good showing was hardly noticed by his countrymen: Pierre Levegh, who had led in his Talbot until shortly before the end, went off the track because of fatigue (he had driven the whole race solo), handing victory to the Mercedes 300 SL pairings, Lang/Riess and Helfrich/Niedermayer. Three years later, both Levegh and Simon would line up at Le Mans in the Mercedes team.

This was an age of countless non-championship races on French soil, whose prize money nevertheless provided a lure to many of the big works teams. In two of these events Simon was well placed but again (as in Switzerland) was forced to hand over to Farina and Ascari when they retired. At Montlhéry, Farina went on to take second, and at Saint-Gaudens Ascari won, leaving Simon with the meagre consolation of knowing he had driven the cars up until their handover, and the famous names had then taken the glory. At the Monza Grand Prix Simon came home second to Farina having driven his car without interruption, but this race was also a non-championship event. In the 1952 Italian Grand

Prix Simon once more took an unrewarded sixth position in his Ferrari Tipo 500 – the World Championship points were distributed among the top five placings with an additional point for fastest lap. Then at the season's end, Ferrari informed the Frenchman that he would have to seek alternative employment – Mike Hawthorn, the up-and-coming Englishman, was deemed to be a better prospect, and was recommended by Tony Vandervell to boot. There was a certain amount of log-rolling going on here: Ferrari's *Thinwall* engine bearings were manufactured by Vandervell Products Limited.

André Simon was left high and dry. He continued in sports car racing with Gordini, but there was no vacant Grand Prix seat for the time being. He was out of luck again at Le Mans in 1954. Sharing a drive with Jean Behra he was forced to retire shortly before midnight with ignition failure.

A year later at Monaco in 1955 he was down to drive a private Maserati in the Grand Prix. His chance to drive the Mercedes W 196 came when Hans Herrmann had his serious accident in practice on the Thursday. He had to make do with the longer chassis regular version, by contrast with the special cars driven by Fangio and Moss. To his credit, he started from the fourth row (four seconds slower than Fangio and Ascari, the two fastest men), in a completely unfamiliar car. In the race itself he managed 25 laps before retiring with engine failure. At first Neubauer and Uhlenhaut suspected that the young man had over-revved his engine, but when Moss and Fangio retired with the same fault (cam follower shaft retaining screw failure in the valve gear) Simon was rehabilitated. He was unlucky that on this occasion the proverbial Mercedes reliability was absent.

Simon was nominated by Mercedes to drive at the Le Mans 24 Hours in a 300 SLR shared with Karl Kling. In practice he was always up among the leaders – he wanted to grab this opportunity by the scruff of the neck. After one hour of the race Kling/Simon were in sixth place and after two hours they were in fifth. Shortly afterwards Pierre Levegh had his terrible accident and the Daimler-Benz team was withdrawn from the race – they had no desire to win an event at which more than 80 people had been killed. Thus, Simon was denied a good showing, but Mercedes rewarded him generously in any case. They based their calculations on a likely finish in fourth place, and he was given 5000 DM. His name

André Simon in the Grand Prix of Europe at Monaco in 1955.

was on the entry list for the German Grand Prix, but this race was among the many events to be cancelled in the wake of the Le Mans disaster and thus the opportunity eluded him.

Simon did drive the 300 SLR again, though sharing with Wolfgang von Trips in the Tourist Trophy in Ireland. It was a good day for Mercedes, who took the top three placings with Moss/Fitch (Moss driving all but a half hour of the event), Fangio/Kling and Simon/von Trips. In practice, there was an unfortunate incident involving Simon. When reconnoitreing the 12 km route in Neubauer's

company car (a Mercedes 220S, registration number W 21-6164), he had an incident with a lorry in which he damaged a front wing, broke the headlights and crumpled a bumper. The Daimler dealership in Belfast offered to pay for the damage to the Morris truck and Simon, who wanted to buy Neubauer's car in any case, was to bear the cost of damage to the Mercedes. Eventually, however, the insurance company was brought in after the police had got wind of the accident.

Simon then took delivery of the car over six months later, on 6th June 1956, from

109

Untertürkheim. He still had 3634 DM in his personal account at Stuttgart and because the car was to cost him 6000 DM, he was asked to pay the balance to the used car department. Simon only handed over French francs equivalent to 1473 DM, leaving almost 900 DM outstanding.

More than six months later Professor Nallinger wrote requesting settlement of the account, even threatening legal proceedings, but to no avail. The letters were returned because Simon had moved from La Varenne leaving no forwarding address. Eventually the Paris dealership of Mercedes-Benz tracked Simon down. He was living in the Avenue de Versailles in Paris. Alfred Neubauer had learned that Simon's financial outlook was less than healthy and in mid-December 1957 he settled the matter in his own fashion. He suggested to Nallinger that the sum should be transferred to the race department's account as a "miscellaneous expense" in recognition of Simon's service.

He lined up for two Grands Prix in 1956. At the French Grand Prix at Reims he started from last place on the grid in a Maserati 250F, even slower than the "undriveable" Bugatti 251 with Trintignant at the wheel. Simon retired from the race but was classified twelfth.

In Monza he drove for Gordini again, likewise starting from last position but finishing ninth. In the Caen Grand Prix he split the Maseratis of Harry Schell and Roy Salvadori to take second. In Sweden at the sports car Grand Prix he drove a Maserati but the car was retired by his partner, Musy, after going half the distance.

At Le Mans in 1957 he shared a Maserati with Jean Behra. After four hours the car with the trident badge took command of the race, but shortly after, with Simon at the wheel, the car retired with transmission failure.

Simon drove in a number of French rallies until his return to Le Mans in 1962. In a Ferrari shared with Tavano he was lying fifth when once again, this time in the 17th hour, he was put out with mechanical failure. A year later, with Cassner, he drove a Maserati Tipo 151, in 2nd place on the grid, which had been entered by the French Maserati importer Johnny Simone. One hour into the race, Simon was placed amazingly ahead of the whole Ferrari pack including John Surtees, Pedro Rodriguez, Mike Parkes, Lorenzo Bandini, Pierre Noblet and Dan Gurney. But dreams of victory were shattered once again when the Maserati went out with a gearbox breakage. In 1964 (sharing with Trintignant this time) Simon again retired the Maserati 151 with an electrical fault.

At the Nürburgring in the 1965 1000 Kilometres, Simon contested his last big international race crewing a Cobra (in Daytona Coupé form) with Jo Schlesser (the man in whose memory all current Ligier Formula 1 cars receive the designation "JS"). He retired on this occasion too. He continued to drive in the odd rally but increasingly avoided the racing scene. Anyone who wanted to know (or would listen) could hear his tale of bad luck and unjust treatment: he would have been World Champion, no question, but he was given bad equipment. And because he repeated the story over and over and became more and more embittered, he soon came to be ignored even by his closest friends. Which explains why no one knows exactly where André Simon is these days, and hardly anyone who is asked is really interested to find out.

DESIGN
&
CONSTRUCTION

The Power Plant

The engine of the W 196

In 1952 Daimler-Benz had already begun to consider a return to Grand Prix racing. That year the Fédération Internationale de L'Automobile (FIA) endorsed a new set of regulations for Formula 1 to be effective from 1954. The old rules (allowing unsupercharged engines up to 4.5 litres and supercharged units up to 1.5 litres) had been self-destructive. Alfa-Romeo's withdrawal at the end of 1951 had sounded the death knell of this formula. Organizers were forced to run races to Formula 2 regulations. In Formula 1, only Ferrari remained as a manufacturer with any chance of winning. And who wanted to see a race where, firstly there were hardly any cars taking part, and secondly where it was obvious who the winner would be? Thus in 1952 and 1953, the World Championship was run under regulations allowing cars with engine capacity of up to 2 litres unsupercharged (500cc supercharged).

After the pre-World War II experience of supercharging, which came to dominate engine technology and allowed power output to soar to unprecedented heights, the new formula was designed to put blown units at a clear disadvantage. Whereas unsupercharged engines were allowed up to 2500 cc, supercharged ones were allowed up to only 750 cc. The disadvantage was so obvious that throughout the whole of the formula's span, only one constructor, the Frenchman René Bonnet, attempted to build a supercharged engine and that was in any case completely uncompetitive.

The 2.5-litre unit was regarded as the only option for building a competitive engine by Mercedes, a firm that had perfected the art of supercharging before the war (Daimler had registered a patent for a supercharger as early as 1885). Overall control of development work and the racing department was in the hands of Dr Fritz Nallinger, the development representative on the board. He had done some competition driving himself and had also worked on the development of the legendary Silver Arrows in the 1930s as technical director. Design and costing was under the control of the director of overall design, passenger vehicles and racing cars, Dr Hans Scherenberg. Leader of his racing car design department was senior engineer Ludwig Kraus (later appointed by Daimler-Benz AG to be chief of technical development of Auto-Union). Hans Gassmann led the subgroup for engine construction. Helmut Weller and Werner Bruder were responsible for work on the chassis and the gearbox specialist was Hans Nedwidek. Within his research department Rudolf Uhlenhaut created a racing department of which, naturally, he was in charge. Uhlenhaut was able to employ his vast wealth of experience gained in this department before the war.

Hans Gassmann, also an experienced pre-war engine designer, began sketching out ideas for the final shape of the new Mercedes engine as soon as the new regulations were announced. According to the rules, there were no restrictions on fuel and thus there would be no disadvantage for a supercharged engine which requires a considerable percentage of alcohol for its fuel for internal cooling.

To be competitive, an output of 260PS would be required. This was the limit of output from Mercedes, most powerful engine to date (in terms of power per litre), the M 165. This was a 1.5-litre V-8 supercharged engine built to contest the race at the Mellaha circuit near Tripoli on 7th May 1939. The Italians had done some last minute rigging of the rules for the race (a sizeable lottery was to be run in connection with it) so as to favour the Alfa Romeos and Maseratis. After only six months of development the W 165 was ready and Hermann Lang and Rudolf Caracciola scored a one-two victory ahead of the Alfa driven by Emilio Villoresi, the brother of Luigi Villoresi (Emilio was killed in an accident later in the 1939 season).

But now, 15 years later, that engine's specific output per litre of 175PS would have to be doubled by an engine of half the capacity if the 750cc supercharged option of the new Formula 1 was to be followed. Prospects for this did not look good as the power band would have been in the upper reaches of the rev range and would probably have been very narrow. Good torque characteristics are necessary in a racing engine to ensure decent acceleration out of corners. Uhlenhaut liked to allow his drivers a reasonable rev range where there was usable power. Besides these considerations the resulting weight handicap would have been enormous, because the fuel consumption for such a small supercharged engine would have been so high. Overall, then, there was but a single way out: a "normal" unsupercharged engine.

But Daimler-Benz did not intend to venture on to the track in an entirely primitive fashion. Superchargers might be out, but the new engine would at least be fuel injected. This was another area where the Stuttgart firm had garnered many years of experience: its aero engines had been equipped with fuel injection in the 1930s, and it had become standardized by 1935.

Application to racing would put new demands on such a system. In 1952 a team from those aero engine days had come back to Daimler-Benz along with Hans Scherenberg. The small team of specialists had worked on the first series production fuel injection system under Scherenberg's direction at Gutbrod (1949 to 1951). On the M 196*, it was Scherenberg's colleague of many years, Karlheinz Göschel (later chief of passenger vehicle research), who would be in charge of development work on the fuel system. In collaboration with Bosch, who built the complete system, countless tests were undertaken within given parameters, such as variations of engine speed and load in order to determine the correct adjustment for fuel injection pump, injector delivery pipe system/injector nozzles and intake tract. Mercedes was the first manufacturer to build a fuel-injected Grand Prix racing car.

Plans to use this system, which had not as yet found widespread use in passenger cars, were based on the very same premise that had dictated the shelving of the small supercharged engine: concern at the provision of as wide a usable rev range as possible. Up to this time, racing engines had tended to be gutless at low revs, and would produce their power only when they had reached 50 to 70 per cent of their peak engine speed. The use of carburettors was unable to solve the problem posed by this technical fact. Carburettor choke diameter (and, therefore, airflow) could be increased, but would result in problems at lower revs when fuel has a tendency to form droplets in the inlet tract – but power in the higher rev ranges would then suffer proportionally if the choke diameter was decreased to ensure delivery of enough power at lower revs.

By using fuel injection, such problems do not arise. The inlet tract diameter can be very large without prejudicing either high- or low-speed power outputs. Other advantages are that even at low revs, there is plenty of torque, pick-up is good after gear changes, and acceleration therefore benefits.

*M = *Motor* (the prefix W was applied to the *car* type number)

Mercedes chose direct fuel injection, a system in which fuel is injected directly into the cylinders (as on the aero engines and the Gutbrod Superior) rather than being introduced into the inlet tract. The final position was just below the inlet valve and inclined 12.5° upwards. The result was good charge distribution around the combustion chamber, with a very rich mixture near the spark plugs and correspondingly lean mixture elsewhere. Fuel was delivered at a pressure of 85 bar.

With fuel injection comes the advantage of maximum power extraction. One of its disadvantages, of lesser importance in the case of racing

Side view of the M 196: the total of sixteen sparking plugs can be clearly seen, as can the injection system mounted on the top of the engine.

machines, is that the cylinder walls are flooded with fuel spray. On the bonus side, however, each cylinder receives precisely the same amount of fuel. Variations in fuel distribution that occur with carburettors are therefore ruled out. A further benefit is the reduction in fuel consumption, for smaller tanks mean less weight and less weight means faster times. The high compression ratio also ensures higher efficiency – greater power output and reduced fuel consumption.

Up until three weeks before the first race, all test sessions were run with four Italian-made twin-choke Weber carburettors. The Mercedes people wanted to hedge their bets in case the injection system gave problems under race conditions.

Assessment of the optimum construction for the engine was the next consideration of concern to the designers. Should they take the pre-war course and build a 12-cylinder, or should they be looking at an 8-, a 6- or even a 4-cylinder unit? With a 12-cylinder, valve area could be maximized relative to cylinder capacity, enabli · highest possible revs to be attained. On tł ⁄ʰer hand the car's centre of gravity would be puₐhed relatively high, unless a "flat" angle was chosen for the V (about 120°). A very short front section could have been designed for the car had the V layout been chosen, but this was not deemed a relevant factor. Besides this, the 12-cylinder would have been a highly complex and very heavy piece of equipment.

Finally the engineers decided on an 8-cylinder as a compromise. V-6, V-8 and straight-eight engines were investigated and calculations were carried out (especially on vibration characteristics), the choice finally falling on the straight-eight. Vibration characteristics determined that power take-off would not be at the end of the block, but centrally. Thus the crankshaft only had to withstand forces similar to those in a 4-cylinder engine, besides which there was a saving in weight. The design was therefore like two 4-cylinder units coupled together.

After this decision was reached, a single-cylinder was built for the test bed. Its capacity was 310 cc and consisted of a combustion chamber with four valves (two inlet and two exhaust) and valve springs, welded to a steel cylinder. A dozen such single-cylinders were built over the months allowing observation of the progress of development.

The past soon caught up with the engineers. At engine speeds of up to 8000 rpm, which were common in the 1930s, tappet bounce limited engine power and breakage of highly stressed valve springs frequently caused engine failure. Good cylinder charging at peak revs was also necessary to reach required power outputs. Valves therefore had to be fully opened and fully closed as quickly as possible. If the story is to be believed then Hans Gassmann, the engine specialist, must be credited with an excellent solution that he arrived at on the tram one morning. His idea was to force the valves open and shut. He imagined two cams for each valve, one that would open it and another that would slam it shut via a lever. The desmodromic system, known in German as *Zwangs-Ventilsteuerung* or *Z-Steuerung*, was born.

The discovery was far from new. In the French Grand Prix of 1914, the race where Mercedes scored a one-two-three, two of the rivals (Delage and Th. Schneider) were fitted with this sort of valve gear, although with modest success. The system, which made possible considerably higher revs and an increased compression ratio, was fully developed to race standard by Mercedes. With a possible maximum of about 13,000 rpm, the engine speeds that could be reached with this valve system were phenomenal.

Bearing in mind the success and the power outputs achieved by Daimler-Benz in Formula 1 with this system in 1954 and 1955, it is perhaps a wonder that *Z-Steuerung* was not taken any further. The reason is that the great strides made in the precise calculation of cams with lower accelerations meant that the desmodromic system was no longer essential. The Italian motorcycle manufacturers Ducati continue to build engines with the system known colloquially as *Desmo*.

Welding work on a cylinder block.

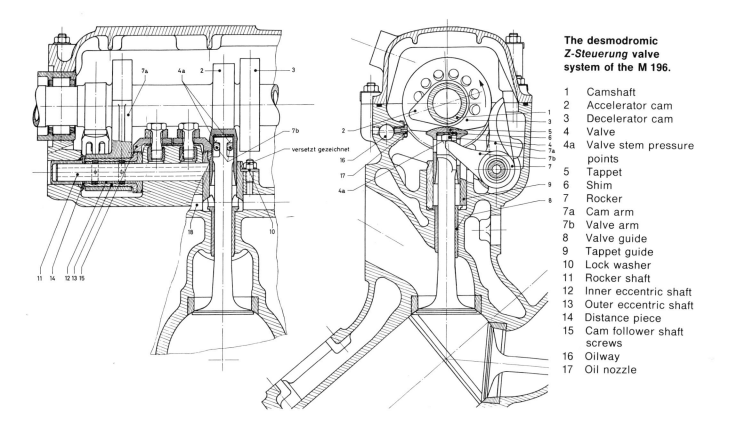

**The desmodromic
Z-Steuerung valve
system of the M 196.**

1 Camshaft
2 Accelerator cam
3 Decelerator cam
4 Valve
4a Valve stem pressure
   points
5 Tappet
6 Shim
7 Rocker
7a Cam arm
7b Valve arm
8 Valve guide
9 Tappet guide
10 Lock washer
11 Rocker shaft
12 Inner eccentric shaft
13 Outer eccentric shaft
14 Distance piece
15 Cam follower shaft
   screws
16 Oilway
17 Oil nozzle

versetzt gezeichnet

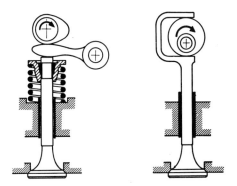

Normal (spring) system   Desmodromic system

Schematic diagram of desmodromic system.

117

In 1986 Renault introduced a new valve system in its Formula 1 engines. On the French company's EF15B engine valve springs were omitted, as on the M 196 thirty years before. Instead of normal twin valve springs, the French engine has piston-cylinder units, the pistons attached to the valve stems and, when the valve is open, compressing nitrogen gas within a closed circuit which then expands again to close the valve.

The new Mercedes arrangement brought revisions to the valve system itself. The engine was originally designed to have four valves per cylinder, but the desmodromic system allowed the valve size and weight to be increased and had the added bonus of allowing a deep hemispherical combustion chamber to be used.

After successful test-bed trials, work could now start on the complete 8-cylinder. The engine had four camshafts (the unit being, in effect, two 4-cylinders). Each camshaft operated four valves. The inlet valves measured 50mm in diameter and the exhausts 43mm. The exhaust valves were sodium-filled to improve cooling (a well-proven technique). Valve lift, originally set at 10mm for both inlet and exhaust, was later increased to 13mm (inlet) and 12mm (exhaust). Precise bore and stroke measurements were 76 x 68.8mm. These figures show how generous the valve head dimensions were. Total capacity of the unit was exactly 2496 cc.

In the earliest stages of the car's overall design, it was decided that in order to keep the centre of gravity as low as possible, the engine would be installed at an angle in the chassis. This was another reason for the choice of an in-line power unit.

The inlet tracts were at a very steep angle corresponding to the engine's 53° tilt to the right. The original BMW 328 and later Veritas Meteor 2-litre Formula 2 engine designed by Ernst Heinkel had similar steeply inclined inlet ports. This latter power unit had been designed for Germany's first (but now, defunct) postwar racing car manufacturer after BMW in Munich had failed to put its 328 engine at the disposal of Veritas. As on the Mercedes, this particular inlet port layout had been chosen because it kept the incoming mixture away from the exhaust valve, reducing the loss of charge density from heating by contact.

Daimler-Benz contracted crankshaft manufacture to the firm of Hirth whose bolted-up roller-bearing crankshafts had been most recently installed in Porsche and Veritas cars with good results. Both ends of the crankshaft were fitted with vibration dampers, each consisting of a dozen balance weights embedded in rubber. When the first engine was run on the test bed, the vibration was clearly visible to the naked eye. The problem lay not in incorrect calculation of the balance weights but in the crankcase, whose construction was not robust enough. The immediate solution was a supplementary cast aluminium 'bridge' spanning longitudinally the gap between the paired covers on inlet and exhaust camboxes and thereby the cylinder heads which made the crankcase more rigid; the final cure came when material thicknesses were bolstered and additional ribbing provided.

Pistons were made by Mahle. The material was a special alloy to Mahle's own recipe and each weighed 475 gm. They were fitted with two oil scraper rings, one above the gudgeon pin and one below. Average oil consumption was 20 to 21 litres of Castrol-Racing per 1000 km. In coming second in the 1955 Italian Grand Prix Piero Taruffi used 23.3 litres per 1000 km, while the winner, Fangio, used 27.5. In the Belgian Grand Prix, another full-throttle circuit like Monza, Fangio's winning engine used only 19.1 litres per 1000 km. This data was accurately recorded after each and every race and practice session, as were fuel consumption figures and rate of wear on front and rear brakes. Because the cars carried 40 litres of engine oil there was always a sufficient reserve of lubricant on board.

Mixing of fuel was the responsibility of Esso's research laboratory in Hamburg. After countless tests the final potent cocktail was designated RD1: 45% benzol, 25% methyl alcohol, 25% high octane petrol, 3% acetone and 2% nitro-benzine. Fuel for test sessions and races was delivered to Stuttgart from Hamburg. In the case of the two races in Argentina in January 1955, Esso delivered direct – but had to agree that all drums sent to Beunos Aires would carry the logo of the Argentina state oil company, YPF, although they contained quite different products.

The final matters to be decided were the firing order and valve timing for the new unit. Theoretically there were three possible firing orders, the choice being the one guaranteeing constant high output in prolonged running at highest possible revs: 1, 4, 7, 6, 8, 5, 2, 3. Once chosen, the valve timing remained unaltered throughout the racing life of the

The Mercedes-Benz Formula 1 engine on the test bed.

engine from 1954 to the end of 1955. Inlets opened 20° before TDC and closed 56° after BDC; exhaust valves opened 50° before BDC and closed 14° after TDC.

The exhaust manifolds (47mm diam) led into two tail pipes (65mm dim). The induction pipes were each 235mm long and were fed from a common air box/plenum chamber.

At the start of their racing life in 1954 (French GP, 4th July), the engines developed 257PS at 8250rpm. As intended, strong torque was delivered over a wide rev range: at 6300rpm engine power was 220PS, and at this speed, peak torque was also produced (25.2 mkg). The complete engine weighed 204kg. There were tests involving a crankcase made of magnesium but the material proved so flexible that extensive reworking would have been necessary after every race. Because the weight advantage over the normal component was only 7kg, the engineers abandoned attempts to use this material.

Transmission was via a 240mm single dry-plate clutch. The propeller shaft angled to the left went beneath the driver's seat to the rear of the car where the gearbox was located. The gearbox itself had five forward speeds and reverse, which was fitted with a catch to prevent accidental engagement. The limited slip differential had a range of final drive ratios; a choice of nine available between 2.167 and 3.154:1.

The 1955 version of the Grand Prix engine with modified inlet rampipes.

Except for 1st, all were fitted with Porsche synchronizer rings and there was a plethora of ratios – three for 1st, two each for 2nd and 3rd, four for 4th and seven for 5th. The transmission used oil from the engine's oil tank and was fitted with its own feed and scavenge pumps.

Of course the W 196 engine underwent constant development. At the end of its career output had risen to 280PS and maximum revs to between 8500 and 8700 rpm; in practice for the British GP at Aintree in 1955, Piero Taruffi missed a gear and buzzed the engine well over 9000rpm without it suffering any ill effects. Valve seats were a vulnerable point; the hardening process used on them often gave problems. Otherwise the Daimler unit proved to be robust, reliable and superior to its rivals in terms of power extraction. Mercedes suffered total retirement due to engine failure in only one of the

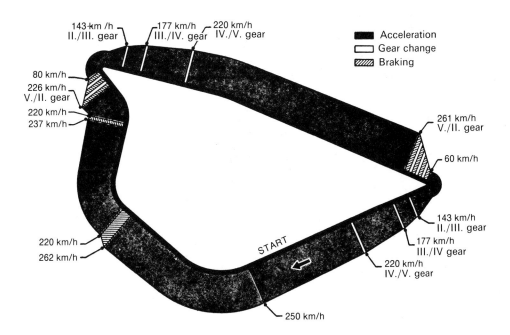

Performance chart for the W 196 in the race at Reims in 1954.

twelve Grands Prix its team contested; at Monaco in 1955, the engines of Fangio, Moss and Simon (numbers 19, 20 and 22) all broke the retaining screws on the cam follower shaft of the valve gear.

In 1955 the 300 SLR sports cars were fitted with a 3-litre cast aluminium block version of the straight-eight engine, which powered Mercedes to the World Championship in this category too.

121

The Structure

The W 196 chassis

In line with the practice of the day, the chassis of the W 196 consisted of a tubular spaceframe on which were mounted all assemblies such as engine, transmission, brakes and the numerous pipes and tanks. The diameters of the tubes were 20 and 25mm, and wall thickness varied between 0.8 and 1.0mm. The frame was designed precisely to the *Cremona-plan*, that is to say, all members were subjected to either tension or compression. Calculations were based on a possible load of up to 4.0G, i.e. four times the car's own weight.

A similar chassis arrangement was to be found on the 300 SL sports car of 1952, and also the series production 300 SL; on the W 196, however, there was no need to consider provision of door or passenger accommodation. Thus, the sides of the frame around the cockpit were very robust and built up high. The complete framework weighed no more than 36kg. In spite of its low weight, it was considerably stiffer than the twin-tube frame of the pre-war W 154 and also torsionally stronger than that of the 300 SL of 1952.

The radiator was mounted at the front of the chassis and the fuel tank at the rear. On the first versions of the W 196 the oil tank was mounted to the driver's left as there was ample room for it within the voluminous streamlined bodywork. On the later narrow-body version there was no such "luggage space" because the bodywork hugged the chassis more closely. A new position therefore had to be found for the oil tank, which contained the lubricant for transmission as well as the engine; its 40-litre capacity made it quite a large item. Eventually it gravitated to the very back of the chassis, behind and below the fuel tank.

A number of different fuel tanks were used. According to circuit characteristics and closely related fuel consumption, larger or smaller tanks could be fitted in order to avoid unnecessary additional weight. The fuel tank was mounted rigidly to the chassis by tubes running through the tank from side to side. The early days of the W 196 racing career were plagued by persistent vapour locks in the fuel system, which gave Mercedes technicians a number of headaches. Eventually the cause was isolated during testing: the fuel tank was absorbing heat radiated from the track surface (in sunny conditions) which warmed the fuel. The removal of the usual black finish from the fuel tank, leaving bare aluminium, solved the problem once and for all.

At Monaco in 1955 the W 196 appeared with outboard front brakes for the first time. This alteration was forced by a reduction of 20cm in the length of the chassis frame, which meant that there was no longer room for the large brake drums in front of the engine. Relocation of the brakes resulted in an overall weight saving of more than 40kg since the intermediate shafts, universals and the brake drum chassis mountings were unnecessary, and the drums had to be reduced in size to fit inside the front wheels.

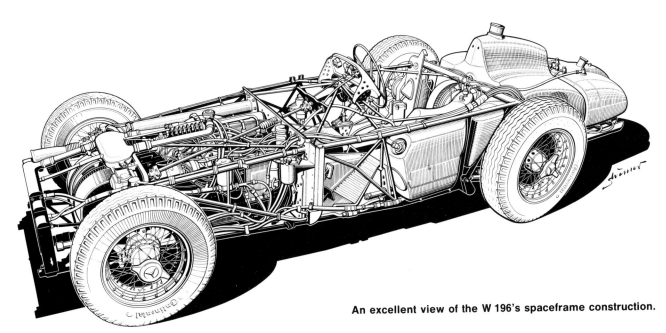

An excellent view of the W 196's spaceframe construction.

A crucial feature of any chassis is its suspension. Its characteristics and the ingenuity of the designer are decisive to the car's handling; and in a racing car, that can be every bit as important as superior engine power. The design of the front suspension on the W 196 was similar to that of the pre-war Grand Prix cars, except that on the new machines more attention was paid to overall slimming down of components in the interests of weight reduction. There were twin wishbones attached to the wheel hubs by ball joints, and a universally-jointed shaft connected the wheel to inboard brakes. Of course this layout results in a greater overall weight than one in which the brake drums are mounted directly on the wheel hubs. On the other hand there is a considerable saving in unsprung weight, which contributes to better handling.

The W 154 had been fitted with rubber stops to restrict steering movement, but on the W 196 these were replaced by a hydraulic damper arrangement. The lower wishbone was fitted with a torsion bar and also hydraulic telescopic dampers. In 1954 this was unusual. Both Ferrari and Maserati (rear) continued to build suspension systems with transverse leaf springs.

At the 1955 Monaco Grand Prix the wishbones, which were made of outrageously expensive titanium, were shortened from 290mm to 190mm, and also became lighter: the upper wishbone now weighed 618gm and the lower 1364gm. A single brake drum weighed 6870gm and, by comparison, a complete wheel and tyre was 16.7kg.

The rims were 16-inch wire-spoked. According to Rudolf Uhlenhaut there were no plans to use disc

124

wheels (as Bugatti had in the 1930s), which would have been both lighter and easier to balance:

"Again it was probably a question of lack of time. We already knew wire wheels from the pre-war era and they had given good results. Throughout the life of the W 196 we had no problems with the wheels."

The tyres were supplied by Continental in Hanover. It was no easy matter for the German company to come up with tyres that could withstand speeds up to 300km/h as well as race distances of up to 500km. Pirelli in Italy and Englebert in Belgium

Klenk, who was victim of a serious accident in testing at the Nürburgring in the 300 SL in 1953 and was a former co-driver to Karl Kling.

In the Grand Prix of Europe at the Nürburgring in 1954, new tyres were available with 9mm tread thickness. Despite the enormous demands of that circuit, which was notoriously harsh on tyres, wear was no more than 45%, and thus the same tyres could easily have been used for another race over the same distance. The tyres developed for the race in the Eifel were therefore designated *Typ Nürburg*.

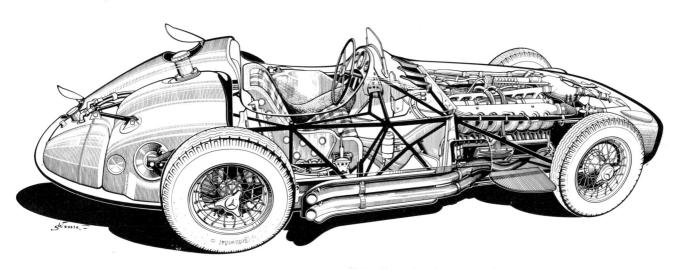

This offset view from rear shows fuel and oil tanks (rearmost). The holes in the driver's seat illustrate the type of weight-saving measures employed.

had a head start of many years when it came to the development of racing tyres. The first trials of the Continental products were carried out only in May 1954 and they immediately showed promise under extreme conditions. At Reims on 20th June, the day of the tests, track surface temperature was at a phenomenal 60°C. Despite these adverse conditions and the very high average speeds the tyres held their own. Dimensions at the front were 6.00 x 16 with tread depth of 5.5mm, and at the rear 7.00 x 16 with tread depth of 6.5mm. The rubber was designated *Typ Monza*.

After the 1954 British Grand Prix, which was run for some distance in pouring rain, there was evidence that the Continental technicians had quite a bit of ground to make up on their rivals. Conti in the meantime had secured the services of Karl

At Monza the divers were far from satisfied with the performance of their Continental tyres. On the Monday following the race a parallel test with Pirellis showed that the W 196 was considerably faster on Italian than on German rubber. Reduction of air pressure on the Continentals then resulted in times a second or so better even than the Pirellis. The lesson was learned: in future pressure would not necessarily have to be constant but could be varied according to track characteristics and lap times to give optimum results.

For the Avus race in Berlin the *Typ Avus* tyres, with shallower tread depth were used (front 3.5mm, rear 4.5mm). The decisive factor here was the nature of the high-speed track which had only one tight bend, the Südkehre, but otherwise consisted of flat-out straights and the famous banked Nordkurve. After the Spanish GP, where the tyres performed without problem, there was a test session at the Nürburgring; with data from this test, the Continental engineers prepared to develop a new "Universal" tyre for the 1955 season which would be usable in all weather conditions. The new tyres were ready for use by the time the two Argentinian races came around in January. Throughout the 1955 season there were no further tyre problems. The Conti rubber was a match for all its rivals and was even superior in some respects. Before the team's withdrawal, the 300 SLRs at Le Mans in 1955 covered the astonishing distance of 1700 kilometres without a single tyre change.

Because of the forces to which the tyres were subjected on banked circuits, a new type with reinforced carcass was used at Monza in 1955. By contrast with, for example, the Lancias, which were dogged by tyre failures throughout practice, the Continental products gave no problems whatsoever.

To return to the chassis of the W 196, the choice of rear suspension design was a surprising one. Whereas most other constructors in the Fifties went for a de Dion rear axle, the Daimler engineers chose a swing axle with very low pivot point. The idea behind the "lower pivot point" was explained by Dr Hans Scherenberg (who was also credited with numerous patents for the new axle) in a talk on the W 196 in mid-1955:

"In a normal swing axle the final drive housing is fixed firmly to the chassis via rubber mountings. The two half shafts are fitted to the housing, the universal-joint pivots being coaxial with the shafts. On the single-jointed swing axle, a single common lower pivot point is fixed to the chassis and the shafts are likewise joined by a single central universal joint. Thus the final drive housing swings with the right-hand shaft. The car's cornering attitude is directly related to this lowering of the pivot point, and the consequent lengthening of the swing axles."

At the very time of the W 196 design, Scherenberg

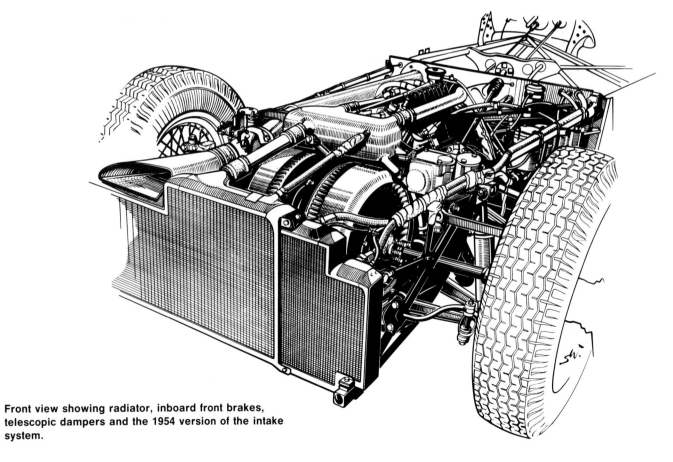

Front view showing radiator, inboard front brakes, telescopic dampers and the 1954 version of the intake system.

126

was doing very advanced pioneer work on pre-calculation of the behaviour of cars and alterations that could be made at the design stage. In analysing the behaviour of a fast-moving vehicle, lateral forces on tyres play a crucial role, forming as they do the link between vehicle and road.

On examining the graphs obtained from the

of as near equal a wheel load as possible becomes clear when you consider that in an extreme case, a wheel that jumps off the track under cornering can withstand no more lateral force. Because centrifugal force is still present, the result in this case will be a skid."

The new swing axle construction of the W 196

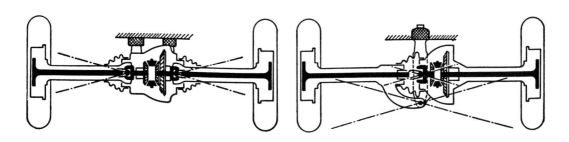

Normal swing axle   Single-jointed axle

Simplified outline of swing axle with low pivot point, compared with a normal swing axle.

calculations, the Mercedes engineers found that lateral forces do not rise in proportion to load on the wheel, but rather rise to a maximum value and then tail off rapidly. Besides this they had to bear in mind that in fast cornering, load distribution was unequal on inner and outer wheels. As load on the inner wheel reduced, so the outer wheel became more heavily loaded. Thus load distribution over the four wheels had to be kept as near equal as possible to ensure high lateral forces on all four wheels.

For these theoretical reasons a de Dion axle was ruled out for the new car. Such an arrangement had been used on the pre-war cars and very soon it became clear that, firstly, it was incapable of putting down the raw power of the supercharged engines (as Uhlenhaut put it, "Under acceleration from the Klostertalkurve up to the Karussell it was possible to see exactly where the car was gripping properly. There was a black line, broken in many places. The gaps were the places where the axle was unable to put the power through the tyres and was bouncing off the track"); and that secondly the de Dion layout translated any isolated unevenness in the track surface into a vibration affecting the whole axle, which was not greatly reduced even with well-adjusted springing.

In a talk in Brunswick at the VDI Conference in October 1955, Ludwig Kraus said, "The importance

shifted the roll centre to a point less than two centimetres above the surface of the track. Further design features, such as the inclined engine install-ation, the low clutch and low driver's seating position made possible by the diagonal propshaft, allowed the car's overall centre of gravity to be lowered to just 310mm above ground level, compared with almost twice that height on the Mercedes 220 S.

The forged inner ends of the rear swing axles were machined to H section in the interests of weight saving. The welded outer tubular ends were fixed to the wheel hub housings. The engineers built in three degrees of negative camber at the rear, that is to say, the top inner edge of the wheel rim tilted inwards slightly. In order to retain this desirable wheel angle even under conditions of reduced fuel load (a full load of 220 litres weighed 175kg), auxiliary springing was fitted starting with the British GP at Aintree in 1955. After covering half the distance, the driver could operate the mechanism which reduced the hardness of the springing and restored wheel camber to the intended figure. The auxiliary spring was worked by releasing a piston under oil pressure.

Steering was a compact Daimler-Benz worm and roller assembly fixed to the top of the chassis and offset to the left. The steering column was relatively long and kinked to the left via a universal joint behind the engine compartment bulkhead. Steering ratio was 12.65:1.

The steering wheel was also of Mercedes' own make, consisting of aluminium hub and spokes with a wooden rim. The steering wheels were normally four-spoked but Stirling Moss's special request for a three-spoked one was quickly satisfied.

The driver was seated comfortably behind the wheel, almost as though on a sofa. His legs were spread quite wide because the pedals were spaced far apart. Throttle and brake pedal were on the cockpit floor on the right, the clutch on the left. The seat itself consisted of individual pieces of varying thicknesses which could be swapped and combined according to the size of driver. The original upholstery was in a blue, orange and yellow check

which was considered very dashing at the time. That material was changed for 1955 and the various cars had likewise various seat coverings. The new pattern, which is also that to be seen on most W 196s in existence today (one exception being the car at the Motor Museum at Beaulieu), was a green and red check.

As already mentioned, the car was fitted with drum brakes. Although disc brakes had been tried with some success, especially in Britain from the early 1950s, and had also given good results in racing (the victorious C-Type Jaguars at Le Mans in 1953 had disc brakes), the Mercedes engineers opted to continue with drums. This decision may also have been prompted by the lack of time available for the preparation of a raceworthy car.

The rear axle of the W 196.

A W 196 chassis without its rear axle in the racing department workshop.

Because of their location within the body of the car itself, the brake drums were very generously proportioned and far larger than would have been possible had they been mounted on the wheel hubs (as the outboard brake layout proved at Monaco in 1955). Using the Alfin process, the Silumin alloy finning was cast directly around the inner cast-iron ring. The fins served a dual purpose: firstly they increased the flow of air and secondly they conducted heat better and more rapidly. Ventilation was further improved by a sheet aluminium shroud surrounding the whole of the drum. Measurements showed that this design gave precisely the results that had been calculated beforehand: in braking from 300km/h the temperature of the drums rose by 150°C (temperature of the smaller outboard drums rose by 195°). At an ambient temperature of 80° the final maximum values were 230 and 275° respectively.

Even under conditions of constant harsh braking, the heat was dissipated rapidly thanks to the ventilation. The result was very low wear on the brake linings (Textar PV65, width 90mm) over race distances of about 500 kilometres: the average values were between 0.18 (Nürburgring 1954) and 1.03mm (Monaco 1955) on the rear brakes, and between 0.15 (Spa 1955) and 0.84mm (Aintree 1955) at the front. The smaller narrower drums on the short-wheelbase cars were fitted with Textar linings of 68mm width. On these linings, a similar spread of readings were recorded as on the larger brakes.

The 1955 season saw the incorporation of a brake servo from the Frankfurt firm of Alfred Teves: another first in modern Grand Prix racing.

The racing department was planning to introduce disc brakes on the successor to the W 196 for the 1956 season, but, unfortunately, the car was never produced. In conclusion it should be noted that

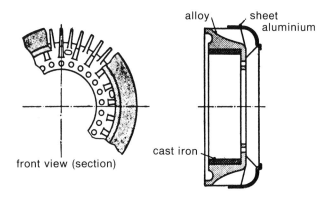

alloy sheet aluminium

cast iron

front view (section)

Detail of brake drum

Walter Kosteletzky, racing workshop manager.

overall, the chassis was a pointer to future passenger car design trends. The new swing axle concept later found applications on the series 220, 180, 180 D, 300 SL and 190 SL Mercedes. The telescopic dampers as used on the front axle soon became *de rigueur* on all racing cars. The racing engineers at Daimler-Benz managed to build a car in a short space of time that was not, however, without its teething troubles, some of which became especially apparent in the races at Monza and Pedralbes in 1954. Conscientious chassis development (including further work on the Continental tyres) resulted in the superiority over allcomers that the W 196 enjoyed in 1955, once the engine had established itself as a dominant force in its first season.

Once the short-wheelbase cars (2210 and 2150mm) had been produced, giving the optimum chassis for all circuits, Mercedes' rivals were virtually powerless. Only Lancia made positive progress at the start of the 1955 season to break the Mercedes stranglehold, but after the death of Ascari in May and the withdrawal of the Turin team, the Germans had the rest of the field at their mercy.

Fangio's record lap time at the Nürburgring in October 1955 (9:33.3 minutes), which served to mark the end of the W 196's racing career was an impressive underlining of the quality of the chassis. Particularly on the twisting Nordschleife there, carving more than 16 seconds from the lap record within a single year (given an unaltered circuit) must imply concentrated development work on the chassis in the interval.

130

Two chassis at
different stages of
completion.

A W 196 chassis under construction.

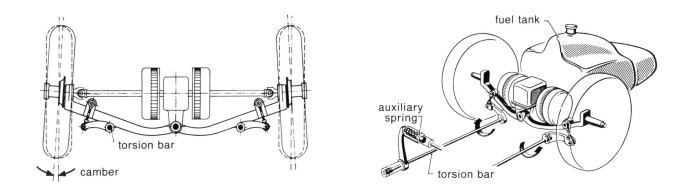

The new auxiliary spring system introduced at the British Grand Prix and its installation in the rear axle.

An unattainable dream
for many: the cockpit
of the W 196.

The External Skin

W 196 bodywork

The Mercedes-Benz W 196 caused a real stir on its début. Long before the French Grand Prix of 1954 any number of photos of the new German car had been published showing its streamlined body. But it was only when the cars appeared at Reims that everyone was finally convinced that the projected body shape would actually be used.

The idea of building an all-enveloping shell for a Grand Prix chassis instead of an open wheel version had been around even before the Mercedes engineers got to work in the early 1950s. The cars intended for the 1940 season were to have been built with streamlined bodywork. The slippery shape had been developed by Mercedes-Benz and Auto-Union engineers in the battle for the world speed record which came to a head at the end of the 1930s. Early in 1938 Bernd Rosemeyer became a victim of the engineers' incomplete knowledge of the workings of these record attempt vehicles when he crashed his Auto-Union on the Frankfurt-Darmstadt motor-

way. The outbreak of World War II put an end to all further plans to introduce streamlined vehicles in races outside those held on the Avus in Berlin.

In 1954 there were to be Grands Prix held on a number of very high-speed circuits. Reims was one such track, Silverstone, Monza and Pedralbes, with its very long straights, were others. Only the Nürburgring and the Bremgarten circuit at Bern appeared to confer no advantage on a streamlined car.

Thus the Stuttgart team opted for the all-enveloping body. Using magnesium and aluminium, panels were beaten out over wooden blocks. Walter Schüller was a true artist of the craft and was in charge of production of body panels. Before work started on the first shell, detailed studies were conducted in the small wind tunnel at the Motor Vehicle Research Institute at Stuttgart Technical College using a 1:5 scale wooden model. The first complete body to be unveiled to the press early in

A wooden model for the streamlined shell . . .

1954 was without the small windscreen that was added later after the first test sessions to protect the driver from the slipstream. This first model was also without rear-view mirrors in the bulge in front of the cockpit. The radiator entry carried a Mercedes star. The car certainly looked the part, being very low especially between the front wheels, thanks to the inclined installation of the power unit. The wings at all four corners followed the contours of the wheels and above the wheel arches at the front, additional horizontal fins protruded, which were intended as an aid to straight-line stability. The rear wings extended far back to the tail as did the central head rest.

At the test session at Reims and also in practice for the French Grand Prix the Mercedes star was retained and was fixed to a narrow horizontal chrome strip. In the race the badgework was abandoned to be used only once subsequently, 13 days after the race at Reims, at the British GP at Silverstone in 1954, when the ambient temperature was so low that the slight air turbulence resulting had no detrimental effect on cooling.

In Britain the engineers realized that the second, open-wheeled body type was urgently needed. From the cockpit of the streamlined car, the drivers were blind to anything at track level less than 2^1/2 metres from the car. Such visibility was, however, crucial to precise cornering. On fast tracks this feature was no great problem, but on slower circuits an unrestricted view of the front wheels was desirable to allow more accurate cornering.

The second version of the car had also been planned long in advance, but its preparation was overtaken in the rush to prepare for the race at Reims. One wooden mock-up, a cross between streamlined and open-wheel versions, had open front wheels but enclosed rear wheels. This layout was rejected, as was another proposal for total enclosure of the cockpit with a type of turret.

Much midnight oil was burned in preparing the open wheel version of the W 196 in time for the Grand Prix of Europe at the Nürburgring. The week after the British Grand Prix one car had been finished, but in the rush its oil tank was still mounted outside the bodywork. By the time of the race itself, three open wheel cars had been built and the oil tank repositioned at the rear and inside the bodywork. Fangio's car had a small rectangular vent in the right-hand side in front of the bonnet designed to improve the supply of intake air; the cars driven by Karl Kling and Hermann Lang had no vents, and all three cars carried a Mercedes star painted in black on the nose. All the open wheel cars (Hans Herrmann drove a streamlined version) had long shields fitted behind the exhausts to protect the right-hand rear tyres from the heat.

136

At Bern the cars were unchanged – at least in terms of bodywork – except that the vent on Fangio's car had disappeared since the race at the Nürburgring. It was destined to reappear in another guise in 1955. At Monza, too, the W 196 appeared in its recognized form (Fangio and Kling driving the streamlined cars and Herrmann the open-wheeler).

Two modifications were tried out at the Avus which were never to reappear: in practice Kling's car carried covers over the rear wheel arches which were removed by the time the race came around, and Fangio's cockpit was adorned with circular intakes.

At Pedralbes the heat shields were removed from the exhausts as it had been found during testing that the tyres were unaffected by heat from this source.

The Argentinian Grand Prix saw the Mercedes team equipped with a completely revised W 196 on which the bodywork had also undergone a number of changes. Because of the modification to the intake tract and the repositioning of the rampipes a bulge was built into the engine cover on the right hand side (the inlet "side" of the engine). At the front of this bulge there was a fine mesh grille preventing the ingress of foreign bodies. The Mercedes engineers had become especially aware of this danger after the episode with the newspaper at Pedralbes. For this very reason a hinged wire mesh grille was also fitted at the front of the radiator duct (see p.142).

The large vents in the cockpit surround were deleted and replaced by a small flap which the driver could open and close at will. At the Grand Prix of Buenos Aires on 30th January the W 196 was very strangely clad. Because of the abnormally high temperatures that had been experienced in the previous fortnight, Rudolf Uhlenhaut, Walter Kosteletzky and the team gladly fulfilled each driver's wishes for extra cockpit cooling. After the modifications, Moss's car resembled a fighting fish: extra vents had been cut in the cockpit surround which were then fitted with scoops to direct the air as required. A metal shield about 50cm long and 20cm wide was fitted to the right of the car, to protect not the tyres, but the driver from the heat.

As if to round off the whole story, Fangio, Moss and Kling drove cars powered by the 3-litre engine from the 300 SLR sports car which required an extra-large bulge in the bonnet. This was necessary because the 3-litre unit could not be inclined to the same degree as the 2.5-litre Grand Prix engine. Additional vents were cut in this bulge to provide

. . . and the finished product at the beginning of 1954 (without windscreen as yet).

A very quirky version of the "monoposto" body.

more cooling air to the engine.

Fangio's car was not cut about as much as Moss's (the Argentinian was the most resistant to heat) but the mechanics nevertheless took the shears to the cockpit of the World Champion's car, cutting a sizeable portion away from the surround to allow more air to enter.

In May 1955 at Monaco a further two revised versions of the W 196 appeared, the short-wheelbase cars. Outwardly these cars could be recognized by the cockpit surround which was no longer ventilated. Instead on the right and left there were

This model already bears close resemblance to the final article.

The first open-wheel version nears completion in the racing department workshop at Untertürkheim.

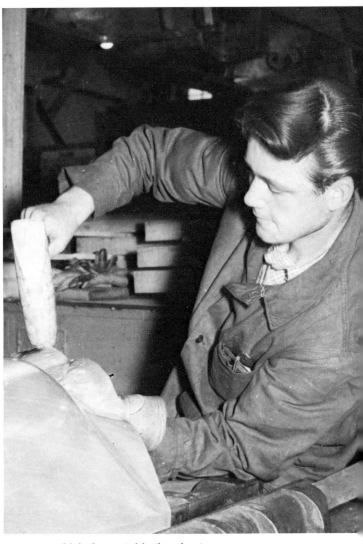

Before work begins with the sheet metal, a wooden form is first produced . . .

. . . over which the metal is then beaten.

two flaps integrated into the bodywork at the back end of the bonnet which the driver operated by a lever.

For the British Grand Prix at Aintree, Moss had a new nose on his car. The shape was exactly as before but the whole front consisted of a single panel, hinged at the front, which could be swung forwards. This allowed the mechanics better access to the engine. The black Mercedes stars had been superseded by chromed metal ones.

In testing prior to the Grand Prix at Monza at the end of August, the streamlined cars were fitted with an air brake. The design was similar to the one used on the 300 SLR at Le Mans, but on the altered high-speed circuit with its new banked section it proved superfluous. The streamlined cars, which were used only at Monza in 1955, had undergone detail modifications by comparison with their counterparts from the previous season. The vent in the cockpit surround had gone as it had on the open wheel version, replaced by flaps at the sides. To accommodate the 1955 inlet system, the all-enveloping bodywork was also remodelled and incorporated the hinged wire mesh grille at the front

Final detail work in the front of the cockpit area.

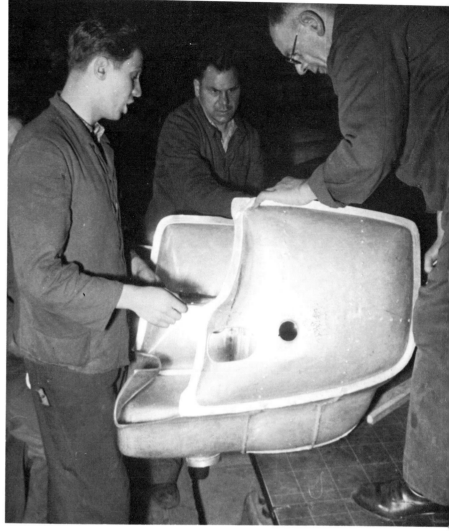

Inspection of a fuel tank.

which, however, was far less noticeable than on the monoposto.

In testing, new front panels were also tried out. One type was flat and tapered towards the front and had a shallower but wider radiator intake; both the other types used a slightly revised form of the earlier intake. Because none of these versions gave any decisive increase in flat-out performance, they were not regarded as essential modifications for future use.

Thus the external shape of the car underwent some modification on practically every outing. The racing department staff were constantly on the lookout for detail improvements. Schüller, the master metalworker, brought his ingenuity to bear on the problem of overcoming the relatively high turnover of body panels: very soon he started making magnesium panels not, as was customary, by beating them over wooden forms, but by stretching them over metal forms which he had machined. Hans Scherenberg recalls Schüller's resourcefulness with considerable pleasure: "He was truly a genius at his craft. His skill as a sheet metal worker was unparalleled." Schüller's metal forms

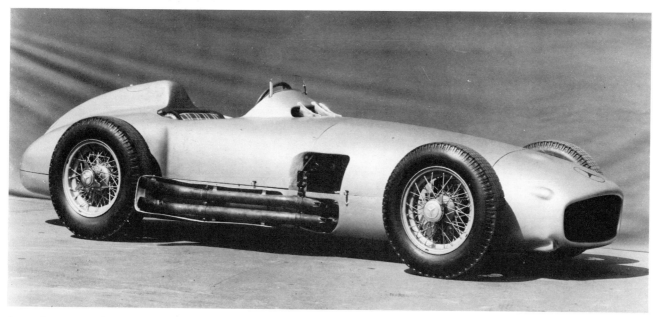

An early monoposto version with large guard over the exhausts.

enabled him to prepare small runs of panels relatively quickly. Here was another area where the Mercedes racing department was ahead of its time.

Design of the 1955 radiator grille.

1 Bowden cable
2 Tubular frame with mesh grille
3 Cable guide
4 Pivot arm
5 Return spring

Karl Kling in practice at the Avus with rear wheel covers: the covers were not used in the race.

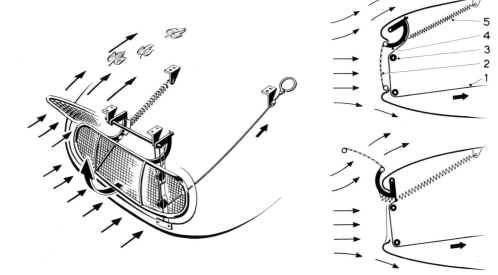

Circular intakes on the cockpit of Fangio's W 196 (Avus 1954)

The air brake similar to the one on the 300 SLR was used
only in test runs prior to the Italian Grand Prix in 1955.

This modified front section was another feature that
remained unused in the final race.

144

THE RIVALS

The Rivals

Challengers to Mercedes 1954-1955

The raiders lying in wait for Mercedes on the Grand Prix trail were mostly old campaigners with a wealth of experience. At the start of the 1954 season, however, all teams were equal in one respect. The new Formula 1 regulations required new cars from all participants. Ferrari and Maserati, Italy's two veteran manufacturers, both had resources in the form of engines and, to a certain extent, chassis from their two preceding seasons in Formula 2. But experience soon showed that use of such available equipment on the building block principle could also have its drawbacks – handing possible advantages to a totally new design.

In 1952 and 1953, the years when the World Championship was run under Formula 2 regulations, Ferrari had enjoyed clear-cut dominance. In the Tipo 500 F2 car, Ascari won consecutive Championships with ease. Given Ferrari's constant financial dramas, what could be more logical than the reworking of the 4-cylinder Formula 2 engine for the 1954 Grand Prix season? New screw-in cylinder liners were fitted to the cylinder heads to give a bore of 94mm (Tipo 500 = 90mm). A new 90mm stroke (78mm) crankshaft completed the basic set-up. This 2.5-litre (Tipo 625) engine was raced in non-formula events in Argentina and Rouen, where it proved very powerful. The twin plug 4-cylinder developed 235PS at 7000rpm. As it turned out, the Tipo 625 was used more often during 1954 than Ferrari had planned. At the same time a totally new car was under

construction which first appeared at Reims, the third round of the championship, and returned in time for the race at Monza. Again, its designer was Aurelio Lampredi.

This model, the 553, was shorter and lighter than its predecessor. Its bore and stroke measured 100 x 79.5mm with valves at an included angle of 100°. The car was very light, weighing between 580 and 600 kg, and a further feature was its side-mounted fuel tanks, fully enclosed by the bodywork which gave it a squat, plump appearance. Very soon the Type 553 became known as the "Squalo", or Whale. There was a de Dion rear axle curving round the front of the differential housing and the pinion was driven by spur gears. Gear ratios were rapidly interchangeable thanks to this design – the mechanics could complete the job in about 20 minutes. The whole of the steering mechanism and the rear axle radius arms were made of light alloy.

On its début in Reims in July, however, the Squalo proved very unreliable. The 625 was dusted down for the next few races, and its engine was fitted with cylinder heads with larger, wide-angled valves derived from the Squalo. This modification resulted in an increase in power to 264PS at 7000rpm.

For the 1955 season, the Squalo was reworked as the Tipo 555 *Supersqualo*, the side-mounted tanks being supplemented by a rear-mounted one. The engine was supplied by two 58mm twin-choke Weber carburettors and its output was now 263PS at

The in-line 4-cylinder
engine of the Ferrari
Super Squalo.

6900rpm, practically identical with the older 625 engine but with a wider power band. In place of the transverse front spring there were coil springs and an anti-roll bar. Simple lack of funds prevented Lampredi from developing the car as he thought correct. When Ferrari took over the Lancia D 50 team in mid-1955 their designer, Vittorio Jano, was also brought to Maranello, whereupon Lampredi quit Ferrari.

Ferraris were raced by a whole range of drivers in the mid-1950s. "Nino" Farina, José Froilan Gonzalez, Mike Hawthorn, Maurice Trintignant, Harry Schell, Luigi Musso and, after Lancia's withdrawal in June 1955, the young Eugenio Castellotti. Among the privateers were Manzon and Rosier as well as the Belgian journalist, Paul Frère, who contested a few races.

With the Alfa Romeo Tipo 158 Farina became the first World Champion in 1950. In 1954 and 1955, however, he posed no real threat to Mercedes. At the start of the 1954 season in Argentina he took a second place behind Fangio (then driving a Maserati), and was on the front of the grid for the Belgian Grand Prix in which he retired. On 27th June he was entered for the Supercortemaggiore race at the Autodromo di Monza.

His practice session lasted less than a lap. On one of the straights where the car was flat out, the propshaft came adrift and severed a fuel line. The red car was immediately engulfed in flame and by the time Farina had braked from 240km/h to a speed at which he could safely escape his legs were already severely burned. His 1954 season was over.

In effect, this accident put an end to Farina's whole racing career. In 1955 he again drove a Ferrari in Argentina, causing himself terrible pain in doing so. His legs were wrapped in asbestos and before the race he had morphine injections in an attempt to overcome the agony. Incredibly, in the searing heat during the Argentinian Grand Prix, he actually managed 2nd place. A few months later at Monaco he was 4th and in Belgium he came 3rd. This, though, was the final race that the driver from Turin was to contest. Ascari's death affected him deeply, and at Ferrari the young lions were in any case getting hungrier. Shortly afterwards Farina retired from racing. In 1960 he was killed in a public road car accident on the Riviera.

For 1954 Gonzalez, the Argentinian, took over as No. 1 at Ferrari after Farina's accident. In Britain he beat the Mercedes and that year was runner-up in the World Championship. The young Argentinian had his fire dampened at the Nürburgring where in practice for the Grand Prix of Europe, his young friend Onofre Marimon was killed at the wheel of his Maserati. Gonzalez himself was injured later that season in the sports car race at Dundrod in Northern Ireland and in 1955 he only took part in his home Grand Prix. Thereafter he raced only four more times in Formula 1: in the Argentinian Grands Prix of 1956 (in a Maserati), 1957 and 1960 (in a Ferrari) and, also in 1956, on his favourite circuit, Silverstone, in the British Grand Prix. He never added to the single victory he scored in 1954.

Mike Hawthorn, readily identifiable by his mop of blond hair and his obligatory polka-dot bow tie, made rapid progress through the ranks to a position among the world's élite. He first raced in 1951 and just two years later he was not only a member of the Ferrari works team, but also a Grand Prix winner, over Fangio at Reims. In 1954 he won the closing round of the season in Pedralbes in Spain to put himself third overall in the Championship behind Fangio and Gonzalez.

The following winter Hawthorn underwent a kidney operation and he continued to suffer as a result well into the 1955 season. That season he had joined the Vanwall team set up by his patron Tony

Vandervell, the man who had prepared his route into the Ferrari team for 1953. Vandervell's business was the manufacture of special bearings and Ferrari was among his customers.

But the Vanwall proved uncompetitive and after the race in Belgium Hawthorn rejoined Scuderia Ferrari – too late to benefit in terms of his World Championship position, since the team were not at peak power that year. He also bore the worst of the flak in the wake of the Le Mans disaster: in the eyes of many, he was chiefly to blame for the horrific accident. In court proceedings his name was cleared. Even at home there was something of a campaign against him: because he had avoided conscription there was even a debate in the House of Commons. There it was argued that he was representing his country as a racing driver and that was why he had been exempted from national service. Three years later, in 1958, Hawthorn became the first World Champion in the post-Farina-Ascari-Fangio period, and the first Briton to take the title. He retired from racing as Champion and a few months later was killed in a road accident in his Jaguar under mysterious circumstances.

In 1954 there was another swift Englishman driving for the other famous Italian stable. Stirling Moss drove the Maserati 250F. Like the Ferrari 625, this was a car derived from a previous Formula 2 car. To build the machine, Giulio Alfieri had taken components from the Formula 2 A6/GCM (the car that Fangio had driven to victory in the 1953 Italian GP). The car's power unit was based on the 2-litre straight-six (bore x stroke, 76.2 x 72mm) with dimensions enlarged to 84 x 75mm to bring the capacity up to 2.5 litres. With compression ratio 12:1 and three twin-choke Weber carburettors the twin plug engine developed 270PS at 8000rpm.

The 250F soon powered Fangio to his first Grand Prix win, in Argentina in 1954, but only because the privateer Musso had his car (an A6/GCM with 250F engine) cannibalized for spares for the works team of Marimon and Fangio. At the Belgian Grand Prix, Fangio and Maserati led the field home again.

Thus the team from Modena played a vital role in Fangio's World Championship triumph. Though it is often said today that he won the Championship in the two years 1954 and 1955 for Mercedes, this is only half true in the case of the first victory.

In 1954, Maserati was hard hit by the death of its top driver, Onofre Marimon, at the Nürburgring.

The pundits had predicted a great future for him as a natural successor to his fellow Argentinian Fangio. At the Italian Grand Prix at Monza Stirling Moss, who had always turned up for races in a British racing green 250F, was taken into the works team. At the end of that season the Englishman packed his bags and headed for Mercedes. The opportunity of driving the best available car had been too good for him to miss, and in this respect he differed from his fellow countryman Jackie Stewart who, in 1971, with the chance of driving for Ferrari, rejected the offer. He argued that he could not go to Maranello or else there would be no competition left for Ferrari.

The Frenchman Jean Behra, who was becoming more and more dissatisfied at Gordini, thus had the chance of driving a competitive car in the World Championship. The former French motorcycle champion stayed with Maserati until 1957; the following season he raced for BRM and the year after he ended up at Ferrari where he soon tangled with the manager Dragoni. Throughout this period, Behra was always among the very fastest drivers but sadly he would seldom make it to the end of a race. In 1959, shortly after the end of his difficult term at Ferrari, the little Frenchman, who never won a single Grand Prix in 52 starts, was killed in a sports car race at the Avus while driving a special car known as the Behra-Porsche (a single-seater precursor of the later Works Formula 2 Porsche). The car went off the banked Nordkurve section and smashed into a flagpole.

Another Maserati driver in 1954 was the "American in Paris", Harry Schell. The handsome, lanky Schell with his playboy image showed real class, especially in Spain where he led for many laps after Ascari's retirement. But his masterful drive ended with a spin and a crunched tail. His only other start for Maserati was in 1955 in Argentina, after which he drove a Ferrari at Monaco before joining Vanwall. In 1957 he returned to Modena before driving for BRM and Cooper (where the language barrier was probably less of a problem). On 13th May 1960 at Silverstone, Harry Schell, whose best ever placing was 2nd at the Dutch GP in 1958, was killed in a Cooper.

It was not until 1957 that Maserati really reaped the benefits of the most popular Formula 1 car of all time, the 250F. Fangio won the World Championship at the wheel of this car which, in an interview with the Italian journalist Corrado Milanta at the end of 1954, he described as that year's best design (despite his experience of the W 196). That Championship was his fifth and last: after a final race with the 12-cylinder 250F at Reims in 1958, he hung up his helmet for good.

By contrast with Fangio's career and the effective life of the 250F, Lancia's term as Grand Prix challengers was brief indeed. The Turin firm had enjoyed considerable success for several years in sports car racing and when the new Formula 1 was announced for 1954, Dr Gianni Lancia decided, in August 1953, to build a Grand Prix contender.

The 63-year-old Vittorio Jano was in overall charge of the project. Engine design was by Ettore Zaccone Mina, chassis and suspension were the responsibility of Francesco Feleo. The first Grand Prix car from the Lancia stable was designated the D50; it had a 90° V8 twin plug engine with four overhead camshafts, two valves per cylinder with dual springs and four twin choke carburettors. Three versions were built, one with bore and stroke 76 x 68.5mm, one with 74 x 72mm and a third with the almost square dimensions, 73.6 x 73.1. Power output from this final version was 250PS at 8000rpm.

The pannier fuel tanks gave the D50 its distinctive shape and were intended to ensure consistent handling characteristics and weight distribution under varying fuel loads as the race progressed. The engine was a stressed member serving to connect the spaceframe rear with the front of the car. A full-length spaceframe was thus unnecessary and the result was a considerable saving in weight. At 600kg, the Lancia was one of the lightest Grand Prix cars in use at the time.

The power unit was inclined at an angle of 12° to the axis of the car, allowing the propshaft to run towards the side of the driver, whose position was thus very low. The Lancia was a very compact vehicle and in fact the most attractive design of all the 1954-55 contenders. The five-speed gearbox was in unit with the differential and the car's wheelbase measured 2280mm, the front track 1290mm and the rear track 1330mm. The rear axle was of the de Dion type with transverse leaf spring and there were outboard drum brakes all round.

On 8th February 1954 the Lancia D 50 was first put through its paces at Turin's Caselle airport. Giuseppe Gigglio, the Lancia test driver, was first to

The straight-six in the Maserati 250F.

drive, after which Alberto Ascari took the wheel. Ascari had signed for Lancia on 21st January, as had Luigi Villoresi. Though the car had been put together in rapid time, the detail work dragged on and on: the D 50 did not make its début until October in Spain.

Ascari's loyalty to Lancia during those months was impressive: after all he was reigning World Champion and would have been keen to defend his title (in 1953 he established the record, which stands to this day, of five consecutive Grand Prix wins) and also to show Fangio in his Mercedes who was boss. Ever since 1951, Fangio had been his great rival. That year the Championship had been decided in the Argentinian's favour in the last round in Spain, when Ascari encountered tyre problems with his 4.5-litre Ferrari.

Gianni Lancia loaned his driver to Maserati and Ferrari on a couple of occasions, but that was no way for the great man from Milan to win a Championship. When Pedralbes came around and Ascari could finally get down to business with the new car, he mauled the opposition both in practice and in the opening laps of the race. But after nine laps his race was run, the machine out with the usual new car problems.

In the first race of the 1955 season in Argentina, the Lancia trio of Ascari, Villoresi and newcomer Eugenio Castellotti were in deep water with the handling of their cars. They all spun time and again, because in fast cornering the tanks tended to accentuate the centrifugal force, which made the D 50s liable to break out without warning, leaving no time for correction to be made. Ascari nonetheless led the race for the first 22 laps until retiring – after a spin.

On 27th March Lancia celebrated its first Formula 1 win. At the non-championship Valentino Grand Prix in Turin (Valentino being the name of the park through which the course passed) Ascari won. Engine output was now 265PS and the engineers had gone a long way to remedying the handling worries.

The young Maserati understudy Sergio Mantovani suffered a horrible accident at the race. His left leg had to be amputated after his car rolled several times. Six months later he was back in the cockpit of a specially built sports car but his Grand Prix career was over.

At the race at Pau in France it looked as if Lancia was heading for a comfortable victory for Ascari but on the 90th lap out of 110 he had to stop to have a leaking oil hose put right. Behra went on to win in his Maserati ahead of Castellotti, whose Lancia team mates Villoresi and Ascari came home 4th and 5th. Ascari won in Naples on 8th May but it was an insignificant victory in a race for only nine cars.

The Lancia team arrived in Monaco with high hopes; the narrow, twisty street circuit seemed tailor-made for the D50s. Ascari put up fastest lap in practice but only after a titanic effort – the revised short-wheelbase Mercedes pressed him hard. On race day the Mercedes pair of Fangio and Moss left their rivals floundering in their wake. Louis Chiron was in the Lancia team after winning the 1954 Monte Carlo rally for Lancia in an Aurelia B 20, but he and his three team mates were never in the hunt. When Mercedes dropped out with trivial faults Ascari inherited the lead after covering four-fifths of the distance. That very lap he skidded at the chicane by the harbour and the car went out of control and into the sea. His nose appeared to be broken but he was otherwise unharmed. The final classification in this race of attrition showed the remaining three Lancias to be 2nd (Castellotti), 5th (Villoresi) and 6th (Chiron, though several laps in arrears).

Four days later Italy was rocked by the death of Ascari during casual testing at Monza. Lancia announced its immediate withdrawal from racing – outside financial pressures also playing their part. Mercedes' most serious likely competitors thus disappeared from the scene before they had really had a chance to show their hand.

On 26th July 1955, to give the exact date, the whole of the Lancia team (but for a single car in Fiat's possession, now the sole surviving D 50) was transferred to Enzo Ferrari. Six Formula 1 cars, two transporters and countless spares changed hands. Even Vittorio Jano went to Maranello and worked on revisions to the D 50 for the 1956 season. That year Fangio won the World Championship in the Lancia-Ferrari, but only after the selfless Peter Collins handed over his car when the Argentinian retired in the deciding race at Monza. If Collins had continued he would have won the title. The former D 50 continued in use as the Ferrari 801/57 until the end of 1957 and was followed by the Ferrari Dino 246.

The young Eugenio Castellotti, who had been just as quick in practice as his team No. 1, drove the last race contested by a works Lancia. In Belgium he was fastest in practice but soon dropped out of the race. He then transferred to Ferrari and by virtue of a 3rd place at Monza and 5th at Zandvoort (to add to his 2nd at Monaco) he emerged as 3rd placed man in the World Championship, best non-Mercedes driver, and in his first season at that.

In 1956 he put his Ferrari on the front row of the grid on five occasions (his team mates were still Fangio, Collins and Luigi Musso) but his points tally was less impressive and he finished 6th in the final ranking. At the first race of 1957 he came away practically unscathed from an accident, but then came 14th March. At the Autodromo di Modena, a circuit consisting of the taxiways of a small airfield, he was doing some private testing. That same day Behra was also testing his Maserati at the circuit, and was timed at less than a minute for a lap.

This naturally fired up Castellotti and once again he climbed aboard his scarlet Ferrari. He never returned from his first lap. Entering a narrow chicane far too quickly the car slid off and into a low concrete wall, the car rolled over and over before finally slamming into the concrete ledge of the small grandstand. Castellotti died from serious head injuries; the impact had torn the helmet from his head.

Cesare Perdisa, who came from a wealthy though unsupportive family and was a friend of Castellotti, was also forced to give up racing after a very short career. In 1955 Perdisa had come third at Monaco on his Grand Prix début behind Castellotti.

The white-haired Luigi "Gigi" Villoresi, team mate and fatherly friend of Ascari for many years

The Lancia D 50 was powered by a V8.

both at Ferrari and Lancia, was another who had to retire from the sport in 1956. He was involved in a serious accident while racing a 2-litre Maserati in a sports car event in the Roman suburb of Castelfusano.

By contrast with the misfortunes and disasters that befell the Italians at the end of the 1950s, the British were positively on the march. The Vanwall, brainchild of Tony Vandervell, first went into action at Monza in the 1954 Italian Grand Prix. Though it first appeared with a 2.3- rather than the maximum allowable 2.5-litre engine the experts cast many an approving glance over the slender green car.

The following year Mike Hawthorn joined Vanwall, but soon left to return to Maranello because of the car's extreme unreliability. The 4-cylinder engine borrowed its cylinder head design from the "Manx" Norton motorcycle engine, a hugely successful design from a company controlled by Tony Vandervell. Like Daimler-Benz, Vandervell had also opted for (indirect) fuel injection. The engine capacity for 1955 was 2490cc (bore/stroke 96 x 86mm), separate Amal carburettor bodies less float chamber controlling air supply to each individual cylinder. Valve gear consisted of twin overhead camshafts and valve springs were of the exposed hairpin type, fitted between the camshafts and the cylinder heads. By mid-1955 the engine was delivering 265PS at 8100rpm. The chassis, originally built by Cooper, had a de Dion rear axle and independent front suspension and there were disc brakes all round (a system vastly more popular in Britain than on the Continent).

After Hawthorn's departure for Maserati, Schell

153

took over the Vanwall seat and in the 1955 British Grand Prix at Aintree he was a sensational seventh fastest in practice, faster than all the Ferraris. His race showing was, however, halted by a leaking brake pipe. Vandervell had to wait until 1957 before his cars finally took the Grand Prix world by storm. His team for 1957/58 consisted of Stirling Moss, Tony Brooks and Stuart Lewis-Evans. Between 1955 and 1960 the green cars took the start in 28 Grands Prix and notched up nine wins – a victory every three races, a record that few marques could match. In fact there was only one car that managed to better that record: Mercedes took nine wins from twelve races.

Alongside these figures, Gordini's roll of honour looked quite pitiful. Amédée Gordini, originally an Italian national who changed his name from Amadeo before taking French citizenship, was Grand Prix racing's true battler. Always on the breadline, his modest means would permit the building of only a few cars which, once made, were constantly on the go in the quest for prize money from non-championship races where the big works teams were only thinly represented, if at all. Thus there was little time for development work to be carried out on the elfin blue cars in the course of a season. This accounts for the fact that they were the only cars which, instead of showing improvement, actually got worse as the season progressed.

The Gordini was the only Grand Prix car with a rigid rear axle and the only one with a single plug engine, the relatively small bore making a second plug unnecessary. The 1954 Grand Prix car was virtually identical with the 1952/53 Formula 2, though with larger capacity. Like Ferrari and Maserati, Gordini simply exchanged cylinder liners.

The straight-six was developed from the four-cylinder 1100, 1300 and 1500cc Simca-based engines. The Gordini had a 4-speed gearbox, a ZF self-locking differential and weighed in at just 580kg. Its weakness lay in the engine which developed only 220PS, far too low to pose a serious threat to the big boys, and in general mechanical unreliability. Jean Behra's performance at the wheel in a number of races is thus the more remarkable. At Silverstone in 1954 he posted fastest lap at 1:50.00, but because the same time was achieved by six other drivers, the otherwise usual point for fastest lap was not awarded. The blue cars took part in 40 Grands Prix between 1950 and 1956 – the reward: just two 5th places.

In 1955 Gordini unveiled a completely new design. But the car was not race-ready until the last round of the season at Monza and the following year the team contested only six races before Gordini turned his back on Formula 1. The 1955 unit was a 2498cc 8-cylinder (bore/stroke 75 x 70mm). The twin overhead camshaft engine had four twin-choke Solex carburettors and the simple Scintilla-Vertex magneto ignition system. Output was 256PS at 7300rpm. The car weighed 650kg and had its gearbox in unit with the engine. The design was also notable for Messier disc brakes, wide, streamlined nose and all-round Watts-linkage independent suspension. The car probably had a great deal of potential but again Gordini's shoestring finances could not stretch to a serious development programme. The quality of the drivers was also somewhat suspect: Bayol, Pollet and Lucas were second division, if that. Behra, the team's best bet, was lost to Maserati at the end of 1954 because Gordini could not afford to pay him.

The 1954 and 1955 seasons were awash with rumours of new Formula 1 projects. The return of Alfa Romeo was a particularly persistent topic and, true enough, in Milan a team of engineers under Dr Giuseppe Busso were working on a Grand Prix car. The engine was ready for use: a 12-cylinder with alloy heads (bore/stroke 68 x 75mm). Two valves per cylinder at 90° to each other operated in hemispherical combustion chambers. Power take-off was from the middle of the roller bearing crankshaft (Hirth System) and there was dry-sump lubrication for the aluminium crankcase. The 5-speed gearbox in unit with the rear axle was driven via a multi-plate dry clutch.

The real surprise was the chassis design for the Tipo 160. Instead of the usual seating position between the axles, the driver was to sit behind the rear axle. A 4-wheel-drive system was being worked on. Preparations got no further than the modification of a Tipo 159 with the driving seat relocated to the rear. After a session at Monza, the Alfa test driver Consalvo Sanesi was impressed, but shortly afterwards the whole team of engineers working on the ambitious project were put back on to series production tasks when the new Giulietta was given priority. The incredible 12-cylinder engine still exists today, but the rest of the car remains a mere paper tiger.

Not so the Bugatti 251, which was unveiled to the press in November 1954 on the airfield at Etzheim in Alsace; its first and last race appearance was then delayed until 1956. The design was the work of Gioachino Colombo whose Milan design firm was contracted to Bugatti. It was a revolutionary design: the 8-cylinder mid-engine was mounted transversely behind the driver and the front wheels were encircled by a vast aerodynamic nose. A lack of financial commitment, a sporadic test programme and a generally half-hearted approach by the Bugatti management marred the chances for a renaissance of the famous marque. The last Grand Prix appearance by a Bugatti was a débâcle and unworthy of the once great name. At Reims in 1956, Trintignant was a whole 17 seconds slower in practice for the French Grand Prix than pole man Fangio in his Lancia-Ferrari. In the race proper the demoralized Frenchman gave up after only 18 laps of the 60-lap race when (besides the car's disastrous handling) the unfiltered inlet tracts became blocked with dust.

Especially in the West German motoring press, there were repeated rumours of a Formula 1 car under construction at EMW, the East German car firm Eisenacher Motoren-Werke. The eastern bloc challenger never materialized. British challengers besides the Vanwall came from Connaught during 1955 – one even had streamlined bodywork – but they proved as uncompetitive as the HWM and the Cooper (whose time came at the end of the decade).

For the non-championship race at Pau, the Italian Arzani turned up, named after its designer. During the race its driver, Alborghetti, crashed through a fence and died in the wreckage; the car was never used again. This race also saw the appearance of two Deutsch-Bonnets. René Bonnet was the only designer to attempt to build a supercharged challenger for the 2.5-litre formula, which allowed such engines a capacity of up to 750cc. The tiny Panhard-based cars had rigid rear axles and front-wheel drive and, as well as diabolical handling, had a hopeless power disadvantage with only 120 or 130PS on tap. The Deutsch-Bonnet vanished as quickly (or should it be, as slowly) as it had appeared.

The lesson to be drawn from this detailed survey of Mercedes' rivals in 1954 and 1955 is this: with all due respect for the technical prowess of the team from Stuttgart, and also the attacking style of their drivers, the team's success came at what was for them a favourable time. Ascari and Farina were out of commission, Ferrari was on the ropes with financial trouble and Maserati was unlucky in that its drivers either deserted to the opposition (Mercedes) or else had accidents (Marimon) – the Germans only needed to pick up the pieces. Such speculation is however contradicted by the facts: the W 196 triumphed on nine of the 12 occasions on which it took part in a Grand Prix. Each win was as difficult as the opposition could possibly make it. The rivals were finally to wake up only after Mercedes had cleaned up and withdrawn from the scene.

The straight-six Gordini engine.

THE TEST
PROGRAMME

The Test Programme

Track testing the W 196

Practice makes perfect. In July 1954 this ancient proverb was proved correct by the Daimler-Benz racing department. But we should also remember the regular testing sessions throughout the winter of 1953-54 that contributed so much to the W 196's later success.

The first time the car turned a wheel under its own power was in December 1953, in bitterly cold conditions and against a backdrop more suitable as the set of a film about industrial espionage than the scene of a new racing car's first trial run. The action took place around the Daimler-Benz factory at Stuttgart-Untertürkheim, between the main gate, the research department buildings and the area where the test track is sited today. The workers going home in the evening after finishing their shift could not believe the sight they saw: a strange, high-speed device hurtling through the darkness making a devilish racket. The spectators were not to know that they were witnessing an historic event – the W 196 was being given its very first try out.

Karl Kling was at the wheel, sitting amid an apparent tangle of tubes, hoses and cables. The car had no bodywork at that time. That was yet to come, in the first few weeks of the New Year. Then it was on to Hockenheim on 18th February; a real circuit could give more accurate first impressions of the car's behaviour than could be observed within the confines of the factory.

Just two months later the team went to Italy, where winter had already given way to early spring and serious testing could be attempted. On 4th and 5th May 1954, W 196 chassis number 1 was taken to Monza for the first test runs with the team's new Continental tyres.

More trials followed on the Autobahn near Schwieberdingen. Getting a motorway closed for special purposes in 1954 was nowhere near as simple as it had been before World War II. In those days the Mercedes people would just put a sign up saying "Beware, race testing", and then unleash the cars. The number of cars using the motorways was so small that there was no need to close a whole one off when testing at speeds of up to 300km/h. There must have been dozens of drivers in their Adler Trumpfs or Hanomag Kommissbrots who were scared half to death when Rudolf Caracciola or Manfred von Brauchitsch went tearing past with superchargers screaming. But in 1954 thorough preparation was needed if Mercedes wanted to do such a test, as on 12th April and 6th and 8th May. The relevant police authorities had to be notified and they then issued times at which the motorway could be used for test purposes. One hour was allotted on each day; there were others who wanted to use the road after all.

Thus the team spent more and more time at Hockenheim, which is only 90km from Untertürkheim. Testing could be carried out with far fewer interruptions on that very fast track (which in those days was driven anti-clockwise and took the

First test session at Hockenheim, Karl Kling at the wheel.

cars through the town itself) and it soon became the team's weekly destination. It was there that Hans Herrmann very nearly lost his life in May 1954 when a burst hose sprayed oil all around the cockpit as he approached the Stadtkurve and he was forced to drive straight on because his foot kept slipping off the brake pedal. The car fetched up in the wall of a house in the town, but the talented youngster escaped with badly burned feet. The team was there on 11th, 12th and 28th May, and also for six days in June (8th-10th, and on the 12th, 13th and 20th). From 28th May the second car, chassis number 2, took part in testing.

Reims on 21st and 22nd June 1954 was the venue for the last preparatory test shortly before the race début of the W 196. The car was still equipped with the four twin-choke Weber carburettors which had been standard throughout the series of tests. Trials on the fuel-injection system continued right up until

the French Grand Prix itself. The final trial went very well but Neubauer advised a postponement of the car's first official appearance. Eventually the decision was reversed and the cars duly took the start at Reims, even though an immediate victory was thought unlikely.

In practice for its first race, the W 196 returned fuel-consumption figures that made a mockery of all the pre-race calculations. As planned, the cars were fitted with fuel injection; it was the first ever appearance of a fuel-injected engine in the history of motor racing and the system was intended to reduce fuel consumption. Experience had shown that this

Testing at Reims in June 1954.

Uhlenhaut with the first "monoposto" version of the W 196. The oil tank is still positioned externally.

160

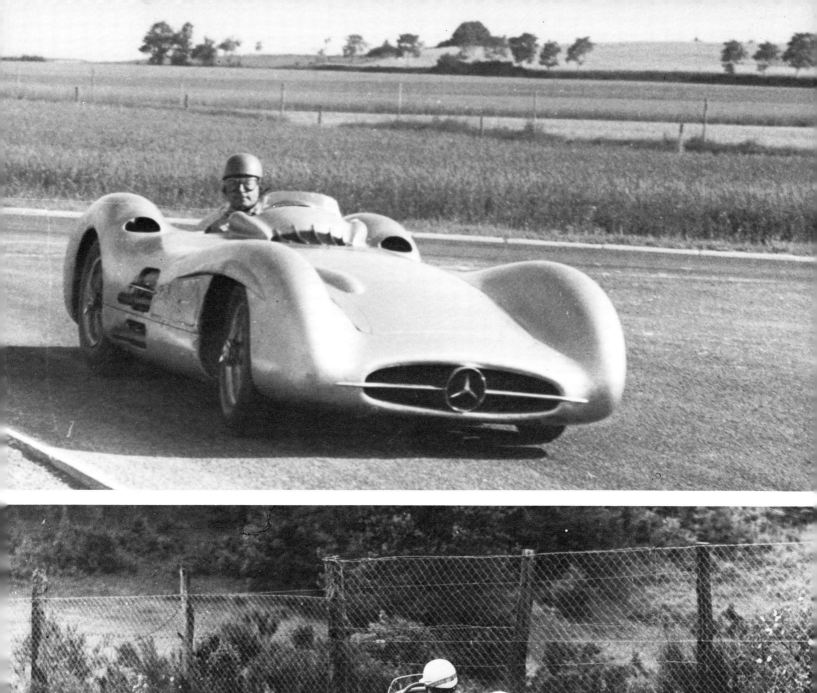

Moss at Hockenheim in 1954. The radiator grille under evaluation here was not used during the 1955 season.

would be the case and so did the calculations prepared by the Daimler-Benz staff. But practice now resulted in a consumption of over 40 litres per 100km instead of the expected 35 litres. This meant that fuel would run out 48km short of the flag, but a refuelling stop would take too long because all the other contenders were well able to go the full distance (just on 500km) without replenishment.

The wet track was believed to be responsible for the car's unexpected thirst; wheelspin was far greater and led to higher engine speeds than would be normal on a dry circuit. Whatever the reason, Uhlenhaut sped back in his 300 SL to Stuttgart,

where extra tanks were hastily built and temporarily installed just before the start on Sunday on the left-hand side of the cockpit.

This was the first and only time that the team's calculations went so wide of the mark. The Reims incident was a one-off in the whole of the W 196's career. In future the results obtained by the calculations staff of Karl-Wilhelm Müller, Hans Enke and Otto Lang were nearly always confirmed. Throughout the car's racing life – and that of the 300 SLR sports-racer – testing naturally became a regular component of the team's timetable: among the sessions were those at the Nürburgring (21st-

This W 196 looks a sight after acceleration tests at Stuttgart – Echterdingen airport.

23rd July 1954, first tests with the open-wheel bodywork, 27th-29th September, 2nd-5th November 1954), at Hockenheim (20th-21st and 24th, 26th and 30th November 1954) and at Monza (22nd-25th August 1955). Practice does indeed make perfect.

THE RACES

The Première

41st Grand Prix de l'ACF, Reims, 4th July 1954

At last the great day arrived. Mercedes-Benz racing cars lined up at the start of a European Grand Prix for the first time since 1939. In 1914 Christian Lautenschlager won the French Grand Prix; in 1934 the Silver Arrows from Auto-Union and Mercedes-Benz marked the return of a German presence to the Grand Prix fray at Montlhéry (though suffering defeat at the hands of Louis Chiron in his Alfa Romeo), and in 1954 it was again the French Grand Prix that had been chosen by the German team, this time for the début of the W 196. The race fans had turned out *en masse* for this one; 300,000 of them came to the triangular circuit near Reims with the prospect of finally seeing an end to years of monotony in Formula 1. Since 1952 only two makes had shared the spoils in Grand Prix racing – Ferrari had 14 wins to its name and Maserati had picked up the remaining three.

Two of these wins had been scored in 1954. In Argentina, and then in Belgium on 20th June, two weeks before Reims, Fangio had been in dominant form with the works Maserati 250F. But the Argentinian ace, who had won the World title in 1951 for Alfa Romeo, had signed for the newly formed Mercedes-Benz team for the remainder of the season. Neubauer had seen him win at the Swiss Grand Prix at Bremgarten in 1951, and from that point onwards, it was clear to the Fat Man that the man known to his compatriots as *El Chueco* (Bandy Legs), would be indispensable for the team from

Stuttgart once Mercedes-Benz was back on the Grand Prix trail.

Fangio thus had a decent points cushion when he arrived at Reims. His victories at Buenos Aires and Spa-Francorchamps, plus the point for fastest lap in Belgium, gave him 17 points. His closest Championship rival at that stage was the Ferrari driver Maurice Trintignant with nine points.

As the three shining silver W 196s were unloaded from the transporters on Thursday, people thronged the paddock to witness the spectacle. Neubauer was visibly enjoying the performance. He took centre stage and, with his vast stomach occupying much of the available space, tugged contentedly at the lapels of his jacket.

Joining Fangio, obviously number one in the Mercedes team, were Karl Kling and the up-and-coming Hans Herrmann. Friday practice was the first occasion on which the W 196 was powered by the engine with fuel injection. Just 10 days before the event on 21st and 22nd June the Mercedes entourage had been at Reims for testing, though the car was still in Weber-carburetted form. Fangio's and Kling's cars (chassis nos. 3 and 5) were fitted with engines that had spent some time running on the bench at Untertürkheim. Herrmann's W 196 (chassis no. 2, a car that had been at Reims 10 days before) was fitted with a power unit which had not yet run as time had become so short.

Onlookers and rivals alike were most interested in

Board member Fritz Nallinger and Alfred Neubauer keep an eye on maintenance in the workshop.

166

the streamlined bodywork sported by all three cars. It was a thoroughly unconventional style of body for Grand Prix racing where cars were traditionally open-wheelers. Even so, the Mercedes engineers had read the rules, and there was nothing in the fine print to forbid fully enclosed wheels (by contrast with today's Formula 1). Because most of the circuits to be used in 1954 were high-speed venues, the designers had decided on a particularly slippery body shape. Externally then, the W 196 was quite different from its French and Italian rivals.

Alberto Ascari, World Champion in 1952 and 1953, was waiting for the Lancia D 50 to be finished and was on loan to Maserati for the French Grand Prix. Another driver contracted to Lancia, Gigi Villoresi, was also driving a Maserati. Other men at the wheel of the 250F were Onofre Marimon, Prince Bira of Siam, Roy Salvadori, Roberto Mières, Ken Wharton and Harry Schell.

Ferrari, the other big Italian team, was without Giuseppe Farina who had burned both legs badly in a serious accident in May. The prancing horse was represented by Fangio's fellow Argentinian José Froilan Gonzalez and the young Mike Hawthorn, both driving the tubby new Tipo 553 *Squalo*, or "Whale". The older Tipo 625 was in the hands of Maurice Trintignant and private Ferraris had been entered for Robert Manzon and Louis Rosier.

Lance Macklin had brought a 2-litre HWM to France, and further back on the grid were four blue Gordinis once again poorly prepared for a race. Jean Behra, Paul Frère, André Pilette and Berger were the drivers, but they posed no threat to the Mercedes.

In practice Fangio had been the only man to break the 200km/h barrier. His effort secured him a prize of 50 bottles of champagne which the organizers had offered to anyone bettering this mark. The 8.301km circuit at Reims-Gueux had been improved since the previous year and the asphalt surface was in fine condition. The track was roughly triangular with two particularly sharp corners. The first after about half lap distance was a 130° bend where maximum speed was about 80km/h. The longest straight followed, which led to the most spectacular point on the course at Thillois. This was a 150° bend where maximuum speed was about 60km/h. Top speed of about 260km/h was reached shortly before Thillois, after which the driver had to change rapidly from 5th to 2nd gear and wipe off 200km/h. At Reims at least as much

was demanded of the brakes as of the engine.

The Mercedes camp was out of sorts after practice. Average fuel consumption had risen from about 35 litres/100km in testing to a figure above 40 litres. They figured that the reason behind their car's unwelcome thirst was the damp track which was causing greater wheelspin on acceleration. Sunday's weather forecast was changeable.

Whatever the reason, the cars would not last the whole 506km distance without refuelling about 50km from the end. They could not afford to lose time with a fuel stop because the races in Argentina and Belgium, had shown that Maserati and Ferrari could easily go the whole distance. After Saturday practice Rudolf Uhlenhaut drove back to Stuttgart, returning to Reims in the early hours of race day with three specially made extra tanks in his Mercedes 300 SL. The tanks were swiftly installed on the left of the cockpit on the W 196s. There had also been concern about oil frothing during practice. Hans Scherenberg instructed the mechanics to fit smaller diameter hoses in a number of places to build up pressure. The potentially damaging frothing problem vanished immediately.

In spite of these niggling faults, unavoidable for most new cars on their début, the two W 196s of Fangio and Kling had given a convincing display in practice and lined up together harmoniously on the front row of the grid. They were joined by third fastest man Alberto Ascari with his Maserati. The Italian was a mere tenth of a second slower than Kling but over a second behind Fangio. First up for Ferrari was Gonzalez, sharing row two with Marimon in his Maserati, and Hans Herrmann in the third Mercedes was sandwiched between Hawthorn and Bira on row three.

Shortly after 2.45pm on Sunday, the ageing Charles Faroux, doyen of the French sporting press, flagged the drivers away for the Grand Prix de l'ACF (Automobile Club de France). Fangio and Kling immediately roared to the front in their silver cars.

Ascari gave chase to the two Stuttgart machines in his Maserati but he was out within a lap. He had already suffered two engine failures in practice and this time his transmission packed up. The first serious contender was already out of the running.

The Ferrari duo of Gonzalez and Hawthorn trailed the Mercedes pair after Ascari's retirement. Herrmann was less than happy with fifth place at this point and stepped up his pace. He displaced Hawthorn after seven laps and Gonzalez after eleven, setting a new lap record on the way and establishing a Mercedes one-two-three.

Gonzalez in his turn was not hanging about either. After twelve laps he crossed the line having retaken his former third place, but he had pushed his car too far. A few kilometres later, the car from Modena rolled to a halt in a welter of smoke. Hawthorn had already been forced to retire by that time and so both works Ferraris were out before one-quarter distance.

Lap 17 provided more drama for the spectators: Hans Herrmann parked his car with a smoking engine, a legacy of insufficient time for bench testing at the factory. The rest of the field saw a chink of light. Was this the beginning of the end for the other Mercedes too? There were still a number of Ferraris and Maseratis in the hunt.

Those who lived in hope were themselves the ones who suffered next: Villoresi's Maserati hobbled around the track with a sick engine and within five laps, another three Maseratis were out. Wharton had a transmission failure, Schell's fuel pump packed up and Mières suffered engine failure. After 36 laps there were only seven cars left after Rosier and Trintignant (Ferrari) dropped out. At the front, Fangio and Kling sped around the track, trading places time and again.

At the end of lap 38 there was a heart-stopping moment for the Germans in the crowd. Kling crossed the line several seconds ahead of his Argentinian team mate after Fangio had spun at Thillois in the drizzle that had begun to fall. Just a few kilometres later the Mercedes were back together and Fangio led the next lap.

On the stroke of 5 pm, as if on a secret command, many of the spectators put their radios to their ears. The World Cup Final had just kicked off in Bern. At 17.06, with ten laps to go at Reims, there came the first cry of 'Goal': Puskás had put Hungary into the lead.

Fangio and Kling continued to play cat and mouse. They drove nose to tail, sometimes side by side and no one knew who was going to be ahead at the finish. At 17.11 the Hungarians stretched their lead to 2:0 with a goal from Czibor. German hopes seemed dashed, but then Hungary had been clear favourites from the start, while here in Reims a remarkable West German success looked to be on the cards.

A minute later as the Mercedes pair crossed the line again there was another goal: Morlock had slipped a penalty in after a foul on Sepp Herberger and that same minute Rahn hit the equalizer.

Back on the track Fangio and Kling were shaping up for the final duel. From Thillois the pair were separated by only a couple of lengths. With two kilometres ahead of them they both poured on the power. Kling edged up on Fangio inch by inch and the spectators on the home straight all leapt from their seats: no one wanted to miss a moment of the battle. The cars neared the line as one, Kling was right on Fangio's shoulder and the cheering drowned the scream of the engines – the race was over.

Fangio won the French Grand Prix by about a metre. The Mercedes men had scored a one-two on their return to international racing. Their rivals were in the dust and licking their wounds. The privateer Robert Manzon was left to uphold the honour of Ferrari, coming 3rd a whole lap in arrears in his home Grand Prix. Bira and Villoresi nursed their Maseratis into 4th and 5th, and the only other cars running were the Gordinis of Behra (5 laps behind) and Peul Frère (11 laps behind).

The uproar had hardly died down, the victory ceremony was just finishing and the odd bottle of bubbly was being cracked in the Mercedes pit, when there was another shout of triumph: with six minutes

Race numbers are painted on the cars before the début.

Scherenberg, Nallinger
and Neubauer wrestle
with the problem of
vapour locks.

169

The jubilant atmosphere after the team's successful practice: Neubauer (seated), Karl Kling and his wife (centre), Nallinger and Uhlenhaut (left).

to go, Helmut Rahn had put West Germany ahead by 3:2. Toni Turek blocked all the Hungarians' best efforts in the final six minutes and that 4th July, the West Germans became World Champions. What a day . . .

The three Mercedes works drivers in consort. Fangio is trying on a new pair of goggles.

Seconds before the off. Tensed in the front row are Fangio (18), Kling (20) and Ascari in his Maserati.

Throughout the race the two W 196s of Fangio and Kling ran nose to tail.

A début victory – Fangio crosses the line just a length ahead of Kling.

Disillusionment

7th British Grand Prix, Silverstone, 17th July 1954

Less than a fortnight after the triumph at Reims, the World Championship brought the Daimler-Benz team to Britain.

At the time there was a ban on most sporting events on Sundays in the United Kingdom (not until the early 1970s did the authorities relent, making Sunday motor racing acceptable). Thus the period between the French Grand Prix and the next round was just 13 days; that mystical figure, which is so often held responsible for misfortune and defeat, was about to acquire a new significance for the team from Stuttgart.

Daimler-Benz had been hoping to bring the second, open-wheeled version of the W 196 to this race, but despite the team's best efforts the car was not ready. Instead the team turned up with its familiar racers as used in France – the by now famous streamlined machines. Two drivers had been nominated: Juan Manuel Fangio and Karl Kling who, fittingly, were allocated race numbers 1 and 2 in recognition of their one-two at Reims – or perhaps that should be unfittingly, as events turned out.

Silverstone, a former Royal Air Force base, is situated in an area of wide-open fields about 70 miles northwest of London. The squat, black hangars dotted around the track reveal Silverstone's former importance as a World War II bomber station operating against Hitler's Germany. Soon after the war the squadrons were redeployed, the ends of the crossed runways joined with a tarmac road and another permanent circuit was ready for use.

The circuit differed in character from Spa-Francorchamps and Reims, the other two tracks visited so far in 1954. Instead of the long flat-out sections of the Belgian and French courses, the straights at Silverstone are comparatively short. The drivers must constantly lift off to negotiate curves then accelerate and brake again.

Fangio had posted fastest time in practice, but was unhappy for all that. On one of his last laps he had a brush with one of the small, sand-filled oil drums that marked the course. The left-hand front wing was punched in and streaks of yellow paint bore witness to the force of the impact. Anyone who knows Fangio will be aware that it caused the man almost physical distress whenever he damaged one of his cars.

That evening in the Five Arrows Hotel in Waddesdon, near Aylesbury, serious team discussions were held. Fangio and Kling told Neubauer and Uhlenhaut that at this circuit, the streamlined bodywork was more of a hindrance than a help. The drivers had to be able to see the apex of each bend in order to drive at the limit, but the bodywork on the W 196 did not allow it. Whereas other drivers had a clear view of their wheels and could position their cars to within a millimetre of the track markers, the Mercedes men always had to leave a margin of safety. As well as being costly in time it was unsettling to the drivers.

Neubauer and Uhlenhaut could only scratch their heads. Their new car, if only it had been ready, would have been the right weapon for their two pilots in this situation. The best they could do was to console Fangio and Kling with the coming race at the Nürburgring: here in England they would have to make the best of a bad lot.

The supporting programme to the British Grand Prix organized by the RAC consisted of a sports car event and a 500cc Formula 3 race. The sports car event was won by a certain Colin Chapman in his Lotus, and in the single-seater race a lanky timber merchant by the name of Ken Tyrrell took the laurels.

The Grand Prix itself was timed to start at 12 noon. The event of the year in the British racing calendar was going to start under a leaden sky that threatened to drench the circuit again as it had done the night before. Puddles stood in a number of places around the track and oil spillage from the supporting events made conditions more slippery still.

The dreary weather predictions did not bother the 100,000 spectators in the slightest. Just as they had waited in stoic indifference at the ticket booths, now they stood ankle deep in mud to await the contest to come. Practically every last one of them carried three essential items: an umbrella, a thermos flask

full of tea and the programme. The detailed knowledge displayed by the British in motor racing matters is no matter of chance but is solidly based. They read the articles in the programme (which in 1954 included a piece on the de Dion axle) very closely, and the conversations among the crowd showed that the race was being witnessed by many thousands of true *cognoscenti*.

There are just a few seconds to go before the off, so to capture the true flavour of the occasion we will go over to the BBC radio commentary team, with Raymond Baxter at the start and finish: ". . . and we can see the clouds of exhaust smoke blowing back over the drivers' heads. There is a stiff breeze down here at Woodcote and on my right, all eyes are on the starter. Cameras are aimed at the drivers. One or two are trained on the starter who is consulting his watch. The drivers are motionless. One or two cars are rolling forwards. A few seconds to go – and they're off! Just listen!

"They're already under the bridge and approaching Copse Corner. Gonzalez leads in the works Ferrari. Moss is 2nd in the private Maserati and 3rd is Fangio in the works Mercedes. As they head towards Maggots, Gonzalez is well on his way, Stirling is 2nd and then comes another red car. The first Mercedes with Fangio is lying 4th. So it's Gonzalez and Hawthorn. Or rather, Gonzalez 1st, Stirling Moss 2nd, Mike Hawthorn 3rd followed by Fangio. That's the order as they stream through Becketts and head off down Hangar Straight, the fastest part of the course. At the end of the straight is

The new Mercedes was making headlines in Britain, too.

176

Stowe Corner, where Eric Tobitt is waiting. So, over to Stowe!" Tobitt: "From Stowe we can see then rounding Chapel Curve with Gonzalez still in the lead and pulling away. Hawthorn passes Moss on the run up to the bend. Just before the bend . . . Gonzalez 1st, Hawthorn 2nd, Moss 3rd, Fangio 4th . . . all through the bend now. Jean Behra following in 5th. Kling. That's the order as they go through Abbey Curve – the right-hander. The odd puddle still standing at that point. Now they're on their way out of my range so it's back to Raymond Baxter."

And so on. The opening laps of the British Grand Prix were not short of excitement. Fangio was naturally unhappy with his 4th place and put on a charge which soon brought him up to 2nd.

Behra's showing in the blue Gordini was astounding. The Frenchman was right in the thick of it in 5th place, up with the world's élite. The Maseratis, which had to start from the back row of the grid because they missed practice, were cutting through the field like dogs through a flock of startled sheep. After two laps Onofre Marimon was running 6th with Ascari keeping pace.

Four great marques were represented here in Britain, two Italian and one each from Germany and France. And they were holding the top six placings: two Ferraris, two Maseratis, a Mercedes and a Gordini. The drivers were an international bunch too: three Argentinians, two Englishmen and a Frenchman, followed by a German and an Italian.

With 30 laps of the 5 kilometre course gone in this 90-lap race, it started to rain and the track became more and more slippery. Fangio, who appeared to be controlling the race from his 2nd position, tangled with the oil drums yet again. With a loud crunch he sent one spinning out of his path. The front right-hand section of the car was punched in. Shortly afterwards the incident was repeated, the left of the car suffering this time. The Mercedes was in the wars but the Argentinian still held on to 2nd.

On lap 50 he finally had to admit that this was not his day. The car jumped out of 4th gear and from then on he had to keep his hand on the lever. Soon the same happened with 3rd gear and with circumstances against him – restricted forward vision, rain and oil on the track and now trouble with the gearbox – it was almost too much even for Fangio. As the race wore on he gradually slipped back.

But he was not the only unfortunate man that day. Nine laps before the end Stirling Moss retired. In full

Even in practice the expression on Fangio's face (pictured during practice) says that something is amiss.

view of thousands of his disappointed British fans, he struggled back to his pit in the green Maserati 250F and parked the car with a broken rear axle. Even in gear the machine could easily be rolled backwards and forwards. His disappointment was plain to see but at least he received a standing ovation for his bravura performance.

Behra was another who had to drop out. Once again, the ambitious Amédée Gordini and his blue cars left the track empty-handed. Behra had finally played a starring role, but there were no celebrations on the journey back to France.

We can follow the closing stages of the British Grand Prix with the BBC commentary team. Eric Tobitt, himself drenched to the skin, reporting from Stowe Corner:

"The leader Gonzalez is approaching, past the hoardings with the hangars in the background and spectators in front. They've been glued to the spot all afternoon, not wanting to miss a moment of this, in my opinion the most exciting race ever to be held here. He slows, takes Stowe Corner very gently. Trintignant is in front of him and now he accelerates. Past me for the final time, the car slides a little, his hand is in the air. He makes to go past. And now he is past Trintignant. In front of Trintignant he accelerates out of Club Corner towards Abbey

The start of the British Grand Prix. Gonzalez is already in front with Moss on the outside (7) in 2nd.

Curve and very soon he will be with Raymond Baxter. So now over to the finish line."

"The photographers are massing on the finish line and the chequered flag is out. All eyes are to the right, awaiting Gonzalez's Ferrari. He comes over the runway, past the hangars on the wet track. Through Woodcote in his works Ferrari, the last corner, to win the 7th RAC British Grand Prix. His gloved hand reaches for the sky, Trintignant in his identical car crosses the line for 5th place and

Gonzalez has won after 261 exciting miles of the 7th RAC British Grand Prix."

And what of Fangio? Despite serious difficulties he held on to 4th place. A terrific performance in the circumstances, but the event had shown that not every appearance by the Mercedes team could be crowned with glory like its début at Reims. Ferrari had fought back, in a way almost more impressive than Mercedes in France. Gonzalez had driven a faultless flag-to-flag victory, his colleague Mike

Fangio's W 196 is still undamaged here before his argument with the oil drums.

At Silverstone Herrmann was the reserve: he is pictured here with Rudolf Uhlenhaut.

Hawthorn had come 2nd and Trintignant was 5th in the private Ferrari. Marimon was 3rd, an excellent showing by Fangio's young fellow Argentinian – but no one could guess that this would be the last Grand Prix for the carefree Maserati driver.

Kling also had difficulties with the conditions. He was lapped twice, so it would have been pointless for Fangio to have taken over his car. At the end of the race both Mercedes were running on only seven of their eight cylinders (Fangio's car had three slight piston seizures and the other pistons were worn to a greater or lesser extent while the crankshaft showed signs of cracking: Memorandum by Uhlenhaut dated 23rd July). The blue oil smoke following the cars had not escaped the attention of ther rivals. After a depressing defeat at Reims, the Italians were bouncing back.

The next round was over the Nürburgring. Ferrari and Maserati were well-equipped for the battle, whereas Mercedes had only work to look forward to. Fangio, Kling, Uhlenhaut and Neubauer set off back to Germany in reflective mood. They had no time to lose because the race at "the Ring", the home circuit, was particularly important for them. German expectations ran high.

Gradually the Stuttgart men were realizing what they had let themselves in for. The competition would not sleep if their new cars were not victorious (like Ferrari at Reims); they would simply bring out their more reliable earlier cars. Not every race would be a whitewash like the French Grand Prix. Stress began to tell. In their minds Neubauer and Uhlenhaut were already feverishly at work – the storm warnings were up. Even the Channel crossing was appropriately rough, with high seas and lashing rain.

The effervescent mood that had reigned 13 days before had turned to one of bitter disillusionment.

The Home Game

Grand Prix of Europe, Nürburgring, 1st August 1954

"The night before the Grand Prix was unforgettable. I drove slowly around the Ring, past countless tents, caravans and camp fires which were burning at the Hatzenbach and the Karussell, at Wippermann, Brünnchen, Pflanzgarten and all the other famous bends at the Nürburgring. As usual throughout this strange summer it was a cool night. The woods of the Eifel kept their dark watch, like a backdrop for a production of *Wallenstein*. Up in the paddock work was under way in nearly all the pits. Here and there mechanics were lifting out engines, repairing faults from the practice sessions, or giving their charges a final tune-up before the Sunday's event."

Thus ran the opening paragraph of the report on the 1954 Grand Prix of Europe, penned by the Chief Editor of the magazine *das AUTO, MOTOR und SPORT*, Hans-Ulrich Wieselmann. On the eve of the big race at the famous Nordschleife, the mood for the most part was cheerful. Several hundred thousand spectators had come to the Eifel circuit, nearly all of them hopeful of a homewin for the new Silver Arrows from Mercedes-Benz, praying for a repeat of countless pre-war victories when Caracciola, von Brauchitsch, Lang and Seaman were the Titans of the Nürburgring. Years later with a twinkle in their eyes, they would be able to give their friends an animated account of the race: "I was there in 1954 when Mercedes won."

That same night when there was so much gleeful anticipation of the race, a tearful old man was making his way from the Nürburgring to Italy. His first visit to Europe from Argentina had been to see his son take part in a Grand Prix. His son was Onofre Marimon, and he had been dead a few hours. In his mourning, the father was returning to Milan to be at his daughter-in-law's side at that time of grief.

Marimon was killed at Wehrseifen on Saturday afternoon while attempting to improve his time, and therefore his grid position. The left front brake on his Maserati had locked, the machine skidded off the track, through a hedge and into an embankment. The Argentinian did not survive the impact.

When the sad news reached the pit lane, Juan Fangio and José Gonzalez, both Argentinians like Marimon, embraced each other. The photo of the tough racing drivers, bitter tears in their eyes saying more than words, went all around the world.

By now Fangio was tossing and turning in his bed in the Sporthotel. Down in the paddock, where most pits were still humming with activity, that of Maserati lay silent. The Italian team had withdrawn its entry for the Grand Prix of Europe after the accident, and only the private Maseratis would start the race.

Thus Mercedes' opposition was reduced: Ascari, a three times winner of the German Grand Prix (a feat shared with Rudolf Caracciola) was a master of the Nürburgring and would be absent. Ferrari, with wins in France and England, would be the Germans' chief rival. For its part Mercedes was well-armed with four cars taking the start. On 10th July Neubauer had registered his team of four drivers for the race with the organizing body, the Automobil-club von Deutschland (AvD). They were Juan Manuel Fangio, Karl Kling, Hermann Lang and Fritz Riess. Hans Herrmann and Rudolf Uhlenhaut were down as reserve drivers.

In practice Neubauer preferred Herrmann over Riess, the man from Nuremberg, though the young driver had to make do with a streamlined car (chassis number 2, the same machine he had driven at Reims), whereas his three colleagues would have the open-wheeled W 196.

Work on the new type continued until just before the weekend of the race. At the factory the machine was known as the *Monoposto*, somewhat confusingly since the streamlined W 196 was a single-seater too, and thus also deserving of the title.

The team had been to the circuit in the week following the race at Silverstone and put the car through a series of detailed tests, with Karl Kling and Uhlenhaut doing most of the driving. The oil tank was still mounted externally at this time, by the cockpit of the open-wheeled car. On the streamlined machine, of course, the tank in this position was fully enclosed by the bodywork but on the open-wheeler, whose shell hugged the spaceframe closely, another position had to be found. Eventually it was moved right to the back under the fuel tank. The

new Mercedes arrived for the race proper late on Saturday. The newest chassis (number 6) was allocated to Fangio, Kling took over the machine used by Fangio at Reims and Silverstone (number 3) and Lang used chassis number 5 as driven by Kling at Reims. The two latter cars were thus converted streamlined chassis. Fangio immediately showed the opposition just what to expect from Mercedes' latest offering, lapping at 9:50.1, more than three seconds faster than Hawthorn in the first Ferrari. Moss in his green Maserati had driven the 22.8km course in just over 10 minutes, closely followed by Hans Herrmann in the streamlined W 196 which, despite its poor all-round vision, also showed it was no slouch. Hermann Lang on his Grand Prix comeback started 10th on the grid.

The name of Kling did not appear at all in the official list of practice times. Late on Saturday on his first practice lap his right-hand front wheel came off on the home straight, the Antoniusbuche, the fastest part of the course: this is just another indication of the haste in which the cars had been prepared. Kling's perfect mastery of the wildly lurching machine is all the more astonishing since he did not even have a brake drum to skate along on, this component being buried in the nose of the car. Becaue he had failed to complete a timed practice lap, the incident landed him on the back row of the grid, an unaccustomed position for Kling.

At a quarter past one on Sunday, Silverstone victor Froilan Gonzalez catapulted into the lead from row two of the grid. The old campaigner Lang had done even better: as the pack streamed into the Südkurve he was 4th behind Gonzalez, Fangio and Moss, and had Herrmann in his wake.

At the end of lap 1 there was a wild cheer from the German spectators on the home straight whose expectations were running so high. Fangio was in the lead. The roar from 300,000 throats shook the old pine forests. A swashbuckling drive from Kling had brought him up to 10th at the end of lap 1 from his back row position on the grid. After two laps he was 8th and on lap 3 he crossed the line in 5th, a points-scoring placing.

Herrmann Lang, European Champion of 1939, held 2nd behind Fangio from lap 5 onwards. Up hill and down dale he flew around the Eifel circuit like the good old days and fully justified his selection. For 100km he was comfortable in 2nd place until his team mate Kling began to attack. By this time a

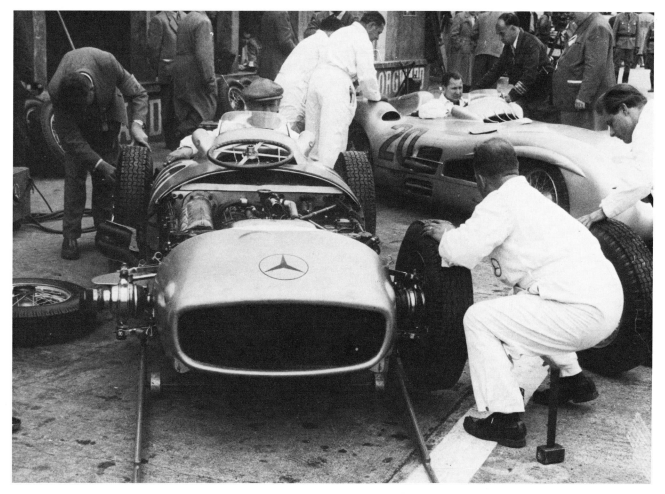

The open-wheel version of the W 196 made its first race appearance at the Nürburgring.

faulty injection pump had sidelined Hans Herrmann. The spectators appeared unbothered for Herrmann had already been victorious in the sports car event in his Porsche (another driver in the production sports car race was a certain "Axel Linther" from Cologne – the pseudonym of Wolfgang von Trips). On laps 9 and 10, three Mercedes were ahead of the rest of the world, Fangio in the lead followed by the two Germans Kling and Lang.

Shortly after, however, "Hermännle" had to retire. Kling had passed him driving like a demon and, in his effort to keep the younger man in his sights, Lang left the track near Flugplatz, that spot where the course traverses a bridge across the main road and the car seems to be heading into thin air.

The engine refused to restart and that was the end of a remarkable drive; Lang's comeback, so keenly anticipated by so many, lasted just a single race. In the next race but one, the Italian Grand Prix at Monza, Lang attempted to qualify in a practice run off against Hans Herrmann but was just pipped by his team mate.

Events unfolded rapidly. Two Mercedes were leading, chased by Gonzalez, Trintignant and Mantovani. Moss and Hawthorn, the two speedy Englishmen, had already dropped out and the spectators were cheering Kling on his incredible drive. Lap by lap he was gaining on Fangio and in the Mercedes pit, where one or two board members were watching, the mood was one of annoyance. Fangio was meant to win here and take another step

Fangio takes the lead the moment the flag drops. The German spectators cheer him to the echo.

towards the World Championship, but now Kling, his own team mate, was putting the screws on.

In the pit there were long faces each time he crossed the finish line. Only Uhlenhaut knew the difficulties facing Kling, which he was trying to indicate by wild gesticulations on every lap. A weld in the fuel tank had split shortly after the start of the race and Kling had been alerted by a fine mist of spray from the right-hand rear of the cockpit. His ill fortune was going to force him to make an unscheduled stop for fuel, and now he was trying to make up time in anticipation.

As he scorched round he put up fastest lap at 9:55.1, an average speed of 138.8km/h.

With six laps to go, many thought the race was over. Hardly a soul doubted that Kling would win his first Grand Prix – in his third race in the W 196. Suddenly the news came from the Karussell that

Fangio was back in the lead. What had happened?

At the end of the lap, Kling coasted to a halt in the pits with a two minute deficit. A transmission mounting had given up under the strain and was hastily patched with wire while the car was refuelled. Kling stood helplessly by as he was passed first by Hawthorn (driving Gonzalez's car, who had retired with stomach cramps, still suffering after Marimon's death) and then Trintignant in the second works Ferrari. The German had suddenly slipped back to 4th.

Thereafter positions remained stable until the end of just over 500km of racing. Fangio crossed the line ahead of the Ferrari duo of Hawthorn and Trintignant and then Kling who picked up the extra point for fastest lap and moved up to 5th in the table with 10 points.

Despite his win, Fangio could not rejoice. He

Beneath the landmark of Nürburg castle, Fangio leads from Gonzalez, the winner at Silverstone.

stepped sadly from his car, trudged to the victory rostrum and waited for the ceremony to end. His thoughts were on his dead friend. Onofre Marimon. His performance had almost been too much for him. He had pulled himself together and taken the start but it had required an almost superhuman effort. The great Fangio was deeply saddened and would never fully recover from Marimon's death.

After the race several thousand cars made their way from the circuit through the traffic bottlenecks. Volkswagens, Opel Kapitäns and Rekords, little BMW-Isettas and Messerschmitt bubble cars, and also Mercedes 170s and 180s carried happy race-

After a punishing struggle and a short spell in the lead the unlucky Karl Kling was forced into the pits. Top right: The disappointment is written all over Kling's face.

Hermann Lang, European Champion of 1939 contests his last Grand Prix at the Nürburgring.

goers away from the Eifel. They had witnessed the first victory for Mercedes in a Grand Prix on the Nürburgring for nearly 20 years. Maybe it was not the German Grand Prix, but the Grand Prix of Europe must surely count for more? Defeat at Silverstone was all but forgotten, the newly rebodied W 196 had fought back and shown its mettle. They could look forward contentedly to the Swiss Grand Prix in three weeks' time.

The following Monday a special telegram of good wishes was received in Stuttgart. It was addressed to the board of Daimler-Benz. None other than the federal Chancellor, Konrad Adenauer, was sending his congratulations for the racing department's great triumph at the Nürburgring. Following the success of the West German football team in Bern a month before, Germany had another sporting victory to celebrate. It was sure to boost the reputation of the young Bundesrepublik, and the Chancellor was a proud man.

187

After Kling's stop, Fangio was once again unchallenged at the front . . .

188

. . . and won the Grand Prix or Europe. Germany celebrates his victory.

The Jubilee

Swiss Grand Prix, Bern, 22nd August 1954

The city of Bern was in festive mood; it was 20 years since the first Swiss Grand Prix, held in 1934. Motor racing had been at a new high point that year, with the German Mercedes and Auto-Unions challenging the Italian Alfa Romeos and Maseratis and the French Bugattis. International motor racing had been given new impetus. After only a few races the German cars had shown their superiority and so in the first Swiss Grand Prix, Hans Stuck took the laurels in his Auto-Union. His team mate August Momberger was 2nd while the Mercedes encountered a number of difficulties.

Mercedes were once again on the grid 20 years on, and once again it was the first year of a new set of regulations. In 1934 the 750 kilogram formula merely laid down a maximum weight, leaving the designer an otherwise free rein. The generosity of the regulations soon led to engine outputs in excess of 600PS, which proved beyond the control of many drivers. As time went by more and more rules were brought in to regulate the design of racing machines. The weight formula was soon abandoned in favour of capacity restrictions, which in the short term were the only means of keeping a check on soaring power outputs.

A new formula for Grand Prix racing had been drawn up for 1954. Atmospheric engines were restricted to a maximum of 2.5 litres and supercharged units were allowed up to a maximum of 750 cc. Daimler-Benz was back on the scene notching up two wins in the three races so far contested. With bated breath the Swiss awaited events at the Bremgarten track on the outskirts of Bern, the capital.

The two practice sessions were scheduled for Thursday and Friday. The Saturday preceding the Grand Prix was devoted to motorcycle and national sports car events. Formula 1 practice was to take place in the early evening, between 17.15 and 19.00 on Friday. At the height of the summer there was no

Slight adjustments in wet practice: Kling in the pits.

reason to worry about the lateness of the sessions, but the summer of 1954 had been rainy and the organizers were destined to be unlucky. Thursday practice had been dry but overcast; on Friday, however, it was bucketing down. It was futile to hope for improvements over the times of the first session, and the drivers in any case brought their cars in before seven o'clock because those sections of the course that ran through the woods were too dark to be driven safely in cars which, after all, were not equipped with headlights.

The adverse conditions soon dashed the hopes of one driver. The Frenchman Robert Manzon skated off the wet track at a corner and collected two concrete bollards and three small trees in the process. The Ferrari looked a mess and Manzon

suffered injuries to his legs and a few broken ribs. His misfortune created the opening for Umberto Maglioli, a driver who had contested several sports car events for Ferrari.

Thus Thursday's times determined the grid placings. Fangio, no newcomer to the Bremgarten track, had lapped the 7.28km course in 2:39.7. Even so, the Mercedes driver was not fastest. His fellow Argentinian Gonzalez had played musical chairs throughout practice, swapping between four different chassis and in the narrow-bodied version (without side-mounted tanks) the Ferrari number 1 lapped two-tenths faster than Fangio.

In the wake of Marimon's death, Stirling Moss had been signed by Maserati and now, instead of his private green 250F, was driving a red one with a

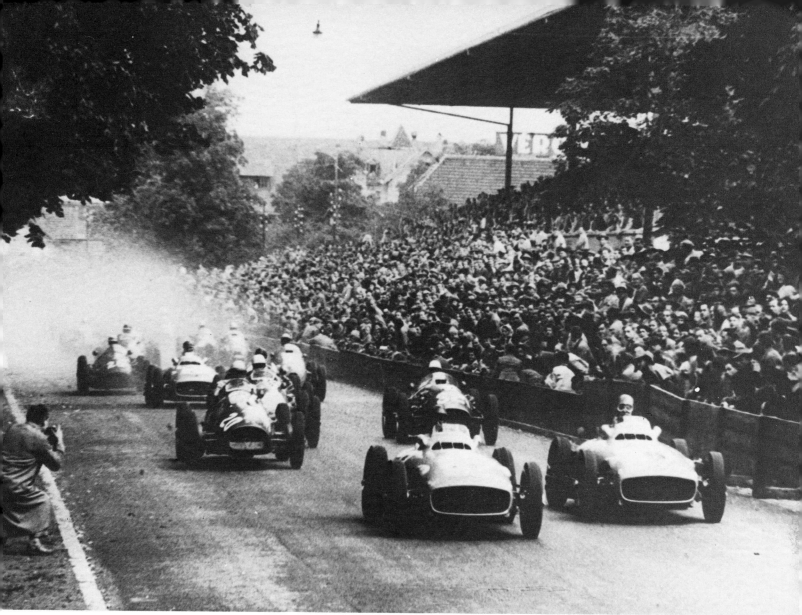

The start of the last
ever Swiss Grand Prix
at Bern's Bremgarten
circuit. From the
front . . .

. . . and from behind.
Once again the
Mercedes lead the
field away.

A motor racing idyll. Fangio at full throttle on the Bremgarten circuit.

narrow green band painted on the nose – even the proud Italians were ready to make this small concession to British racing colours. Moss put his car on the front row, albeit nearly two seconds in arrears of Gonzalez.

Next up was Trintignant (Ferrari), whose good showing at the Nürburgring had given him a boost, Kling (Mercedes), Hawthorn (Ferrari), Herrmann (Mercedes), and Wharton (Maserati). The three big marques thus shared the front three rows of the grid. This was Hans Herrmann's first visit to the Swiss circuit and on Monday and Tuesday he had driven several slow laps in a 220 to learn the course and its salient features. Ken Wharton had taken over Moss's private Maserati and was going splendidly; in the wet session on Friday he stood out with third best time. Moss had been fastest ahead of Kling. If the race was wet on Sunday, the pundits were predicting a victory for Moss in the works Maserati, who was expected to shine in the rain. As an Englishman he was after all used to persistent rain.

There was a notable absentee from the Swiss race: reigning World Champion Alberto Ascari. The man from Milan, who had been loaned to Maserati by Dr Gianni Lancia for the previous races, now had to concentrate on the new Lancia D 50. The car was ready but there was a lot of fine tuning to be done before its race début, which was planned for the Italian Grand Prix at Monza in September.

At 15.15 on Sunday the Swiss Grand Prix got under way. The organizers had long since gone grey – the only question that remained unanswered was whether their financial losses would stay in five figures or increase to six. The dreadful weather that had prevailed for the last few days had kept many people away from the track. Sunday morning dawned overcast and dull but gradually the dark, looming rain clouds vanished. Despite this, only 30,000 spectators had ventured out, less than a third of the number hoped for by the organizers. The circuit was drying out fast and when the starter dropped his flag, conditions were almost perfect, with a damp surface only in one or two of the wooded sections.

The race had been lengthened by one lap over the previous year's 65. Regulations for World Championship events dictated that they should be either 500km in length or of three hours' duration. The winning time in 1953 had been just a minute and a half over the three hour mark, and that was with the

Kling overcooks it. He goes into a spin at the Forsthauskurve . . .

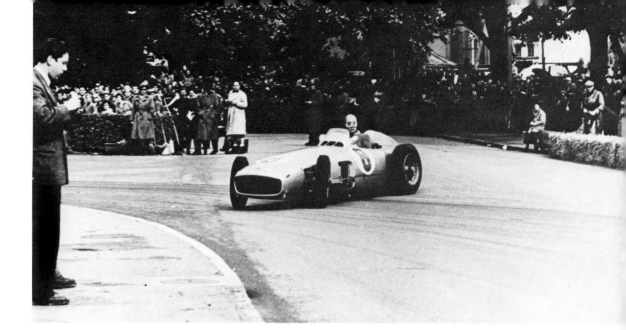

. . . comes to rest facing the wrong way . . .

. . . and has to push start the car.

less powerful 2-litre Formula 2 cars.

Kling made a scorching start and when the pack streamed into the Jordenrampe after about 2km, the two Mercedes of Fangio and Kling were ahead of Gonzalez, Moss, Trintignant, Hawthorn and Herrmann. Kling held his 2nd place only as far as the tight Forsthauskurve. At that point, where the cars scream out of the Bremgarten woods and brake for the corner (where maximum speed was 70-75km/h), it was still a bit slippery. Kling spun and, to add insult to injury, his engine stalled. He had to leap from the cockpit, turn the car to face the right direction and then push start it. All this had to be accomplished unaided to avoid disqualification for using outside assistance. Thus he crossed the line two minutes in arrears of Fangio at the end of his first lap.

At the front, Fangio went merrily on his way. He was extending his lead over Gonzalez by a second a lap. Moss had his sights on Gonzalez and took 2nd and Hawthorn was keeping up with the leading faction, too. The spectators kept a close watch on the group consisting of Moss, Gonzalez and Hawthorn. Could they reel in Fangio?

Hawthorn spurred on his Ferrari mount a little too zealously and after 22 laps, number 22 made a visit to the pits with a sick engine. Hawthorn took the car out for a couple more exploratory laps, but five laps later he retired from 6th position.

The other speedy Englishman, Stirling Moss, also got no further than lap 21. His Maserati was suffering from low oil pressure and Harry Schell's car developed the same fault. Maserati had upped the compression ratio on these two cars to squeeze some extra horsepower from the engine (about 250PS instead of 230), but at the expense of reliability. The unaltered Maseratis of Mières and Mantovani went the whole distance without a murmur.

Kling meanwhile had put his foot hard down and was equalling the pace of the leader Fangio, though the German was encountering backmarkers all the while, which slowed him up. Another good race from the German: if only he had not spun at the Forsthauskurve. After 27 laps he was lying 5th, after 32 laps he was 4th and after 34 laps, 3rd.

Then the PA at Eymatt Corner relayed some unwelcome news, "Kling is missing. We don't know what has happened." Luckily Kling soon coasted past the commentator on the home straight and was able to disclose the reason for his retirement. The engine had revved well above 9000rpm, and the screeching machinery cried enough.

Another Mercedes driver was the beneficiary of Kling's misfortune. Hans Herrmann had been making his way quietly up the order (also helped by the retirements ahead of him). The youngster of the team had never been so far forward in a Grand Prix. In the pits Neubauer folded his arms happily about his girth: after all, it was he who had drafted the 27-year-old into the Daimler team.

The leading trio of Fangio, Gonzalez and Herrmann held station for the final 27 laps of the race. Gonzalez attempted to catch Fangio and brought the gap down to 12 seconds, but then Neubauer gave his man the "V" signal (for veloce, "faster"). The Ferrari driver's resistance was broken and the Mercedes crossed the line a minute to the good. The organizers at least got something right: their decision to extend the race by a lap proved correct. Fangio completing the 66 laps in 3 hr 00 min 34.5 sec.

At the victory ceremony the two Argentinians, who had long been accustomed to such formalities, were joined by a self-effacing Herrmann. He was still unable to believe that he was sharing the rostrum with two of the Sport's greats.

The Zürich magazine Sport described the ceremony like this, "Little Herrmann was invisible, obscured by a particularly bulky official with a large nose who always makes it his business to muscle in on photos of prizegivings." Who does that remind you of? One thing has not changed since 1954 and that is the publicity-seeking functionary. FISA president Jean-Marie Balestre nearly always features prominently in today's photos, just like his counterpart in Bern.

The victory in Switzerland was Mercedes' third in four races. More to the point, Fangio was now unbeatable in the World Championship. Even if Gonzalez were to win the last two rounds at Monza and Barcelona, Fangio would still take the title even if he went home empty-handed. Fangio had his two wins for Maserati at Buenos Aires and Spa to thank for his happy position, but they were all but forgotten. Daimler-Benz had achieved its ambitious aim at the very first attempt. Champagne corks were popping around the Mercedes pit and that evening at the Golfhotel in Berne-Wabern, the celebrations continued in fine style. Chairman of the Daimler-

Top left: A great day for Hans Herrmann: 3rd place. Bottom left: Fangio scores another convincing win.
Right: Gonzalez embraces Fangio on the rostrum, watched by a smiling Herrmann.

Benz board, Dr Fritz Könecke, sent a telegram of congratulations from Stuttgart. He more than anyone knew what effect the World Championship would have on the firm's fortunes in years to come.

At the time no one could guess that this Grand Prix at the Bremgarten would be the very last motor race on Swiss soil. A year later, after the Le Mans disaster, the Federal Assembly in Bern voted to ban all future car and motorcycle events in Switzerland. The ban continues to the present day and this was the last big race ever held there. If all those spectators who had stayed at home could have foretold the future, the organizers would have been unable to satisfy the demand for tickets.

The Challenge

Italian Grand Prix, Monza, 5th September 1954

The 25th Italian Grand Prix had all the makings of a spectacular battle. The victory of the silver-liveried pretenders from Stuttgart meant that the Italians would have to fight back to uphold their honour. Alfa Romeo, Maserati and Ferrari had held sway for years and their victories were almost taken for granted. Suddenly Mercedes was there trying to steamroller the opposition, as in the 1930s. At Monza the gauntlet was down. Victory at Monza was crucial to anyone in motor racing with any ambition.

The fans all agreed that at the race in the royal park the front lines would be redrawn. Ferrari had dealt Mercedes a body blow at Silverstone and taken 2nd place both at Bern and the Nürburgring. Victory would surely follow in Italy.

The preparations made by Ferrari and Maserati were rather like plans for an offensive on a broad front. Quantity was as important a factor in their assault on the German position as quality. Five

works Ferraris were entered and Maserati fielded six cars. Lancia was still absent: its opponents believed that the incredible times reported during testing did not accurately reflect the state of readiness of the team from Turin. Lancia had no wish to expose its team to a home crowd which, though generous in victory, could also be scathing in defeat. Ferrari and Maserati kept their thoughts to themselves, however, for Dr Gianni Lancia still held the wild card, Alberto Ascari. This time it was Ferrari who benefited from the World Champion's services. It was something of a wonder that the prodigal son was welcomed back by Ferrari, but it also shows just how seriously the Mercedes threat was viewed.

Luigi Villoresi, the other driver contracted to Lancia, was loaned to Maserati for the Monza race. The way the Italians closed ranks made the occasion almost like a national mission. The eleven works cars were to be driven by the following drivers: Ascari, Gonzalez, Trintignant, Hawthorn, Maglioli

**Hermann Lang was unable to fend off Hans Herrmann, his youngest team mate, in the practice run-off.
Kling battles with the treacherous cobbled bend.**

(all Ferrari) and Moss, Villoresi, Mières, Mantovani, Musso and Rosier (Maserati).

Confronting the Italians were three Mercedes and three Gordinis. As at Reims and Bern, Fangio, Kling and Herrmann would make up the German challenge. The official race programme also listed Hermann Lang in car number 12, but the ex-European Champion was eliminated in a practice run-off against his young team mate Hans Herrmann on the Thursday. The decision to select the third driver in this way, which is more reminiscent of the machinations at Ferrari, betrays the Mercedes management's uncertainty over its choice. The simplest solution would have been to field four cars (as at the Nürburgring), but the team preferred to concentrate on preparing three ma-

chines as well as possible for the battle with the Italians.

The matter of the third W 196 was decided by one second, and also marked the end of Hermann Lang's racing career. As "Hermännle" admits, without rancour, "I just couldn't find the right line through the Lesmo bend and that cost me those vital few tenths." Hans Herrmann on the other hand had no idea of the significance of the run-off. Talking about the joust with Lang before his death he said, "I just drove in my usual way, quite calmly. It was only later that it dawned on me that I could have been a spectator at the race – I would only have had to be a fraction slower."

All that remains is to say who in the German team drove which version of the car in the race. The team was equipped with two cars of each type at Monza and the decision was quickly reached. Fangio and Kling drove the streamlined version and Herrmann had the open-wheeled W 196. Monza marked the début of Vanwall, a new British team under its patron, the industrialist Tony Vandervell, with Peter Collins driving. The new car was not yet fast enough to pose a real threat.

The pundits were divided in the naming of a favourite for the race. In the previous races, the Mercedes' superior power had given it the advantage on fast sections, but on tight corners, the Ferraris and Maseratis had fared better, thanks to their roadholding characteristics. Timings taken during practice confirmed the impression. The Mercedes drivers were losing several tenths in the two Lesmo curves and anything up to a full second in the Porfido. The Mercedes on the other hand had gained on the Italians on the faster sections, such as the home straight and the sweeping Curva Grande with its 300 metre radius.

The two tight Porfido curves were treacherous indeed. Instead of having a grippy asphalt surface, they were cobbled. This surface was slippery enough at the best of times, but during a race the oil blown out of the cars' engines settled in a fine film over the road and transformed it into a skating rink. Their position just before the long straight in front of the main grandstand made this a decisive section of the course.

That Sunday there was bedlam in the venerable old Parco di Monza. More than 100,000 *tifosi* thronged the track in the shade of the ancient trees and awaited a Ferrari or Maserati victory. Whole

This photo clearly shows the transition from the cobbled surface of the second Porfido curve to the tarmac of the home straight.

households turned out to witness the memorable event. Children charged about, older members of the family sought the shade offered by the beech trees and tablecloths were spread out on the springy turf. Picnics with *pane, formaggio* and *vino* were all part of the entertainment. Half of Milan had trekked to the *Autodromo* and those who could afford it had reserved tables in one of the restaurants dotted about the park. Here in Italy it would be unthinkable to flag the cars off before 15.00 – such a procedure would cause all manner of disruption to the way of life.

There was dynamite in the air at the start. Flags waved in their thousands, either the green, white and red – or Italy's other national flag on such occasions, the Ferrari prancing horse.

Kling made the start of his lifetime. Fourth in

practice, he shot past Fangio, Ascari and Moss to lead a Grand Prix for the second time since Reims. Fangio soon came under attack from Ascari and was forced to push the pace. At the front, Kling had to follow suit to retain his position. On the third lap he approached the Lesmo too fast and, though keeping control of his tail-happy car, had to watch as some of his rivals went through. The Italian fans were ecstatic: things were going to their liking – but there was better to come.

On lap 5 Ascari in his red Ferrari hit the front. The fans were in their seventh heaven and their thunderous reception echoed through the woods. Ascari held the lead until lap 22 when Fangio made his challenge. A few kilometres later the Italian had retaken the lead and Fangio appeared to be having difficulty in keeping pace. Lap 47 brought an abrupt

201

Left: Villoresi in Maserati number 22 battles with Fangio . . .
Above: . . . and Hawthorn in the Ferrari fights it out with Kling.

end to Ascari's race when he missed a downchange and buzzed his engine well past the red line. A damaged valve resulted and the fans were beginning to look longer in the face.

There was still an Italian car up front, however. Stirling Moss had been in the front pack and had even challenged Ascari for the lead on one lap (a duel that may have forced Ascari into his fatal mistake). The Englishman was winning as he pleased, the car taking every corner in a four-wheel drift. With all his powers Fangio tried to keep the lead from getting out of proportion, but the effort forced even him to exceed the limitations of his car. The cobbled Porfido curves had become coated with oil and rubber and were by now too slippery for the Mercedes. Several times Fangio went flying off the track and on to the grass and had to describe a wide arc to get the car back on the tarmac.

On lap 37 Kling had already made a spectacular exit. When an oil hose started leaking his face and goggles were sprayed with oil mist. He ripped his goggles off and had to rely on the tiny windscreen to offer some protection from the slipstream. Still on the same lap, the ailing hose finally burst and Kling was blinded by a thick jet of hot oil. Luckily the straw bales at the Lesmo curve cushioned the inevitable impact and the Mercedes wound up stuck in a hedge. Amazingly, Kling was unharmed apart from the burns from the oil. He was rushed to a doctor who treated his suffering eyes.

At the front Moss was extending his lead, which had grown to 22 seconds by lap 67. Villoresi was also driving like a man possessed and attacked Fangio. But soon it was all over for the two Maseratis: the rear axle on Villoresi's machine packed up and Moss's oil tank started leaking. The two of them rolled to a halt but the applause could not make up for their unrewarded showing. The best chance of beating Mercedes had slipped from their grasp. Alfred Neubauer had been keeping tabs on Moss's sterling effort, however, and was cooking up a scheme of his own.

Thus Fangio inherited the lead which he held until the end of the race. Daimler-Benz press releases the following week described the winner's tactics, "He remained unflustered by repeated attacks and lapped calmly and consistently at top speed." There was no mention of the fact that his lap times would have been insufficient to reel in the flying Moss and

that this victory could be ascribed to a generous helping of good fortune.

Mike Hawthorn crossed the line a lap behind Fangio and 3rd was the second Ferrari driven by Gonzalez (who had taken over Maglioli's machine around half distance when his own engine developed a fault). Hans Herrmann was next home. He had had to visit the pits as early as the 7th lap to have a faulty spark plug changed. The stop cost him a full lap and a possible 3rd place in the final classification, as in Bern.

There was some disappointment among the many thousands of racegoers as they made their way home after the event. Their hopes had been dashed that day and in the fight between Mercedes and the Italians since Reims the score was 4:1. But the Daimler-Benz team was not resting on its laurels after this most recent win which underlined the previous victories. Fangio had mauled Ferrari and Maserati in the lion's den at Monza, but the weaknesses of the W 196's chassis had become very apparent to the Italians. Mercedes would have to come up with something if it was to remain competitive in the coming season.

Rudolf Uhlenhaut had timetabled a tyre testing session for the Monday after the race. The W 196 would run on Italian Pirelli tyres. The result raised some eyebrows: lap times were up to two seconds faster than had been achieved on the German Continental rubber. The result was simply grist to the mill of drivers who had wanted to drive on Pirellis or the Belgian Englebert tyres since day one. However, the ties between Daimler-Benz in Stuttgart and Continental in Hanover were stronger than the wishes of the drivers. Dr Fritz Könecke, chairman of the board of Daimler-Benz, had after all been on the board of Continental before World War II, and such things create strong bonds.

Victory slips from his grasp again. Moss, an enforced spectator, can only regret his missed chance . . .

. . . as Fangio takes another victory, though heavily favoured by fortune.

The Day Out

Grand Prix of Berlin, Avus, 19th September 1954

In 1954 in Berlin, 27th May was postponed until September. It happened thus: the AvD (Automobilklub von Deutschland) planned to stage a race in the spring on the famous Avus, and of course, wanted Mercedes to be in attendance. However, the AvD did not know for what category of car the race should be run, so in December 1953 the sports president of the club, Paul de Bruyn, wrote to Daimler-Benz in Stuttgart to outline his plan.

An unequivocal reply was not long in coming. "The date set for the race at the Avus on 27th May would be unsuitable because of its coinciding with preparations for Le Mans," wrote team manager Alfred Neubauer, who suggested a date in September and also proposed a name for the event. " ... The Formula race that we propose over a distance of 500km could be called the 'Grand Prix of Berlin'."

In January 1954 another letter, this time from Fritz Nallinger of the board of Daimler-Benz, was delivered to the AvD headquarters in Fürstenberg-strasse in Frankfurt. "I wish to stress that we have decided to send a team of 2.5-litre cars conforming to the new international Formula 1 and for this reason we request that the race be run to these regulations."

In Stuttgart the team had already made detailed pre-race preparations, but wanted to await the outcome of the Reims event on 4th July, the début of the Silver Arrows. Mercedes hoped to be able to ascertain the most suitable race distance from the point of view of tyre wear. Nallinger wrote, "It is also possible, however, that, after the French Grand Prix, we might prefer a single race of longer duration. I therefore request that this be left open until the appointed time (after 4th July 1954)."

Two important reasons for the rejection of the May date do not appear in the letter. Firstly, there was doubt in Stuttgart about whether the new cars would be ready (as it turned out, 4th July came around almost too quickly), and secondly Daimler-

Three W 196s on the front row: Herrmann (2), Fangio (6) and Kling (4). Lurking behind them are Behra in the Gordini (14) and Swaters in the private Ferrari.

Benz contested no sports car races in 1954, so that Neubauer's mention of preparations for Le Mans, while serving to fuel speculation, should otherwise be regarded as a pretext.

Thus the date was fixed for September, leaving plenty of time for the organizing body to assemble an attractive field of starters. There was a confident announcement from Frankfurt of the invitation of only two cars from each of the works teams, Mercedes, Ferrari, Maserati and Gordini. In addition the best of the privateers, like Moss and Prince Bira, would be there. As the date of the race approached, the organizers saw their hopes for a competitive line-up crumble away. Ferrari pulled out and so did Maserati: even though they had been in touch with the AvD just a fortnight before the race, the faults and damage that had occurred at Monza could not be put right in time. In the end the organizers were happy that Mercedes was prepared

to send a three-car squad to Berlin. Daimler-Benz was guaranteed DM 6000 start money for each car.

In mid-August Neubauer had told Lothar Hennies, the chief of the Daimler-Benz dealership in Berlin-Charlottenburg that the team was planning to "make the event an all-German affair, and Kling and Lang will be nominated as drivers. The choice falls on Lang because he was the last man to win at the Avus and still holds the track record."

This claim was not entirely true either: Lang had been the last victor for Mercedes, although in the meantime, other races had been run on the Avus, for instance in 1952 and 1953. They had been run to Formula 2 regulations, the World Championship category in those years. Victory in 1952 went to the Swiss Rudolf Fischer in a Ferrari ahead of Hans Klenk and Fritz Riess, both in Veritas Meteors, while the following year Jacques Swaters from Belgium won in a Ferrari ahead of Klenk and Theo

208

Two scenes from a boring race. The Mercedes phalanx takes the Nordkurve (chased by Behra) . . .

. . . and brakes for the tight Südkehre.

Helfrich (Veritas Meteor).

The Avus had been planned in 1908, but it was not until 24th September 1921 that the *Automobil-Verkehrs- und Übungsstrasse* (hence *Avus*) was declared open. The industrialist August Stinnes had bought all the shares in the Avus Company by that time. The first race on the new track was won by Fritz von Opel in an NAG. His top speed during the race was 140km/h. In 1926 Rudolf Caracciola won but the track first became the subject of international attention two years later when Fritz von Opel undertook a spectacular record attempt in his rocket car. The golden age of the Avus was the 1930s when Mercedes-Benz and Auto-Union and their drivers, Rudolf Caracciola, Hans Stuck, Manfred von Brauchitsch and Bernd Rosemeyer, had some epic tussles.

In 1937 Hermann Lang drove to victory in a W 125; his average speed in the 154 km final exceeded 261 km/h. At that time the Avus was 20 km long, two endless straights with the steep banked Nordkurve at one end and the tight Südschleife at the other. The old track no longer exists. The zone border cuts right across the Avus and the straights have been shortened to less than half their former length. The lap now measures 8.4 km, which is more fun for the spectators who see the cars more often during a race. The load on the cars is greater, however, because they have to take the cobbled Nordkurve more often where speeds can reach 180 km/h.

The great centrifugal forces the cars experience can cause them to "bottom" very easily, despite the use of the hardest springs. To counter this the W 196s were fitted with pre-loaded springs giving an extra 10mm clearance, which prevented unforgiving contact with the track surface. Hermann Lang also drove five laps in the first practice session. Once the original plan had been changed he was relegated to reserve: Fangio would race after all along with Kling and Herrmann. Lang again watched from the sidelines.

The lack of opposition allowed the three Mercedes to take possession of the front row of the grid without much trouble for the race on Sunday. Jean Behra in the Gordini was more than 10 seconds away and Robert Manzon, fit once again after his accident in Bern, suffered engine damage to his Ferrari which could not be repaired in time for the race. As the flag dropped, Louis Rosier broke the

propshaft on his Maserati.

Thus only nine cars contested the Grand Prix of Berlin, one third of them Mercedes. They naturally played cat and mouse with the opposition. Only Jean Behra was able to keep station during the opening stages, amazingly crossing the line in 2nd place at the end of six laps. But the Frenchman's race was over after 15 laps of the 60-lap race.

From then on, the Mercedes traded places at the front, lapping everyone by one third distance. The 90,000 spectators who had tripped out to the edge of the Grunewald were unbothered. They wanted to see the Mercedes and Fangio, the new World Champion.

The fact that the winner had been decided before the race was something they could not know. The most unlucky man in German sport, Karl Kling, was to win in front of a home crowd. Fangio was planned to come home 2nd with the young Herrmann 3rd. With his 2nd place behind Richard von Frankenberg, Herrmann had won the up to 1.5-litre class of the German Sports Car Championship. Wolfgang von Trips took the 1.6-litre class.

The constant change of order at the front was thus nothing more than well-orchestrated shadow boxing, the whole affair seeming like a works outing to Berlin. How seriously the team's little spree was taken is summed up by the absence of Rudolf Uhlenhaut, the engineer.

Observant spectators noticed that the cars were slower through the Nordkurve than they had been in practice. All three Mercedes drivers were wearing body belts to make the high-speed banking less physically demanding. At 180 km/h, they were clamped into their seats with a force of 2.9G. The load was especially telling on Fangio, who had suffered a damaged vertebra at Monza in 1952. The three men took the bend at just over 160 km/h throughout the race.

Kling, Fangio and Herrmann wanted to achieve one thing at least: to make this the fastest post-World War II race to date. The record at the time was held by the 1954 Indianapolis 500 victor, Bill Vukovich, who won the race in May at an average speed of 210.58 km/h. When after 498 km Kling crossed the line half a second ahead of Fangio, and a further four tenths ahead of Herrmann, all three had completed the course at a speed higher than the American. Kling's average was 213.5 km/h.

The Avus was thus once again holder of the unofficial title "Fastest Race Track in the World", a distinction it had enjoyed before the war.

Thus the excursion had come to a satisfying conclusion. The Mercedes trio shared the prize money (DM 10,000 for 1st, DM 7500 for 2nd and DM 6000 for 3rd) equally among themselves. Hans Herrmann was as rich as Croesus that day after his second place in the sports car event. Though the victory ceremony was held in near darkness, the sun shone nevertheless: the people of Berlin had seen the Mercedes Formula 1 cars, the Avus was once more faster than Indy, and the W 196s had not even broken sweat in winning.

In routine engine inspection back in Stuttgart the Daimler-Benz technicians found some worrying damage to the valves from foreign bodies. Because the air in Berlin was laden with sand and particles of dirt, this was held responsible for the condition of the valves. The Mercedes team had experienced something similar at Monza where Fangio's engine was found to be about 12PS down on its pre-race output. Kling's unit as used on the Avus was down by as much as 20PS, and a thick oil/sand deposit was found in the inlet ports of 6, 7 and 8 cylinders. To prevent a future recurrence, Walter Kosteletzky proposed the installation of an air filter in the inlet tract.

The Italians had been using their time wisely. The Spanish Grand Prix in October was to be the scene of revenge for the painful defeat of Monza. While the Mercedes men were on their outing, the engineers at Ferrari, Maserati, and especially Lancia, had been hard at it.

Kling wins as planned ahead of Fangio and Herrmann.

No one is in any mood for celebration at the victory presentation.

Defeat

8th Spanish Grand Prix, Pedralbes, 24th October 1954

Suddenly they were on the scene. There had been reports in the specialist press all year and speculation had been rife among fans and professionals alike. Photos had been released that spring but now the real thing had arrived. The new Lancia D 50 finally made its début at the last big race of the 1954 season.

The cars from Turin had a magical attraction for spectators, journalists and the engineers on the other teams, and what a sight they beheld. The car was noticeably more compact than its rivals and there were two reasons for this. Firstly, the cherry-red cars were powered by a petite V8 engine and, secondly, the fuel tanks were positioned between the front and rear wheels, giving the machines their unmistakable external appearance. Thus the D 50 was very short, which made the car nimble, as soon became apparent. The novel positioning of the fuel tanks meant that handling remained largely unaffected as fuel loads decreased. By contrast with the other

Formula 1 contenders, whose fuel tanks were situated conventionally behind the driver, the D 50's centre of gravity did not shift forwards or backwards under such conditions.

With Alberto Ascari at the wheel, the Lancia had already lapped Monza at an average of 195.51 km/h according to unofficial reports. In September at the Grand Prix Gonzalez had driven the fastest race lap in his Ferrari at 187.748 km/h, while in practice Fangio took the W 196 around at 190.58 km/h. Claims about Ascari's record lap at Monza were therefore regarded as highly dubious, even in the light of the Lancia's performance at the Ospedaletti circuit in San Remo two weeks before where Ascari set a new lap record. On this occasion Luigi Villoresi had done severe damage to the second D 50 when he went off the track.

The Lancia men themselves were unperturbed. They did not regard the Spanish Grand Prix as a race where they would take centre stage, but rather

The new Lancia D 50 was the sensation in Spain.

as the last serious test in preparation for the coming season. The object of the Barcelona race was not to win straight out of the box but to size up Ferrari, Maserati and Mercedes, and that was something that solo testing sessions could not do accurately. The opposition would soon see and hear a trick or two.

In the very first practice session on Thursday afternoon the two Lancias cut loose as though pursued by the hounds of hell. Ascari drove lap after lap without missing a beat and the timekeepers in the other teams' pits could only gape in amazement

at their stopwatches. No one could approach his best time of 2:18.00. Fangio was exactly one second slower over the 6 km course and Villoresi in the second Lancia was third fastest.

Towards the end of practice Villoresi received the 'GIRI 8200' signal from his pit crew. That meant that he was to run the engine above the 8000 rpm limit set beforehand – the idea was to see what it could take. Villoresi drove on and the engine held together perfectly. On his return to the pits at the end of practice the telltale on his tachometer stood at 8700, but the engine still sounded sweet as a nut.

214

Ascari's engine on the other hand had gone sick, and Villoresi would have to make do with that car for the race on Sunday.

Ferrari had revamped the "Squalo" and Hawthorn was driving the newest version with the modified front suspension. Coil springs had replaced the former leaf-spring suspension. Trintignant was driving the second, unmodified works car.

Maserati turned up in Barcelona with five works cars, for Moss, the young Luigi Musso, Mantovani, Mières and Schell. All the 250Fs had the definitive de Dion rear axles. Gordini had fitted disc brakes to Jean Behra's car but "Jeannot" was not on peak form, being out-qualified by his team mate Jacques Pollet.

Mercedes had brought a whole truckload of streamlined bodywork to the race but, surprisingly, the open-wheeled cars turned out quickest in practice. Practice was a thoroughly unsatisfactory time for the team. The circuit with its long straights (each over $1^1/2$ km in length) should have favoured the W 196, given its power advantage, but try as he might, Fangio remained a second behind Ascari.

More worrying were the practice showings of the other two drivers Kling and Herrmann. Herrmann started 8th and Kling could do not better than 11th. The W 196s had never been so far down the grid.

At the other extreme, Ferrari and Maserati really had the bit between their teeth. Lancia's performance seemed to have spurred on the other Italian teams. Vanwall's second Grand Prix appearance came to an untimely end in practice on Friday when Peter Collins damaged the car so seriously when he went off at a bend that the team had no option but to withdraw.

The field as it lined up for the start on Sunday morning at 11 o'clock was the most select of any Grand Prix that season. The first row was made up of Ascari, Fangio, Hawthorn and Schell, all of them driving different cars with different types of engine. The Lancia had a V8, the Mercedes a straight-eight, the Ferrari a 4-cylinder and the Maserati, a 6-cylinder. Hopes were high for an exciting race, bolstered by the fact that the first 10 men on the grid

In the race itself the open-wheel cars were used.

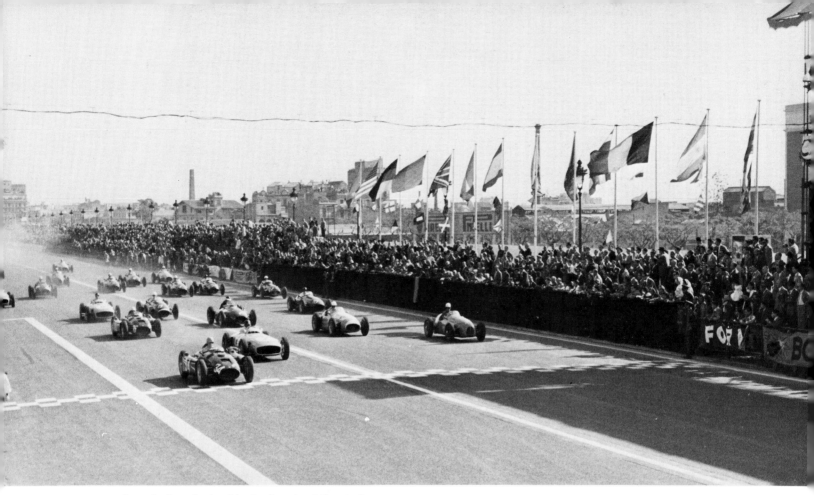

Ascari takes the lead in the Lancia at the start.

were covered by only four seconds (which is very little on a lap time of 2:20).

As the red-gold-red flag of Spain dropped to send the pack on its way, Ascari and Fangio went straight to the front: the first six km of the race were certainly incident-packed. The front men were going at it hammer and tongs as though the race had but a few minutes left to run. When the leading bunch crossed the line after the first lap Harry Schell was leading, with Hawthorn, Ascari, Trintignant, Moss, Fangio and Herrmann thundering along in his wake in close formation. Villoresi had already dropped to the back of the field and retired at the end of lap two. The engine of his Lancia had lost its oil pressure and rather than destroy it, the experienced Villoresi brought the car in.

His team mate's retirement was of no consequence to Ascari. First he displaced Hawthorn's Ferrari and then he dealt with Schell. The new Lancia was leading on its first appearance and seemed quite happy to be there. Ascari was extending his lead by

up to two seconds a lap. It was plain that the twice World Champion was relishing the situation as he drifted the car through virtually every bend: not only was Ascari fast, but he looked it too.

His lead on lap nine was 20 seconds but that same lap, the end came for the second Lancia. The hydraulic clutch had developed a fault and to add to his woes, the oil pump was malfunctioning. The main attraction bowed out but left notice that Dr Gianni Lancia's team would be a force to be reckoned with in the coming season.

Schell automatically took over the lead after Ascari's departure, and was driving a blinder of a race. He appeared unchallenged as far as lap 20 when Trintignant started a charge and ousted the American. A gripping duel ensued at the front until Schell pushed his luck a little too far and spun, damaging the rear of his car. He was able to drive only a few more laps before retiring.

Moss was already out by this time with engine failure, and despite his promise, had failed to score

The Mercedes suffered from overheating because of litter blocking their radiators. This is Kling's car . . .

. . . but Fangio was also affected.

217

in all but one round of the Championship that season – his only points were for 3rd place at Spa. Hawthorn had had a spin in the tumultuous early laps of the race but had not damaged his Ferrari. After battling his way back through practically the whole of the pack he was now lying 2nd behind his team mate Trintignant and ahead of Fangio.

That Sunday Mercedes looked to be on dismal form. Fangio had steadily lost ground in the opening laps and had the retirements of other drivers to thank for his 3rd place. Hans Herrmann had made a good start and had kept ahead of Kling for a long while but was out by this time after repeated pit stops to cure oiled plugs.

The fuel system on the W 196s was adjusted too rich for this race, for reasons of caution. Now they were popping and banging their way round the track, sounding like a great fireworks party. Fangio's engine was not running cleanly and a puff of blue oil smoke emanated from his upper exhaust pipe on every gearchange.

On lap 30 Trintignant's race came to an end when the oil feed to the differential broke. Many were afraid of a repeat of the Monza race where Fangio had won because the whole of the opposition had dropped out ahead of him, but Hawthorn's lead was steady at about 20 seconds, and his car was going like clockwork.

There was a strong wind blowing which had the unwelcome effect of whipping up paper and leaves, and these were lodging in the cars' radiators. Fangio was particularly affected; his engine overheated more and more, the result being that it became rougher and rougher. (After the race the mechanics observed that the oil temperature had reached 150°C and water temperature 110° C.) When Neubauer cautiously signalled Fangio to put pressure on Hawthorn 12 laps from the end, his star driver was fighting with his back to the wall. After the race, everyone was of the opinion that any driver but Fangio would have retired the car. The Argentinian, however, brought his machine home.

Six laps to go and the young Luigi Musso passed him to celebrate the best result in his short racing career: he came 2nd behind the beaming Mike Hawthorn, who lapped Fangio with one lap to go. There was bedlam in the Ferrari pit. Ugolini the manager hugged his victorious driver and with typical Italian exuberance, smothered him in kisses from head to toe.

Understandably there was less rejoicing in the Mercedes camp. Two cars had made it to the finish but there was little comfort in 3rd place for Fangio and 5th for Kling. More importantly, they had never had a ghost of a chance of winning. Even with the cars performing impeccably, their Italian rivals had given them the slip, and if the opposition had not been beset with problems, Fangio might not even have made a top five placing.

At all events there was much to do in the short break before the Argentinian Grand Prix, which would raise the curtain on the new season in January 1955. In particular the team would have to tackle the cars' 100 kg weight handicap over Ferrari, Maserati, and now Lancia, too. The new short wheelbase chassis was close to completion at Untertürkheim. Not only that, but Daimler-Benz planned to contest the big international sports car events in 1955, so the new season would bring additional pressure for the racing department.

Elsewhere among the opposition, heads were held high once more. The German Silver Arrows had been beaten and already voices could be heard (mostly in the Italian motoring press) that claimed to put the Mercedes victories at the Nürburgring, at Bern and at Monza in the right perspective. The Germans were judged to have been on the receiving end of some incredible good fortune, and if Fangio had not been there, it was said, the record would look quite different.

The German counterattack was not slow in coming. Whereas Daimler-Benz for its part – understandably – said nothing, *das AUTO, MOTOR und SPORT* took up the argument. "To wish to ascribe the Mercedes defeat in Spain to an inferiority that has been concealed so far in this 1954 season only by the greatest good luck would seem to any objective, rational person not only far-fetched, but downright absurd."

In all events the prospects at the end of the W 196's début season looked rosy for an exciting year to come. Competition had brought new life to Formula 1 and those who, at the beginning of the year, had predicted a wholesale transfer of public interest to the sports car domain had been made to eat their words. Formula 1 had reached a new high in terms of spectator interest and more manufacturers were putting resources into the sport. All over Europe motor racing leaped up the popularity index, and all the signs were for a buoyant new season.

Fangio could only manage 3rd place but he could still celebrate: he had after all taken the 1954 World title.

Battle in the Heat

Grand Prix of the Republic of Argentina, Buenos Aires, 16th January 1955

In many respects the timing of this race was unfortunate. The Argentinian Grand Prix, opening round of the 1955 World Championship, took place only 2¹/₂ months after the final race of 1954, but four months before the first European Grand Prix, at Monaco. Thus new developments would still be incomplete, and besides this there is another reason that makes the January date far from ideal. This time of year in Argentina is characterized by searing heat, with temperatures often around 30°C in the shade, so sitting in a racing car is no picnic under such conditions.

There had been a number of developments during the winter lay-off. Stirling Moss's transfer to the Mercedes team from Maserati had caused a real stir (especially in Italy and Britain). Sports writers in Italy damned Moss as a traitor, saying he had a contract with Maserati for the new season which he was now breaking. Moss put the record straight in a letter printed in the *Gazetta dello Sport*. The gist of

the letter was that there had indeed been a contract worked out between Maserati and Moss, but Moss had never signed it. What was not widely known was that Alfred Neubauer had also shown a great interest in Jean Behra but the Frenchman, increasingly unhappy with Gordini, had in the meantime signed for Maserati. Thus either Moss or Behra could have ended up at Mercedes rather than Maserati.

Moss still held on to the Maserati that he had bought at the beginning of 1954 even though he would drive for Mercedes. He rented the green six-cylinder out to drivers like Peter Collins or Ken Wharton for some races, while Moss himself drove it in other races (especially the many in Britain itself) in which Mercedes was unrepresented. The astute Moss had even set up his own company, Stirling Moss Ltd which allowed him to claim tax concessions that would have been unavailable if he had been racing as a private individual.

Critical voices were raised in Britain reproaching Moss – and British industry even more – with the fact that he found it necessary to drive a foreign car, because in this respect the country was missing out. This national half-heartedness would have long-term ill effects on the economy because it could not be denied that the Mercedes success on the track benefited their consumer products. Moss soon countered these arguments, too. If Britain would just build a competitive car then he would be happy to make himself immediately available when a fast driver was sought for it.

The other speedy Briton, Mike Hawthorn, had run into a different kind of problem. He went into hospital for a kidney operation during the winter, but suffered a relapse after his release at the end of December and was thus unable to take part in Argentina. Besides this, he had signed on with his patron Tony Vandervell to drive the new Formula 1 Vanwall, thus relinquishing a good position at Ferrari which he had established over the last two years and consolidated with two victories.

Maurice Trintignant had been given the title of French Champion during the break and Hans Herrmann had been awarded the silver laurel by President Theodor Heuss, the highest sporting distinction of the young Federal Republic. Ferrari's months-long deliberations over withdrawing from racing because of constant financial problems ended with the decision to continue in the sport. So had Ferrari's Froilan Gonzalez who had already once decided to hang up his helmet, still suffering in the wake of the death of his friend Onofre Marimon. By the time his home Grand Prix came around he was ready to reverse his decision. He was now dubbed "Big Head" by his fellow Argentinians and not the "Puma", as he was known in Europe.

And what of Mercedes? After the defeat at Pedralbes, the firm had spared no effort throughout the winter which was a time of intensive work rather than a break after the racing season. The W 196 had been shortened and lightened. The wheelbase was down from 2360mm to 2210mm to improve the car's cornering and the engine was modified to maintain the slight edge that the team already had over its rivals in terms of power. Two alterations in particular provided a power increase: new injectors supplied a finer jet of fuel to the combustion chambers, which themselves were given a more rounded shape to achieve better charge stratification and hence improved combustion. Output was now over 280PS and a crash diet had seen the W 196 shed more than 70 kg by comparison with the car raced in Spain. To avoid a repeat of the unwelcome phenomenon observed at Pedralbes, when litter blocked the radiator causing engine overheating, there was a new grille fitted at the front of the cars. A spring held the grille in position which the driver could then raise by means of a cable on a signal from the pits. The slipstream would then blow all the litter away and the driver could release the cable, allowing the spring to return the grille to its original position.

The list of modifications does not stop there. The induction ram pipes, which had previously been curved, had been swapped for shorter, straight items during the winter. All eight were of the same length, 226mm. The new ram pipes forced a change of position for the long plenum chamber which ran at right angles to the ram pipes and linked them and fed them with air. Its new position was responsible for the revised shape of the engine cover. The bulge on the right-hand side of the hood is characteristic of the 1955 version of the W 196; it covers the plenum chamber and is closed by a fine mesh grille intended to keep foreign matter out of the engine. To add to the considerable amount of work done on the Formula 1 cars, the racing department had also been busy on the new Mercedes sports racing car. The 300 SLR was derived from the W 196 (the chassis being practically identical), but logically enough had sports car bodywork and a 3-litre engine made of light alloy (Elektron). This was the new engine which the team hoped to use in the Formula Libre Grand Prix of Buenos Aires, a fortnight after the Argentinian Grand Prix. This kind of race is one in which any type of car of any engine capacity can take part. This gave the Mercedes people the opportunity of trying out the new sports car engine in a race situation in a Formula 1 chassis. Mercedes ran a 564 km trial at Hockenheim on 30th December with Uhlenhaut, Kling and Herrmann to test the durability of the 300 SLR engine. There were no problems; Hans Herrmann drove one of the closing laps in 2:09.5, almost two seconds faster than the existing record. That, of course, can only have been possible with an engine in perfect order.

Because of the planned use of two different engines, the Mercedes-Benz team took enormous trouble over preparations for the two Argentinian races. Whereas the chassis went to South America

The driver (Kling) has no idea of the torture ahead.

At the Argentinian Grand Prix the Lancias proved too difficult to drive. The result: countless accidents in practice and the race.

223

by sea, the engines, which were still being worked on right up to the very last minute, were sent by air freight.

The country was experiencing a heat wave that was unusual for the season and the most ferocious for ten years. At 10 o'clock at night the temperature was regularly around 20°C. By day the whole of Argentina was like a giant furnace that forced everything and everybody to seek refuge from the searing heat. Thus the practice sessions that were scheduled for the whole of the week preceding the race were only sporadically observed – in the slightly cooler evenings if at all.

At the twisty *Autodromo de 17 Octubre,* which has only one short straight in the whole of its 3.9 km length, the Lancia drivers were caught out by the erratic behaviour of their cars. The pannier fuel tanks appeared to be accentuating the centrifugal force on the cars and even a driver of Ascari's genius was unable to guarantee controlled cornering.

Just before the home straight was a very fast left-hander which caused the cars

to come uncomfortably close to the pits each time they passed. In practice – not to mention during the race – the area was thronged with spectators, but such matters of safety were of minor importance so early in the new year. All that would change in five months' time.

There was an incredible atmosphere in Argentina. Fangio was, after all, World Champion and had been given a euphoric welcome on his return from Europe eight weeks beforehand. He was a national hero. His picture was reproduced on the posters that decked all the main streets and squares in Buenos Aires. His team mates Moss, Kling and Herrmann also appeared on the gigantic hoardings advertising the races. The name of Mercedes was on everyone's lips and the three-pointed star badges had become collector's items of such value that drivers were well-advised to remove the emblems whenever they left their cars parked.

At first practice was dominated, surprisingly, by the Italian cars. Gonzalez clocked fastest time (1:43.1) followed by Ascari who has managed a

Moss retires exhausted but is unable to tell the reporters and photographers why.

The almost superhuman demands of this battle in the blazing heat are clearly written on Hans Herrmann's face.

rapid lap despite the quirky behaviour of his car. It took Fangio until the dying minutes of Saturday's practice session to claim a position on the front row of the grid. Less than two seconds covered the ten fastest men: Herrmann in tenth spot had lapped in 1:44.9.

The Autodromo was like a witches' cauldron for Sunday's race. More than 300,000 fanatical spectators packed the circuit which had been built just for them: it was possible to see the whole of the track from any point on its edge. The mercury was reaching dizzying heights. The temperature in the arena, which was hemmed in by grandstands and hence resembled a huge frying pan, was 34°C in the shade and the only place where there was any shade

to be found was in the pits. The temperature of the shimmering track surface was over 60°C. In these conditions the drivers were going to do three hours' hard labour in the cockpits of their cars. Real men were called for on this 16th January.

For the first time since his accident at Monza (in the Ferrari sports car in May 1954) "Nino" Farina was racing again. His burned legs were wrapped in asbestos to protect them from the heat. To relieve the pain a doctor administered two shots of morphine just before the race. Like Fangio, Farina was destined to become one of the heroes of this race.

Fangio took the lead at the start. Gonzalez, Ascari and Moss were in hot pursuit over the

225

Yet another victory for Juan Manuel Fangio.

glowing tarmac. By lap three Ascari had turned the tables and was leading from Fangio, Moss, Gonzalez and Kling. One lap later a number of drivers were forced into retirement. Villoresi spun his Lancia (again) and the Maserati pair of Behra and Schell tangled with Kling's Mercedes at the same corner. Behra collected the other two when he approached the corner too quickly. Only Schell continued after the incident. Behra went straight back to the pits and Kling left his W 196 where it stood.

Ascari was caught out by the wicked handling of the Lancia 40 minutes into the race. He crashed through a debris fence and came to rest only yards in front of a crowd of spectators. Gonzalez now had a narrow lead over Fangio. With two Argentinians in front, the spectators were going wild. This was all soon followed by a merry game of musical chairs. Farina had already handed over his car to Maglioli and now took over Gonzalez's machine after the latter had had another excursion because of the heat but managed to hold the thing together just in time. Fangio continued doggedly on his way.

Shortly after this Moss ground to a halt half way through a corner. The fuel pump was all right but the ignition had packed up. When the marshals asked him why he had stopped there was nothing he could recall. He got out of the car and lay down in the grass for a while and then stumbled back to the pits. Kling set off to take over Moss's machine but he reached the spot only to find that the marshals had wheeled the silver car back to the paddock, whence
Kling returned, bathed in sweat, after his wasted journey.

Meantime Hans Herrmann was suffering the effects of the heat. He had a water bottle mounted in the cockpit which he reached for every ten laps. He calculated that he would make it to the finish without dehydrating, but when he went to take a gulp after forty laps, instead of water he got a mouthful of dirt. In the heat of battle the container had slipped from its mounting, leaked its contents all over the cockpit and then picked up dirt from the surface of the track. Herrmann continued but was soon overtaken by lethargy and fatigue. "I was no longer in control of myself. Sometimes I didn't care whether I steered the car into a corner or simply headed straight on."

In the end his subconscious directed him into the pits where he slumped in a heap and had to be lifted from the car by his mechanics.

Even Fangio did not escape. After half the race was run he brought the car into the pits without warning or prior discussion. When he came to rest Uhlenhaut asked him what the matter was but the driver had no idea why he was there. Neubauer settled things in his own way: he tipped two buckets of water over Fangio who, pleased with the welcome refreshment, pulled himself together. To head off inquisitive journalists and race officials, Neubauer and Uhlenhaut invented the story that Fangio had visited the pits after noticing a suspicious fluctuation in oil pressure.

Gonzalez was back out on the circuit and was catching Fangio and made his bid for the lead on lap 75. But again his attempt was in vain and he returned once more to the Ferrari pit where Farina, who was constantly swapping between two cars, took over. Moss had recovered by this time and drove the last few laps of the race in Herrmann's car. The confusion was so complete that most spectators had no idea who was in what car.

The race was of three hours' duration (the number of laps being determined by the winner's average speed) and so, after 96 laps, Fangio took the chequered flag. He had driven his Mercedes through an inferno for 38 seconds over three hours and was the only driver except Mières to go the full distance unrelieved. His performance was as remarkable as that of Farina who drove one Ferrari to 2nd place (with Trintignant and Gonzalez) and another into 3rd place (with Maglioli and Trintignant). The second Mercedes, driven by Herrmann/Kling/Moss, was 4th, Mières was 5th in his Maserati followed by Schell/Behra and Musso/Behra/Mantovani. The result of this race reads like a sports car event where the drivers change at intervals.

But even Fangio suffered in the wake of his superhuman effort. He was unable to take part in the Mercedes-Benz victory celebrations at the Casino in Buenos Aires, and next morning a doctor diagnosed heart strain. Fangio was certain that he would never, ever forget that race.

The victory also gave Fangio the lead in the 1955 World Championship, the position he had occupied unassailed the year before. Mercedes-Benz had the prospect of a surge in sales to look forward to. There was now a break of a fortnight and then the raceworthiness of the 300 SLR engine would be put to the test.

The Test

Grand Prix of Buenos Aires, 30th January 1955

Exactly two weeks after the start of the 1955 Formula 1 season the *Autodromo de 17 Octubre* played host to a *Formula Libre* race, a type of event that is not often held and generally results from exceptional circumstances.

In 1952 and 1953 there were a great many non-formula races in Europe. The reason for this was that the Drivers' World Championship was run to Formula 2 regulations for those two seasons. At the end of 1951 Alfa Romeo withdrew from Formula 1, having secured the World Championship, leaving Enzo Ferrari's team as the only organization with any hope of winning a Grand Prix. Aurelio Lampredi's 4.5-litre engine was already posing a threat to the Alfa Tipo 159 and it was only with a generous measure of luck that Fangio had managed to take the title at the final race of the 1951 series. Alfa's decision was also influenced by the increasing superiority of the Ferrari.

Such a state of affairs was naturally not welcomed by race organizers. The spectators, whose admission fees contributed so much to the financial success of race meetings, wanted to see some excitement on the track. This seemed improbable for the 1952 season because Ferrari was the only team left with a serious chance of winning.

Thus the choice fell on the smaller, 2-litre maximum, Formula 2 cars for the following year's World Championship. There was any amount of competition in this category. Ferrari, Maserati, Gordini, Connaught, HWM and the German Veritas firm were all represented and exciting racing was in prospect.

But what was to become of Formula 1 cars, so spectacular for their sheer power and speed? What about the 4.5-litre Ferrari and the infernally screaming 1.5-litre 16-cylinder BRM? Such extraordinary products of creative endeavour could not be allowed to become museum pieces overnight.

To keep these cars (and others, like the big

Lago-Talbot) on the tracks there were a number of so-called Formula Libre races in Britain, Italy and France during the 1952 and 1953 seasons. They offered the chance of seeing the Formula 1 racers come out of their semi-retirement to do battle with the smaller Formula 2 cars. Championship points were not awarded for these events but there were usually handsome prize funds. The Albi Grand Prix, where the BRM eventually locked horns with the Ferrari, was one of the great success stories of those two seasons, with professionals and fans alike.

The reason for the 1955 Argentinian Formula Libre race lay elsewhere, however. Fangio was World Champion, having taken the title for Mercedes, and the German marque was highly respected in South America. In preparing for the 1955 Argentinian Grand Prix, Daimler-Benz was mindful of its plans to take part in international sports car racing that season, including events like the Mille Miglia, the Nürburgring 1000 km and the Le Mans 24 Hours. The 300 SLR, based on the Formula 1 W 196, was to contest these races. The chassis were practically identical and the engines were also derived from the 2.5-litre unit, with capacity increased to 3 litres, hence the designation 300 SLR. It was important for Mercedes to put the engine through a tough, competitive test before its first 'real' appearance. The Argentinians had therefore been requested to stage a non-formula race and they had gladly complied – after all two races inside a fortnight were better than only one. The Formula 1 teams were in Buenos Aires anyway so why shouldn't they stay a while longer?

Lancia returned to Italy the week after the Grand Prix, in which the D 50 had behaved so curiously. The team had to get to the bottom of the problem, and also repair the extensive damage from numerous off-track excursions.

Ferrari, Maserati and Gordini remained in Buenos Aires to take part in the second event. Ferrari had also installed a 3-litre sports car engine in Nino Farina's Grand Prix machine which had an output similar to that of the Mercedes, both units developing around 300PS. Although the Ferrari's front end posed no problem when it came to fitting the bigger engine, the Mercedes men had to make several alterations. The 300 SLR unit had to be inclined less acutely than the M 196 to fit in the chassis. The angle chosen, however, left the engine sitting higher in the car than its Formula 1 brother.

To allow clearance for the fuel injection system, a new bulging hood had to be made.

The team prepared three such cars for Fangio, Moss and Kling. Herrmann would drive a "normal" W 196, though it was fitted with an engine whose capacity had been raised to 2502cc by overstepping production tolerances, and was also able to rev up to 400rpm faster than the Formula 1 engine.

The outward shape of the W 196 was also considerably changed. In the light of the weather conditions that had prevailed a fortnight before, the team had done everything possible to protect its long-suffering drivers from radiated heat from the exhaust and the track surface, and had also fitted ducting to direct cooling air through the cockpits. Moss's car sprouted the most additions: being used to a temperate climate at home, he especially had suffered from the effects of heat. The cars looked like mutations when they arrived for practice and even the team declared them to be the ugliest versions of the car that ever lined up for a race. They would certainly never win a concours d'élégance.

The Grand Prix of Buenos Aires was run over two heats. Instead of the course used for the Argentinian Grand Prix two weeks before, the organizers chose Circuit 2, which has more bends. The Autodromo was laid out with a choice of nine different variations on a basic circuit which could be added or taken out at will. For the 1000 km sports car race held between the two Grands Prix the circuit was even extended to include a section of the *Autostrada General Paz,* making a total lap distance of over 17 km. The Buenos Aires 1000 km was won by the Argentinian pair Ibanez and Valiente in a 5-litre Ferrari. Trintignant and Gonzalez, who were in contention throughout the race but disqualified in their new straight-six Ferrari 118LM, and Behra, who came 4th with Bayol in a Gordini, were the only members of the Formula 1 circus to take part in the event.

Along with Farina, the prancing horse was represented by Gonzalez, Trintignant and the Argentinian Bucci in Grand Prix machines. Maglioli raced the new 3.75-litre sports car. Maserati had the largest line-up with cars for Behra, Mières, Mantovani, Musso, Schell (in the car driven to victory by Fangio in the Grand Prix a year before), Menditeguy, Fava and Pian. Whereas Carlos Menditeguy was fairly well known as the captain of the Argentinian national polo team, his two fellow

Fangio casts a critical
eye over the new vents
cut in the car's body.

Of all the cars, Moss's
W 196 carries the most
scoops and vents.

231

countrymen Fava and Pian counted as the real dark horses. The three blue Gordinis were driven by Bayol and the temperamental Argentinians, Iglesias and Birger, as they had been a fortnight previously.

At the start of the first 150 km heat on Sunday afternoon, the temperature was similar to that recorded two weeks before: 33°C and 45% humidity. Against the advice of Hans Klenk, the Conti tyre specialist, team manager Alfred Neubauer sent the four Mercedes into the race on tyres with a tread thickness of 9 mm (Klenk had advised the use of 6.5 mm treads). Neubauer's insistence proved wrong. The tyres were too smooth (a fact that was already known) and thus Farina, in the 3-litre Ferrari, was able to win the first heat by 11 seconds from Fangio, who had himself been leading by ten seconds at the half way mark.

Herrmann dropped out with a fault in the gearbox scavenge pump drive, which was causing oil loss. Kling's engine had slight ignition problems. Moss came in 3rd although his left-hand front brake locked constantly throughout the closing laps. Kling took 4th followed by Gonzalez and Mières. Farina also drove the fastest lap in the first heat.

After a short break, the cars were sent on their way for the second heat. To cure the locking front brake on Moss's car, Uhlenhaut had come up with a rough and ready solution, and poured a whole litre of oil into the brake drum. In a short test on the nearby *Autostrada General Paz* the "repair" seemed to have worked and the brake drum was filled with another litre of oil just before the start. Moss was told that the locking might return again under heavy braking for the first time, sending the car off to the right, but because the first bend was a right-hander, the only problem might be a quick spin into the grass. However, the brake behaved perfectly.

Fangio immediately took the lead from Moss. Mercedes had fitted the tyres with the less pro-nounced tread for this second heat (Monza Type) and they had a positive effect on the car's handling. Unfortunately Farina was unable to mix it in the battle for the overall lead because the wayward Gordini driver Birger drove him off the track at a corner. The shocked and demoralized former champion came into the pits where he handed over to Gonzalez, who was better placed to improve the 3-litre car's placing. Trintignant had taken over Gonzalez, Ferrari and was in hot pursuit of the leaders. Just before the end of the race Moss overtook his team number one and took the flat ahead of Fangio, Trintignant (who crossed the line less than a second behind the Argentinian) and Schell in the first Maserati.

Fangio won on the aggregate of the two heats in a time of 2:23:18.9 ahead of Moss (2:23:30.8) and Trintignant (2:23:53.1). Who could say what the result for Mercedes would have been if Farina had gone the full distance? Anyway, the 300 SLR engines had proved themselves reliable under race conditions (Kling finished both heats to come 4th overall). The exact position would only become clear at the first sports car race when Ferrari, the Jaguar D-Types and the Maseratis lined up to do battle. Even so, the Argentinian expedition had been well worth Mercedes' while and prospects for the rest of the season appeared rosy. A satisfied team, numbering nearly 40 in all, trekked back to Europe where they arrived on 1st February.

No one could have foretold that it was the Daimler-Benz team's last trip to Argentina; nor could anyone have known that Juan Perón, the country's motor racing-mad president, who had invited the Mercedes entourage to a presidential reception at his palace between the two races, would be toppled by a military coup on 16th September 1955.

Just a minute to go to the start of the first heat in the Grand Prix of Buenos Aires. Even Neubauer (on the right-hand half of the track) has to get out of the way.

Fangio and Moss in close formation during the first heat. In the second heat the Briton got his nose in front.

233

Rock Bottom

Grand Prix of Europe, Monaco, 22nd May 1955

The first and second rounds of the 1955 World Championship were separated by a considerable gap in time. In mid-January the Formula 1 circus had been in Argentina and now, in the latter half of May, they had come to Monaco for the Grand Prix of Europe. On the Côte d'Azur the pleasant warmth of early summer was presided over by an intensely blue sky.

The big teams had not, of course, been hibernating since January. There had been numerous non-championship Formula 1 races, for instance in Pau, Bordeaux and Turin. The performances of Maserati and Lancia had been especially impressive – Mercedes took no part in these "city centre races" and Ferrari was having reliability problems.

The fires of speculation had been amply fuelled in the long interval, as indeed they always tended to be about that time. The Italians were noisily proclaiming that Schell had signed for Ferrari. No one really believed it, but by the time the teams arrive in Monaco the Paris-domiciled American was indeed at the wheel of a car from Maranello. The other hot news was that Ascari and Villoresi were abandoning Lancia in favour of Ferrari. At Monaco, however, the situation was normal, the story no more than a fairy tale.

In the meantime (three weeks before Monaco, on 1st May) Mercedes had won the Mille Miglia, with Stirling Moss partnered by the British motor racing journalist, Denis Jenkinson. Shortly after their return from Argentina, some of the Mercedes personnel went to Italy to put the 300 SLR through detailed tests. During the trials, which were driven at racing speeds on the open road, Moss had done considerable damage to the car in two separate incidents (one of which involved a collision with an army truck loaded with bombs). He won the race itself in a new record average, beating the favoured Italians hands down. As well as the Formula 1 W 196, Mercedes also had a red-hot contender in the

235

Hans Herrmann a few minutes before his serious accident. Shortly after the picture was taken his car was embedded in the parapet in the background.

Sports Car World Championship. An accident in the 1000 mile race cost Karl Kling three broken ribs and his place in the Monaco Grand Prix. Hans Herrmann therefore came into the team.

The Automobilclub de Monaco had something special up its sleeve for this race. To boost spectator interest on the holiday before the Grand Prix (Ascension Day was on the Thursday), the first practice session, three days before the race itself, would determine the first three places on the grid. Practice sessions were timetabled for Friday and Saturday too, during which drivers would do battle for places 4 to 20. The tight circuit allowed no more than 20 starters.

The Mercedes drivers naturally had hopes of the front row and Fangio set the fastest lap on Thursday. Ascari soon managed a faster lap and Castellotti in the second Lancia squeezed himself in

front of Moss to take third spot. The Mercedes men were seeing red. Grimly Fangio stepped into his car again and shot off, followed by Moss and Herrmann in quick succession.

For the Monaco race the W 196 had been further shortened, the wheelbase now measuring 2150 mm, that is 60 mm shorter than in Argentina. There were thus three different lengths of wheelbase available, the "original" with 2350 mm between the axles, the "Argentinian" at 2210 mm and now the very short version. Two of the new cars were at the start, driven by Moss and Fangio. Their cars (chassis numbers 12 and 13) had a further modification made necessary by the shortened wheelbase. There was now no longer any room for the brake drums, which had originally been positioned between engine and radiator, and these were now moved outboard and fixed to the wheel hubs themselves. Herrmann was

236

A sea of people throng the hill above the Gasworks Bend.

Only one spectator followed the race from the sea itself.

driving chassis number 4, the 2210 mm wheelbase car driven to victory by Fangio in the Argentinian Grand Prix. On the Wednesday before the first practice session a Daimler-Benz transporter drove up towards the Casino then down to the Mirabeau bend. Before the Station Hairpin, a bend so tight that it has to be taken in second gear, the mechanics unloaded the car. They then experimented to see whether the turning circle was tight enough to allow the car through the bend, which had to be taken at only about 50 km/h. It went, more or less.

Thursday practice was a time of learning for Hans Herrmann, a complete newcomer to Monaco. He did not actually like the labyrinthine course very much. But so what, he thought, and stepped on it. The car did not behave quite to his liking, breaking away all over the place and oversteering badly. But in the pits was Neubauer, and the relationship between the two had been somewhat strained since the Mille Miglia (when Herrmann had arrived back at his hotel at two in the morning). The manager was gesticulating, telling him to get on with it and put in some fast laps.

It was not really very important for Herrmann to go flat out that day, because there was no chance of all three Mercedes getting on the front row together. To achieve that, Moss and Herrmann would have had to go as quickly or quicker than Ascari and everyone could see how unrealistic that was. Herrmann, however, wanted to avoid confrontation and thought to himself, "Well I'll just carry on and probably learn the circuit a bit better. I'll show them."

Herrmann was treading a high-wire, blown one way by his self-esteem and the other by his manager's insistence. At Tabac, down by the

237

The pack hurtles towards the Gasworks Bend after the start.

harbour, the Mercedes got completely crossed up but instead of doing the sensible thing and touring back to the pits, this youngest team member went for another helter-skelter lap of the Principality. He screamed along the home straight, slammed on the brakes for the Gasworks hairpin, drifted through and headed off under full acceleration to St-Dévote, took the corner and thundered up the steep climb to the Casino. It was there, where the road kinks left between the Casino and the Hotel de Paris, that the inevitable occurred.

The back end of the Mercedes snapped out and Herrmann was unable to correct. The right-hand wheels thumped into the kerb (still travelling at 180 km/h) and the car's momentum carried it over the pavement and, with a deafening crash, buried it into the stone parapet separating the sidewalk from the void below. The car demolished two pillars, there was the screech of stone tearing silver metal, and then, just inches from the abyss, car number 4 came to rest.

As he saw the impending crash, Herrmann gripped the wheel with all his might – it broke in the impact. He survived the deceleration through strength and luck, though he was lifted almost a metre out of his seat. As he was hurled back into the

238

Fangio and Moss are in the lead with Ascari in number 26 . . .

. . . and number 44, Trintignant the eventual winner, further down the order.

239

Castellotti (30) could only keep Moss temporarily at bay.

cockpit a vertebra broke and when he tried to climb out of the car he saw what had happened to his right leg. The top of the thighbone was broken and his leg, fractured in six places, had been wrenched about 15 cm sideways out of its socket, so that it no longer appeared to belong to the right-hand side of his body. A single thought now ran through Herrmann's mind, "Please, no fire."

He attempted to hoist himself from the remains of the car and, naturally enough, could not. Eventually he heaved his upper body out on to the tarmac, dragging his crippled leg behind him, and hopped across the road. At last help arrived for the seriously injured driver and he was rushed to hospital in Nice where the doctors diagnosed a broken sacrum and coccyx as well as a dorsal and a lumbar vertebra. He had been incredibly lucky – that Thursday might easily have been Ascension Day in more ways than one.

The accident put a damper on things in the Mercedes camp: no one was in any mood to celebrate the practice success of Fangio and Moss (who had qualified 1st and 3rd). But the show had to go on and thoughts turned to the choice of a driver to take over Herrmann's seat. On 16th April the ONS (Supreme National Sports Commission) in

240

In Monaco, the third Mercedes was driven by André Simon.

Frankfurt had endorsed "Kling, Richard" (an early example of bureaucratic incompetence), "and reserve drivers Herrmann, Hans and Uhlenhaut, Rudolf, for participation in the XIIIth Monaco Grand Prix on 22nd May 1955", although Uhlenhaut would take no part in the race. His ability at the wheel would surely have seen him well up the order, but his knowledge and experience as an engineer were too highly valued by the racing department for them to run the risk of anything happening to him in a race. Safety was uppermost in everyone's minds after Herrmann's accident, so the search went further afield.

Neubauer eventually put his trust in the young André Simon. The dark-haired Frenchman had entered a private Maserati for Monaco, and now he was about to step aboard the car that was every Formula 1 driver's dream. He could hardly believe his luck, but was obviously keen to grasp the opportunity.

At Lancia another Frenchman was celebrating a comeback: he was already 56 years old and a former king of Monaco in his Bugatti (as well as victor in 1930). It was none other than Louis Chiron who had earned the Formula 1 drive in return for his victory at the wheel of a Lancia Aurelia in the 1954 Monte

A race among palms and cactus. Fangio and Moss still head the field.

Carlo Rally. Anyone expecting fireworks from Chiron was in for a disappointment: he was languishing on the last row of the grid with second slowest time.

Here in Monaco the Ferraris were also going through a lean spell. By contrast with the Mercedes team, the Ferrari engineers had actually lengthened their cars for Monaco, and the tight course soon had the last laugh. The twin-cylinder engine that had been expected to appear on this occasion did not (and never did). Trintignant was fastest Ferrari driver in 9th spot, flanked by Simon in the

Mercedes. The fastest Maserati was driven by Behra, who shared row two with the young Castellotti (on the 3-2-3 grid). The Principality had its brightest face on for Sunday, the day of the race. There was blue sky, sunshine, a plethora of dazzling white luxury yachts riding at anchor in the harbour (including that of the shipping magnate Aristotle Onassis) and crowds of happy people thronging the verandas of the hillside villas, champagne glasses at the ready. Even those who had lost at the Casino the night before could raise a smile. The atmosphere at Monaco is always something special.

On the Friday evening a small Mercedes delegation went to the Palace to meet Prince Rainier. Nallinger, Scherenberg and Uhlenhaut presented the gull-wing 300 SL to Rainier, who was duly impressed. Grace Kelly, the American film star, was not in residence at the Palace as the two were yet to meet. The classic *To Catch a Thief* with Grace Kelly and Cary Grant was being filmed on the Côte d'Azur at the time.

More immediately, there was another classic taking place in Monaco: the Grand Prix. As the field roared off on Sunday Ascari got his nose in front briefly, but thereafter it was the Mercedes which set the pace. Castellotti was inspired, passing not only his team leader Ascari, but also Moss. After a few laps, however, the silver cars from Untertürkheim had taken unchallenged control of the race and an element of monotony took over. The drivers dug in: two W 196s leading followed by Castellotti and Ascari in the Lancias; Behra, Mières and Perdisa made up the Maserati delegation and then came Trintignant and Schell in the Ferraris. Hawthorn in the Vanwall and Simon in the Mercedes occupied 10th and 11th places.

It was not long before the runners began dropping like flies. Mières was first to retire, closely followed by Rosier in his Maserati. Taruffi was unhappy with his Ferrari so he handed over to the Belgian journalist, Paul Frère, who trailed the field as the tail light. Castellotti was forced to call at the pits, Chiron was chugging around so slowly that he was lapped time and again, and despite a stout defence Ascari was unable to resist the advances of Behra, who sailed past to make his works Maserati the best-placed Italian car in the field. Simon retired with less than one quarter of the race gone.

The Grand Prix of Europe was scheduled for 100 laps, but in the eyes of many they might just as well have brought out the chequered flag at that point – nothing else was about to happen. But they were mistaken. On lap 50, exactly halfway through the race, Fangio parked his car right outside the station as though he was about to catch a train. His engine had expired. It was the first occasion during his time at Mercedes (and the last, as it turned out) that "El Chueco" had to retire with engine failure.

Mercedes was thus left with Moss as the single iron in the fire. The Englishman was driving superbly. Before Fangio's retirement he had really put his foot down as if telling his team mate, "Look here, here's someone who's just as fast as you." Behind Moss, the opposition was in tatters. Behra inherited 2nd place when Fangio dropped out, but had to visit the pits and take over Perdisa's car and thus fell back to 6th. A few spectators must have been thinking along the lines of "This Moss is really great. First the Mille Miglia only three weeks ago and now Monaco." But just as monotony threatened to grip the race once more, the remaining Mercedes exited the tunnel in a cloud of smoke on lap 80, fumed its way through the chicane, then round Tabac and came to rest in the pits. Moss climbed out, his engine blown. On inspection the following week, it turned out that both Fangio's car and that of Moss had suffered the same failure: a lock nut in the valve gear. As is so often the case, the retirement was caused by a trifling failure.

Moss had almost a lap's lead over Ascari, who was just on the burst up to the Casino as Moss coasted into the pits. There was jubilation among the considerable Italian contingent in the crowd. Just a minute after taking the lead, Ascari shot out of the tunnel and applied the brakes to negotiate the chicane but he was out of luck: oil on the track, probably from Moss's Mercedes, had made the surface into a skating rink. Ascari spun in the Lancia, smashed through the balustrade and dived into the harbour with a tremendous splash to the accompaniment of hysterical shrieks from several thousand onlookers. Anxious seconds passed and then the driver surfaced and was collected by a boat. He was brought into hospital and put in a room right next to Herrmann. The doctor's verdict was that Ascari had suffered no more than a broken nose. A few days later many were questioning whether he had also suffered concussion in the accident.

Suddenly Maurice Trintignant was in the lead; no

Moss comes into the
pits shrouded in smoke
. . .

. . . allows himself the
luxury of a gulp of
water . . .

one had rated his chances but the Frenchman drove to a comfortable victory for Ferrari, whose practice showing had been unpromising, to put it charitably. Castellotti salvaged the honour of Lancia with 2nd, followed by Behra, Farina and Chiron. The number of leading runners who dropped out that day is amply demonstrated by the fact that Chiron came home in 6th place, five laps down on the winner. Moss was classified 9th. Thus in 1955 the race once more justified its reputation as a game of roulette.

Lancia and Ferrari managed to bring home three cars each, proving their reliability if nothing else. The cause of the Mercedes 100% retirement was not yet known, so Ferrari, Lancia and Maserati were in good heart. Perhaps there was a sea change in the offing, with Mercedes heading for the rocks. Just four days later, however, Italian racing fans (and that means practically the whole of the country) had tears in their eyes: Alberto Ascari, Italy's great driver and twice World Champion, was killed in an accident at Monza.

. . . then reports his engine failure to Rudolf Uhlenhaut. Ascari's Lancia in Monaco harbour.

The Procession

Belgian Grand Prix, Spa, 5th June 1955

By the time the Belgian Grand Prix came around, Alberto Ascari was dead. Four days after his accident at Monaco the twice World Champion went to Monza where he met his Lancia stablemates, "Gigi" Villoresi and Eugenio Castellotti. After lunch at a restaurant in the Monza Park Ascari took the wheel of Castellotti's 3-litre Ferrari sports car, just for fun. He even had to borrow a crash helmet because he did not have his own with him: he had not been planning to drive that day.

Ascari had driven less than three laps when the Ferrari rolled over on the long sweeping left-hander that follows the two Lesmo curves. There he was found by Villoresi, Castellotti and Conte Lurani. Ascari died in the arms of his friend Villoresi.

There were no eye witnesses to the accident. The few workers in the park were only alerted by the crash of rending metal. All Italy stood still, Milan went into mourning and flags flew at half mast. That day, 26th May 1955, the performance at the great opera house of La Scala was cancelled. No one wanted to go to the opera on that night of all nights.

Ascari's death was only the beginning of a string of motor racing catastrophes that year. In the United States a few days later, on 30th May, Bill Vukovich, twice winner of Indianapolis, was killed at the Brickyard during the 500. His car rolled over and Vukovich died in the flames because he was unable to free himself. On the horizon was Le Mans.

The mood was subdued when the Formula 1 teams arrived for the Belgian Grand Prix the week after Ascari's death. There was not a single person who disliked Ascari, twice World Champion and a hugely gifted driver. His friendly, winning manner made him enormously popular and he seemed to exude a calming influence. There was no doubt about his ability to whip up the fans when he was out on the circuit either. And now the greatest threat to Mercedes' domination of Formula 1 was lost because Lancia withdrew from racing on Ascari's

At practice on Saturday it was bucketing with rain.

death. With the loss of the finest driver next to Fangio, and the best car – the Lancia D 50 – next to the Daimler-Benz W 196, most observers feared total domination by the silver cars from Untertürkheim: a real procession in fact.

Lancia sent just a single car to Belgium, driven by Eugenio Castellotti. It was to be the Turin firm's final Grand Prix appearance. Ferrari brought three Squalos to the Ardennes hills; these cars had been given some attention by the team's engineer, Lampredi, but were still no match for the front runners when it came to engine power. Instead of Harry Schell, the Belgian journalist Paul Frère took the wheel of one of the works cars for the race at Spa-Francorchamps. Despite new cylinder heads the

Maseratis still lagged behind the Mercedes and the sole remaining Lancia in terms of out-and-out speed on the flat-out circuit.

The track has its tricky sections. One lap of the old circuit measures over 14 kilometres, made up entirely of A-roads that were closed for practice and the race. Crossing the start-finish line, situated close to the casino town of Spa the track continues southwards falling on sweeping curves, many of them leading between houses, to Stavelot. One kilometre before then, just before the fast Masta corner, the cars reach their top speed of about 260 – 270 km/h.

The Stavelot corner is slightly banked and sends the drivers back northwards. A constant gradient

248

The field of 13 just after the start: Fangio leads from Castellotti and Moss, Kling is 4th.

leads for 4 km to the tight hairpin at La Source, taken at about 60 km/h, and then it is on to the home straight between the pits and the main grandstand.

Daimler-Benz had few particularly good memories of the fast circuit. In 1939 Richard Seaman met his death there driving the W 5/163, with its 12-cylinder engine of sheer brute power. He was leading the race in the pouring rain from Hermann Lang, who by that time was holding station in 2nd place. The Englishman tried too hard and went off the track at high speed. He smashed into a tree and perished in the burning wreckage of the car.

In 1955 there was another Englishman driving for the Stuttgart team, Stirling Moss, although it was

Juan Manuel Fangio who was fastest Mercedes driver on the high-speed track. To everyone's surprise it was not Fangio, but the improving Castellotti who starred in practice. On Friday he was faster than Fangio's best (4:18.7) by six tenths of a second, and on Sunday with the track under water he was just four tenths slower than the World Champion (4:53.2 as against 4:52.8). Moss was three seconds adrift of the leading pair. Despite three broken ribs sustained on the Mille Miglia at the beginning of May, which had forced him to miss the race at Monaco, Karl Kling put in an impressive performance at Spa, a track that he was wholly unfamiliar with. Kling was driving a long-wheelbase car, like Fangio, whereas Moss had elected to start

Calculated from these two pit signals . . .

. . . Fangio has an 11 second lead over Moss.

with the medium-wheelbase machine. He liked his car to be slightly more "nervous".

John Fitch, the American, first took the wheel of the W 196 in practice at Spa. Fitch, who had been short on luck with his drives for Mercedes (notably on the Mille Miglia, when he was nominated, only to be displaced by new signing Stirling Moss), was not at home with the unfamiliar car. He was after all only present as substitute, in case one of the first-string drivers should come to grief (after Herrmann's accident at Monaco nothing was being left to chance).

The best times taken by the team's timekeepers for the five Mercedes drivers – Uhlenhaut also did some practice laps – during wet practice on Saturday were as follows: Fangio 4:52.8; Moss 4:55.4; Kling 5:00.2; Uhlenhaut 5:12.0; and Fitch 5:20.6. The lanky American was thus slowest by a considerable margin, but he was still getting acquainted with the car and no one was expecting any miracles of him. Aside from anything else, he would certainly have been taking care to return the car to the pits in pristine condition.

During that rainy session, Fitch and Uhlenhaut had a particular task to perform. They took the cars a whole race distance in an attempt to isolate any faults in the engines or chassis. After the 100% retirement at Monaco the team was taking no more risks. During his stint Uhlenhaut was also able to identify the phenomenon experienced by Fangio and Moss at Monaco. The W 196 behaved best with half-full tanks, but as the load lightened further, oversteer became very pronounced. Uhlenhaut began to consider ways around this problem. The T-car (chassis number 10) was the fifth version of the W 196. So far there had been 2350 mm wheelbase cars (both streamlined and open-wheeled), 2210 mm and 2150 mm wheelbase version (the latter with outboard front brakes): the version used at Spa had the 2210 mm wheelbase and outboard brakes.

With the former King Leopold of Belgium in attendance, the Belgian Grand Prix got under way at precisely 3 pm. Fangio hit the front immediately, closely followed for most of the first lap by Castellotti and then Moss. Approaching the end of the first lap the leaders slowed from high-speed to negotiate La Source, and Castellotti was missing, displaced from 2nd by Moss. He was now lying 3rd, leading a group consisting of Farina, Behra, Kling and Frère. With their man so far up the field in the

Two studies of Moss at La Source: concentrating on the line . . .

. . . and controlling the drift.

The Belgian motoring journalist Paul Frère drove a superb race in his Ferrari to take 4th.

podgy Ferrari, the Belgians were naturally pleased as Punch.

On lap nine Mike Hawthorn's race came to an end, his Vanwall having suffered a broken oil pipe. The man with the flaxen hair was driving his last race for his patron Tony Vandervell; starting in Holland, he would once more line up for his old team Ferrari.

Castellotti held on to 3rd place until lap 17, when he coasted into the pits with a dead engine. This allowed Farina and Kling to edge a place up the order. They were now followed by Luigi Musso who was going well in the first Maserati, then Frère and Jean Behra, who went off the track after only a few laps just before La Source, and then visited the pits to take over from Mières who was suffering from a bruised knuckle.

After lap 17 the places seemed set for the rest of the race, but five laps later there was a Mercedes in the pits. Karl Kling's luck was out again, this time an oil exit/breather pipe on the timing cover was to blame. He had seemed certain to keep 4th spot and

might even have improved his position, because he was edging up on Farina when he was forced out. Once again he was denied a good result.

After Kling dropped out the race simply ran out its remaining 14 laps. Up ahead Fangio and Moss were driving a lonely race, separated by a few seconds, their W 196s running like clockwork. Thus the procession that so many had expected indeed came about and little was happening further down the field either, except that Musso lost a place when he had to pit to change a sparking plug. The Belgian Grand Prix ran to a close in the order Fangio, Moss, Farina, Frère, Behra and Trintignant. The Mercedes had not been just stroking along, however: Fangio improved on his record time set the year before in a Maserati 250F, completing the race more than five minutes faster than in 1954. He had also carved nearly five seconds off the lap record, at least officially, since there must have been a mistake in timekeeping somewhere. If he had driven every single lap five seconds faster than the previous year's record he would have come home only three minutes faster than his winning time of the previous year. The lap record must therefore in fact have been reduced even further.

When the cars crossed the finish line after 36 laps (508.32 km), the spectators – many of them Germans, since the circuit is only about 50 km inside Belgium – surged past the barriers and encircled the victory rostrum. Everyone wanted to be as close to Fangio as possible. There were smiling faces in the Daimler-Benz pit again at last. The cars were in fine fettle once more after Monaco; victory at Spa had redressed the balance. The opposition could not hold a candle to the Mercedes. The points for victory and the fastest lap took Fangio into the lead in the Championship race ahead of Maurice Trintignant, who had led since Monaco. Fangio was on 19 points with Trintignant remaining on 11, followed by Farina (9), Moss (7) and Castellotti (6). There was now a solid foundation for a second World Championship for the Fangio/Mercedes combination.

It was, however, Fangio who was once again the centre of attention for photographers and spectators.

The Lesson

Dutch Grand prix, Zandvoort, 19th June 1955

In 1954 the Dutch Grand Prix had been cancelled but it was held again the following year, when it attained an unforeseeable significance. The 1955 race turned out to be a demonstration by all those with continued faith in and support for motor racing, whether as teams, drivers, organizers or spectators.

One week before, on 11th June, Le Mans had been the scene of the most serious accident in motor racing history. Over 80 spectators and the French driver Pierre Levegh fell victim to the horrific crash. Now, just a few days after the disaster, the investigations and recriminations were naturally at their height. The Briton Mike Hawthorn in particular stood accused of causing the accident by attempting a risky overtaking manoeuvre in front of the pits.

The press excelled themselves, tastelessly printing chilling photographs. Many articles were as malicious as they were uninformed. Everyone with an axe to grind when it came to motor racing (and that was a huge number, as events proved) got down to work immediately. They wanted to see an end to motor sport for good. Suddenly there were any number of concerned parties, but very few who managed to keep a clear head under the circumstances.

Daimler-Benz was in the firing line too: it was one of its cars, a 300 SLR, that had hurtled into the crowd in front of the main grandstand. The old hands knew how to make a story out of that: the car had exploded, they said. The cars were for the most part made of magnesium, said others, who went on to say that the material had ignited on impact, which then caused the disaster. The only thing that these weekend scientists proved was that when it came to matters chemical and physical, they were totally ignorant. Magnesium requires very high temperature conditions (around 600°C) before it ignites. But this is just one example of the type of arguments

255

Just after the start Kling snatches the advantage from Moss.

put forward in the wake of Le Mans.

The week after the accident Daimler-Benz AG invited the press from home and abroad to Stuttgart, showing films and giving talks to clear the firm's name. The upper echelons of the firm were deeply affected by press treatment of the affair (especially within Germany).

Dr Fritz Könecke, the Chairman of the Board, advised Nallinger not to take part in the Dutch Grand Prix. His letter dated 15th June (the Wednesday after Le Mans) contains the following passage: ". . . Just before you leave I would like to say that I have deep reservations about the firm's participation in the Grand Prix next Sunday.

"Even if we convince ourselves in the time available that the circuit is not dangerous and even if there is no accident, which I have reason to believe

will be the case, the public will have doubts about our taking part because they believe that, at such short notice, we will be unable to fulfil our declaration that in future we will not appear at circuits whose safety is in doubt.

"I fear a negative response – even if all goes well – and I believe that, rather than jeopardize our credibility with the public, we should reduce our team's chances for the rest of the Grand Prix season, and that includes the drivers' chances of the World Title. Personally, I would rather see financial compensation for the drivers for any possible losses of prize money that may result."

Nallinger was further advised "to put forward a point of view coinciding with my arguments". Nallinger, however, stated that he did not agree with Könecke's suggestions and the Mercedes team made

Kling at the Hugenholtz Curve. He retired shortly afterwards.

the trip to Holland to take part in the Dutch Grand Prix as planned. As Board representative for passenger vehicle development, Nallinger's stand might have been based on the possibility of the team's withdrawal from the race being misconstrued as a tacit admission of responsibility for the Le Mans disaster.

The Zandvoort circuit sprang up among the sand dunes on the North Sea coast in the middle of World War II. In 1942 a plan for a "training ground with access roads", index no VII/10 was approved, but the town fathers of the Dutch resort managed to keep their true intention concealed from the German occupying forces. It was no training and parade ground that was going to be laid out on the northern edge of the town, but a track for postwar motor racing events. The first Dutch Grand Prix at

Zandvoort took place in 1952, when Ferrari took a clean sweep with Ascari, Farina and Villoresi.

The 4.192km course is not one of the very slowest, like Monaco, but on the other hand it is also far from being among the fastest, like Reims and Monza. At about 150km/h, average speeds around Zandvoort are similar to those possible at the Nürburgring or the Bremgarten circuit at Bern. The Dutch circuit is, however, far less easily learned than other tracks. One corner can look very much like another here, and newcomers can easily be fooled by the monotony of the dunes with their sparse, scrubby vegetation. The atmosphere on the practice days was, not surprisingly, more restrained than was the case a fortnight before in Spa. All those who had turned up to make the Zandvoort race into a demonstration in support of the continuation of motor sport were well aware of the responsibility they bore. That weekend should be free even of the slightest incident, otherwise it could be disastrous for the sport. Notification of the cancellation of the Grands Prix planned for Switzerland and Spain had already been given. Even in France, the cradle of the sport, there was talk of at least a postponement of the race at Reims.

Once again, as in Belgium, John Fitch took part in practice. His best time was 1:48.3. The T-car (chassis number 3, the medium-wheelbase machine driven at Monaco by André Simon) was driven by all the team's nominated drivers. Fangio, Moss and Kling, and also Rudolf Uhlenhaut, all drove some spirited laps in it, setting the following times: Fangio 1:41.5, Moss 1:42.2 and Kling 1:43.0. Uhlenhaut's best was a very fine 1:43.5 late on Saturday afternoon. Fitch the American was thus the slowest, seeming far happier in the sports car than in the Formula 1 machine.

The T-car was originally put down as Fangio's race car but in the course of the two practice days, the Argentinian realized that the shorter version of the W 196 suited him better on this course. He drove the same car he had used at Monaco (chassis number 13), the one with outboard brakes. Moss drove the 2210mm wheelbase car (chassis number 10, his Belgian Grand Prix mount) with inboard brakes and Kling took the wheel of the fourth W 196 type, with its medium wheelbase and outboard brakes.

For the first time in the W 196 era, all three Mercedes were on the front row. Musso was next in the first of the Maseratis, with Hawthorn back in a Ferrari and, just a week after Le Mans, seeming far less outgoing than usual. The race programme had Hawthorn down under his old team's entry, which the Dutch – mindful, perhaps, of their claim on the name – had spelled "v. d. Vell", which went down well as might be imagined.

Fangio almost gave the impression of having jumped the start as he shot to the front to put daylight between himself and the rest of the pack. Musso had exploited the gap in front of him left by the rapid-starting Fangio and got ahead of Moss, Behra and Kling. He held on for just one lap until Moss caught and passed him. What followed was the most boring race in years. Practically nothing happened except when Kling, in fifth place between Behra and Mières, made a misjudgement out in the

Fangio in the Zandvoort dunes.

country and slid off into the soft sand. Unable to free the car he had to return to the pits by Shanks' pony. Fangio and Moss drove in close formation at the front, the young Englishman occasionally playing parson's nose to the World Champion.

If the apprentice Moss still had anything to learn, then he picked it up at Zandvoort as he shadowed his tutor Fangio in the Dutch Grand Prix. Lap after lap they drove round on the invisible ideal line, paring down the unnecessary centimetres. Initially there were many who still believed that internecine rivalry existed in the Mercedes team, but there was no evidence of that here. Moss remained stoically behind Fangio and made no attempts to overtake him. The procession witnessed at Spa continued in a more blatant form here.

Behind the Mercedes nothing happened. Only Musso managed to spin his Maserati at Tarzan, with a radius of 40m the tightest bend on the track, after three-quarters of the distance (it was a 100-lap race). Fangio and Moss who were exiting the same bend at the time, calmly turned their heads to observe the event.

The whole field was lapped at least once by the two Mercedes and Musso in 3rd place crossed the

The scoreboard crew had little to do: for most of the race there was no change in the order, Fangio, Moss, Musso.

line with Fangio three-tenths of a second ahead of his English lieutenant. Castellotti, driving the Ferrari that was still new to him came in 5th, three

As they exit Tarzan, Fangio and Moss calmly turn around to watch the spinning Musso.

At the finish Fangio is greeted with a kiss by his wife Andrea . . . and then congratulates Moss on his 2nd place.

laps down. The Dutch Grand Prix ran its entire distance without any noteworthy incident; the stalwarts, aware of their responsibility, attempted nothing rash.

Routine inspection of the cars after the Dutch event revealed considerable damage to Moss's race engine: "On inspection of the cars and engines on their return from the race it was observed that whereas Fangio's engine was completely clean, Moss's unit was full of sand...

"The inspection of Moss's engine, after oil fouling of one cylinder towards the end of the race, showed that the inlet valves of the rear cylinder block portion were badly damaged. Besides this, cylinders 6, 7 and 8 show signs of excessive wear which can be traced back only to the large amounts of sand entering the engine.

"May we ask you [the letter was addressed to manager Alfred Neubauer] to alert the drivers to the unacceptability of "nose-to-tail running" when this is not strictly demanded by racing conditions. This applies especially to particularly dusty or sandy circuits. This instruction must be adhered to at all times for the sake of technical reliability."

The memo is signed by the power unit engineer Lamm, Uhlenhaut and the chief of the racing workshop, Kosteletzky, who added a handwritten note concerning the distance that should be observed, about 30-50 metres.

Such damage never occurred again in the racing life of the W 196 but in ensuing years, Zandvoort was the scene of a number of races where team mates shadowed each other to the finish, where they were separated by only seconds, or even tenths. Wolfgang von Trips beat Phil Hill by nine-tenths in 1961 (both driving Ferrari 156s); in 1973 Jackie Stewart led François Cevert (in Tyrrell-Fords); the following year it was Niki Lauda and Clay Regazzoni (in Ferraris); and in 1978 the Lotus drivers Mario Andretti and Ronnie Peterson crossed the line separated by just three-tenths, Fangio's winning margin over Moss in 1955. In 1985 the spectators watched a bitter cut-and-thrust duel between the McLaren pair Niki Lauda and Alain Prost, whose challenge was ruthlessly crushed by the Austrian.

A Troucing

8th RAC British Grand Prix, Aintree, 16th July 1955

In Britain there was no argument after the disaster at Le Mans. Instead there was universal agreement: the race would go on as planned. By contrast with West Germany, where the press mounted a full-scale anti-motor racing campaign, the British Grand Prix found a sponsor in *The Daily Telegraph*. In Britain all was well with motor racing.

Elsewhere in Europe things were different. The French Grand Prix at Reims, timetabled for 3rd July, had been cancelled. It was still unclear whether the French round would be entirely struck off the list of Championship events for 1955 or if it would merely be postponed.

The German Grand Prix on the other hand had been cancelled. On the afternoon of 2nd July Dr Nallinger received a phone call from AvD sporting president Count Sandizell: "The German Grand Prix at the Nürburgring has been cancelled because the safety measures demanded by the Supreme National Sports Council cannot be completed before 31.7.55."

A tour of inspection of the North Loop of the Nürburgring had been carried out by Herr Döhmer (of the Automobilclub von Deutschland) and Herr Heinemann (ADAC Area Representative for Hessen and the organizer of the Hessenfahrten). After only 9 km they had compiled a list of faults so long that the AvD was faced with no option but to cancel the German Grand Prix.

The inspection had been forced by an instruction issued by the Federal Ministry of Transport on 21st June, which laid down that all circuits on West German soil should be subject to new surveys by the Supreme National Sports Council before being reopened for racing. The reason: the accident at Le Mans.

The move came in for some particularly harsh criticism from those who still supported motor racing. Richard von Frankenberg, a journalist and himself an accomplished racing driver, wrote con-

The Mercedes pit crew taking a breather in the shade of a parasol during a break in practice.

cerning the competence of Döhmer and Heinemann when it came to judging the safety or otherwise of race tracks. "Let me first say that I have the greatest respect for these two men . . . This respect does not, however, prevent me from stating quite openly that I do not consider them competent to inspect a circuit for today's racing and sports cars – in other words to judge whether and to what degree cars with a maximum speed of 280 km/h may be driven safely on some circuits but less safely on others, thereby constituting a danger. Such judgements cannot be made from the comfort of the boardroom but only from practical experience. They can only be made by a commission at least half of whose members are active in the sport, and furthermore, have personal racing experience of the behaviour of cars with a power-weight ratio of 1PS/5 kg or less."

In his article "Cowardice in the face of the enemy"

in *das AUTO, MOTOR und SPORT* issue no. 15/1955, Frankenberg went on to say: "I sometimes get the impression that many of those in positions of responsibility – within motor racing as well as government – have simply lost their nerve in the face of the disgraceful press campaign following Le Mans, and no longer wish to accept responsibility. Unfortunately this happens all too often in this country and is nothing new – when situations become unpleasant and what is at stake is real responsibility rather than the wearing of an armband just for show or the affectation of a self-important air, then we witness retreat."

Such was the situation in West Germany, with both sides entrenched. The cancellation stood, however. Later on, in 1970 for instance, when the German Grand Prix was switched to Hockenheim from the Nürburgring, and in 1976 when Niki

Four W 196s in the front two rows of the grid, pictured against the decorative main grandstand as a backdrop.

Lauda declared the Nürburgring too dangerous, there were harsh words and recriminations once again, but on those occasions it was the drivers themselves, who according to von Frankenberg should have been consulted in 1955, that started the ball rolling.

In 1955 the atmosphere in Britain was definitely pro-racing. Twenty-five cars were entered for the Grand Prix – an all-time record (just 13 cars had taken part in the race in Belgium), and the race was to be held on a new circuit. A Grand Prix had never been held in the north of England – Silverstone had always been the scene of this most important of races. In 1955, however, the Formula 1 circus trekked to Liverpool, to Aintree, a suburb of the great industrial port, where the most important race of the steeplechase season, the Grand National, is held every year. That race had been instigated in

1839, when it was run as "The Grand Liverpool Steeplechase". When E.W. Topham took over the course in 1848 he came up with the memorable name Grand National and thus was born a sporting event that has remained as magnificent as ever right up to the present day, when it even becomes a destination for members of the Royal Family, who often go to see one of their own horses compete. The 1900 Aintree winner was Ambush II, a horse belonging to King Edward VII.

The course then belonged to the immensely rich Mirabelle D. Topham, the great-granddaughter of E.W. That far-sighted woman had a motor racing circuit built in 1954, using the access roads around the racecourse. It was no small matter, swallowing up £100,000, but Mrs Topham knew what she was doing. Fans of motor racing in the Midlands and up in the north of England had long been denied the

265

opportunity of seeing the world's fastest cars on their doorstep and the trip down to Silverstone, the former RAF airfield, was too long for many to make.

The Aintree course was opened with a sports car race in May 1954, which Duncan Hamilton won in a C-Type Jaguar. The following October Stirling Moss won a race in his green Maserati, and he held the lap record for the 4.828 km course which consisted of five very tight bends and four other corners, connected by a number of straights of varying length. He was just shy of the two minute mark (2:00.6) and was presented with a trophy topped with a huge gold figure. Along with Mike Hawthorn and Harry Schell, Moss was the only Formula 1 driver who knew Aintree. For the others it was completely uncharted territory.

The Italian Piero Taruffi, who had driven a Ferrari at Monaco, had been brought into the Mercedes team for the British race. The firm wanted to field four cars for the races in Britain and Italy. At the age of 48 (which made him the oldest of the Mercedes drivers) Taruffi was a highly experienced campaigner. Three years before he had won the Swiss Grand Prix and finished 3rd overall in the Championship. All the cars for the British Grand Prix were short-wheelbase versions (2150 mm) and therefore had outboard front brakes. The cars had

another new feature for the race at Aintree, all of them being equipped with auxiliary springing for their rear axles. A piston normally held by oil pressure could be released to remove the rigid stop on the rear torsion bars. An additional coil spring was thereby brought into operation to restore the three degrees of negative camber on the rear wheels. Previously this angle would gradually disappear after the start as the 180 kg of fuel were consumed; the cars would usually complete the race with their wheels at an angle only slightly over one degree of negative camber. This accentuated the car's unwelcome tendency to oversteer. The new auxiliary system was operated by the drivers after half the race was gone and made the handling of the W 196 virtually constant throughout the race.

On the first day of practice, Thursday (race day was Saturday in keeping with the British custom), Stirling Moss showed everyone a clean pair of heels. His time of 2:00.4 was two-tenths faster than his lap record and even in the T-car he was faster than the rest of his team (2:01.4). Fangio was next fastest with a time of 2:01.8 in the T-car and 2:02.4 in his race car, then came Behra with 2:02.8 in his Maserati 250 F, Kling on 2:03.6 and three drivers all on 2:04.4: Roberto Mières and André Simon in Maseratis and Piero Taruffi in the fourth Mercedes.

The Italian's performance was excellent and in

Whereas the Le Mans accident prompted a press campaign against motor racing in the rest of Europe, a national daily was the chief sponsor of the race at Aintree.

final practice he improved by more than one second to occupy 5th on the grid. Up at the front were Moss, Fangio (who had improved to 2:00.6) and Behra, with the second row made up of Kling and Taruffi. Harry Schell was an astonishing 7th in the Vanwall, having signed with Tony Vandervell's team when the constant musical chairs at Ferrari got beyond a joke. The Ferraris themselves were way back: by returning to Ferrari from Vanwall, Mike Hawthorn seemed to have jumped out of the frying pan and into the fire and could manage no better than 12th. Even Robert Manzon in the little blue Gordini was faster than the Englishman.

Aintree was also the scene of the Grand Prix début of the new Connaught. The car was powered by a fuel-injected 4-cylinder Alta engine and had a streamlined body which was, however, far less attractive than the Mercedes shape. The car also seemed rather heavy, because Kenneth McAlpine was outqualified by fellow Connaught driver Tony Rolt in an open-wheeled machine that was entered by Rob Walker. There was also a Cooper with all-enveloping bodywork (in fact it was a sports car) at Aintree, but with its 2.2-litre Bristol engine it was left for dead by the rest of the field: Jack Brabham, the Australian, driving in his first season of European racing, was slowest by a considerable margin. The golden age for the Cooper marque would follow three or four years later.

When the field was unleashed at 2.30 pm on Saturday the weather was, untypically, perfect. Mirabelle Topham had really done her homework, for more than 100,000 spectators thronged the circuit to witness a familiar sight. The Mercedes pair of Moss and Fangio shot to the front with Behra's Maserati a couple of metres in arrears. Kling, Taruffi and Musso followed, snapping at each other's heels. The race at Aintree was slightly different from the Spa and Zandvoort processions in that Stirling Moss, to the cheers of his countrymen, passed his team mate Fangio to take the lead on lap three. The pace was too hot for Behra, who retired on lap 10 with engine failure. He parked his red Ferrari on the Waterway, a long, sweeping right-hander after the home straight. Eugenio Castellotti, best placed Ferrari driver up to that point, visited the pits to change sparking plugs.

After Behra was forced out by what transpired to be a broken oil pipe, there were four Mercedes in the top five. Roberto Mières was ahead of Kling with

At last Kling managed a points-scoring finish again.

Taruffi chasing. The Italian was forced to give way shortly afterwards by an attacking Luigi Musso in the works Maserati. On lap 20 Fangio retook the lead from Moss, but held on for only five laps before losing the advantage again to the Englishman. The first ten places after 40 laps out of 90 were as

Newcomer Taruffi ensured the top four placings went to Mercedes.

They crossed the line that close . . . the winner Moss raises his right arm in jubilation (below).

follows: Moss, Fangio, Kling, Mières, Musso, Taruffi, Hawthorn, Trintignant, Macklin and Sparken.

Lance Macklin, who had been involved in the Le Mans disaster in his Austin-Healey, was driving Moss's Maserati 250F, now painted grey but bearing a green-painted nose to comply with the colour regulations then in force. His fellow Briton, Mike Sparken, who had won a sports car race in Agadir in February driving a Ferrari 750S, was in the third Gordini here at Aintree.

Lap 44 (just under the half distance) brought the retirement of Mières in the Maserati, which had suffered damaged valves. In his tireless pursuit of Kling he had overstretched the machinery. Piero Taruffi soon overtook Luigi Musso and Hawthorn handed over his Ferrari to Castellotti. The race was over but the spectators remained transfixed by the action on the track: would Moss really win or would he be forced to relinquish the lead to his team number one, Fangio?

On lap 50 Neubauer signalled "RE" (*Regulare*, or hold station) and the drivers were told to cut the pace a fraction. Only Moss, Fangio and Kling remained on the same lap, with the rest of the field at least one lap adrift – including Taruffi, who kept pace with the leading duo when they lapped him, but then gradually fell behind.

Shortly before the end of the race Fangio really put his foot down and was running only centimetres from Moss. The spectators leaped from their seats. Screaming and waving handkerchiefs and programmes they whipped their driver on. The result was that Moss crossed the line by the slimmest of margins, at two-tenths of a second even slimmer than the winning margin at Zandvoort. Thunderous applause swept down on Moss; he had kept his nose ahead for the first time in a Grand Prix and had become the first Briton to win his home Grand Prix.

The British, however, were far too sporting not to acknowledge that Fangio had been keeping his distance that day. Some newspapers the following day carried the headline "Moss wins – but Fangio helps". No matter, Moss had won his second big

Winner at last in a Grand Prix: Stirling Moss.

race of the season, following on from his victory in the Mille Miglia, and he was the happiest man alive. He also drove fastest lap, allowing him to retain the special trophy for a while longer.

With a clean sweep of the top four positions, Mercedes entered the history books. Only Ferrari had achieved such a thing when Ascari, Farina, the Swiss Rudolph Fischer and Taruffi came home in line astern at the Nürburgring in 1952. The Italians were at rock bottom now, however. The way in which Mercedes outclassed the opposition at Aintree was unprecedented either in 1954 or 1955. Four cars at the start and four cars in the top four places at the finish. With 100% success, Daimler-Benz was left with nothing more to prove.

269

Swansong

Italian Grand Prix, Monza, 11th September 1955

There was a new-look Monza for the closing round of the 1955 Grand Prix season. The body in charge of the old-established circuit running through the former royal park, the SIAS *(Società Incremento Automobilismo e Sport)*, had rebuilt the banking which had been destroyed during World War II. The construction of the curves is, however, considerably different to that of the old ones.

On all other banked corners, for instance at Montlhéry in Paris, on the Avus in Berlin and also the old curves here at Monza, it was normal for the inner edge of the track to be on ground level. This was fundamentally changed in the new design. The Italian designers had realized that it was senseless if a vehicle travelling at maximum speed in a straight line was forced to deviate from its path on entering the curve simply in order to reach the upper edge of the banking, the very area where maximum speed was possible. Such a manoeuvre forces the faster car to travel a greater distance through the curve than a slower one. Besides this, an unavoidable loss of speed had to be taken into account, because the car would first have to climb up the banking, and this all meant that banked tracks were not as fast as they might be. Thus the designers of the Monza track came up with a novel situation. On the Curva Sud, the inner edge of the track (the inside radius) lay 2.4 m below ground level. The base of the northern banked section was sunk only 40 cm below ground level because after about two-thirds of its length it had to cross the road circuit between the Lesmo Curves and the Vialone Curve.

On their inside edges the corners were very flat; the first five metres of their width were practically level, and then began the increase in banking which, on the Curva Sud, reached a gradient of 62% at the point corresponding to the original ground level. The highest point of the curves was 6.2 m above the base but (again only in the case of the Curva Sud) only 3 metres above ground level. Width of the

In Monza the Silver Arrows were in the forefront once more.

banking itself was 13.8 m. The gradient on the outer 3m was 80%. The curves were intended to allow far higher speeds than could be achieved on the older ones destroyed during the war. Whereas 180 km/h used to be possible, speeds around the 260 km/h mark were anticipated.

The banked corners were of differing radii, so the high-speed oval was not an exact oval. Radius of the north curve was 318.20 m, followed by a 873.60 m straight running not quite parallel to the home straight resulting in a radius of 312.32 m for the Curva Sud. The high-speed track measured exactly 4250 m.

The oval was not the only new feature of the circuit. The two cobbled corners had given way to a new curve known as the Curvetta (Little Curve) Sud, which was later dubbed the Parabolica because of its characteristic shape. The addition of the new corner shortened the road circuit to 4750 m and thus the total length of the track was exactly 10 km. The combined banked and road circuit was of course great for the spectators, who could see the cars pass the main grandstand and the pits twice every lap.

The new track was first opened for testing at the end of August and the Daimler-Benz team, as well as Ferrari and Maserati, made use of the opportunity to do some detail investigation of the course before official practice. Mercedes turned up with five cars, both streamlined and monoposto versions with varying wheelbases, as well as the 300 SLR coupé.

There was no shortage of driving to be done either in the test sessions, which were held on 22nd, 24th and 25th August in sunny conditions with temperatures between 28 and 30°C in the shade. Fangio, Moss, Kling, Taruffi, Simon and Fitch took turns at the wheel, with Uhlenhaut doing the odd stint for good measure. Fitch once again proved to be the slowest of the Mercedes men by some margin while André Simon put in a reasonable showing. The Frenchman was entered as reserve driver for the race

272

The new attraction at Monza was the new banked sections.

Three Mercedes in close formation on the banking during practice.

273

Here at the Lesmo Curves the four W 196s are already leading. Moss ahead of Kling, Fangio and Taruffi.

itself whereas Fitch was again just along for the ride.

A variety of nose sections were tried on the streamlined car. One of these had a smaller radiator vent (reducing the flow of air, which had an adverse effect on the drag coefficient), another was low and sharp and was intended to cleave the air better on the one hand, but also reduce lift on the other. Both versions were discarded by the time official practice came around two and a half weeks later. Uhlenhaut also ordered tests on an air brake similar to the one used on the 300 SLR at Le Mans. This test was also no more than a shakedown: the extra panel on the car's tail caused turbulence in the air flow and thus prevented the attainment of top speed. Besides this, there was only a single corner at Monza where the air brake could have earned its keep (the Parabolica); everywhere else the normal brakes did the job well enough without assistance. By the time the Mercedes entourage arrived at the Grand Prix, the air brake had also vanished.

274

The Stuttgart team still had something new up its sleeve, however. Three short-wheelbase (2150 mm) cars had been fitted with streamlined bodywork. In the three days of practice a total of eight cars were used. There were three long-wheelbase cars (2350 mm), two with streamlined bodies and one in open-wheel guise (chassis numbers 2, 6 and 9); there was one example (chassis number 10) of a medium-wheelbase (2210 mm) car with outboard front brakes and streamlined bodywork and four short-wheelbase cars with outboard front brakes, two of which were open-wheelers (chassis numbers 12, 13, 14 and 15).

Practice showed, however, that the short chassis was too frail on the banked sections. Driving the short car, Fangio was almost able to match his time set in the long-wheelbase version, but then it was known that Fangio could wring a halfway decent time out of practically anything that moved, and his effort could not hide the fact that the short car with streamlined bodywork was not suitable for Monza. It was not all down to the car, but lay rather in the track conditions themselves. The joints between the concrete segments making up the banked portions of the track were not precisely flush with one another. At high speed (Fangio averaged over 253 km/h on the high-speed oval on Thursday in practice) the small unevenness at each joint was amplified into a springboard effect: at certain points the car looked about to come unstuck and would hang poised with its front wheels a few centimetres above the surface until it crashed down again on to the track.

The Lancias, under the aegis of Ferrari for the first time here at Monza, had more dangerous waters to negotiate. The extreme loads on the high-speed sections proved too much for their tyres (forces up to three times the cars' weight, or 3G, could be experienced). Driving the D 50 in practice for his home Grand Prix, Farina's car threw a tread at over 250 km/h on the Curva Sud. Suddenly robbed of the necessary force to keep it stuck to the road, the Lancia careered across the track before Farina managed to gather it all up again.

This was not the end of the story: on Saturday he suffered the same misfortune and Castellotti had a front tyre burst shortly after. Ferrari immediately withdrew the entries because of the evident danger of running the D 50s at Monza. The consequences of a Lancia bursting a tyre in the middle of a mass slipstreaming battle at high speed are best left unimagined. Mercedes was ready to supply the Lancias with Continental tyres, which were equipped with a double-strength carcass for the race at Monza, but unfortunately there was not enough of the rubber available.

A Ferrari Super Squalo was hastily prepared for Castellotti but Farina and Villoresi were left as spectators. No one could have predicted that Farina would never again line up for a Grand Prix. With his Ferrari, Castellotti did a magnificent job and managed to snatch 4th place on the grid in the final session of practice to take his position as fastest Ferrari driver behind Fangio, Moss and Kling.

For this home race Maserati had prepared a special car. Jean Behra was at the wheel of a 250F with streamlined bodywork, whose wheels were half covered by the aerodynamic nose and side-mounted fuel tanks. The upper 10 cm of the tyres were unenclosed by the bodywork. The special car was hardly any quicker than its conventional stablemate;

Fangio leads from Moss and Kling on the banking.

275

we may rest assured that Behra would have been the fastest Maserati driver even with the normal car. John Fitch made it to the start of a Grand Prix after all here at Monza, driving not for Mercedes but in a private Maserati.

Well over 100,000 spectators thronged the park on Sunday. They wanted to witness the opening of the new track with the Italian Grand Prix and they were hoping to see "their" teams beat the silver cars from Germany at least. It would be their last chance, after all.

At 3 pm the flag dropped and the last round of the 1955 World Championship was under way (some still believed that the French Grand Prix would be held in October, but it never materialized). The Mercedes of Fangio, Moss, Kling and Taruffi came past the main grandstand after half a lap with a considerable lead over their rivals. The streamlined cars were first up, followed by the open-wheelers. While the German cars strolled away from the rest

of the bunch, the competition soon started to fall by the wayside. Ken Wharton retired the Vanwall on the first lap and Harry Schell in Tony Vandervell's second car managed only a further seven laps. The three Gordinis did not get far either. Lucas was first to retire in the new 8-cylinder which was contesting its first race, followed by da Silva Ramos and finally, on lap 27, Pollet.

Lap 19 saw a surprise pit stop for Stirling Moss. The W 196 had not suffered any sort of failure to bring him in for this stop: a flying stone had shattered his windscreen. The mechanics worked feverishly but by the time Moss returned to the fray, he had been overtaken by 10 of his opponents and was half a lap in arrears of the leading bunch, consisting of Fangio, Kling and Taruffi. Moss was flying after them and in the process set a new lap record of 2:46.9 on lap 21, which remained unbeaten to the end of the race (as the combined circuit was new there was no previously existing lap record). As

While Fangio, Kling and Taruffi exit the Parabolica, Moss is half a lap down and just coming off the banking in pursuit of Hawthorn (Ferrari).

As at the car's début, it was the streamlined W 196 that won its last race, too.

he gave chase he managed to fight his way up to 7th place but then, on lap 29, he returned to the pits on foot. A drive shaft had been unable to withstand the torture on the high-speed section and thus Moss saw his hopes of a victory at Monza dashed, as they had been the year before.

On lap 33, with the general excitement at their first retirement still fresh, came the second disappointment for Mercedes. Directly opposite the pits, which he was unable to reach because he had just exited the banking, Karl Kling coasted to a halt with a broken propshaft after holding a secure 2nd place. In assembling the shaft, the mechanics had omitted to fit a locating dowel. It was a truly maddening defect which was something of a surprise given Mercedes' overall standards of precision. Karl Kling was naturally most disappointed to be on the receiving end of such cruel luck once again.

Many of the spectators were in good heart by

now. Perhaps Ferrari and Maserati were still in with a fighting chance. The Maseratis of Musso, Gould and Collins and the Ferrari Super Squalo of Mike Hawthorn were all out by this stage, but Castellotti was holding on to 3rd and Behra was following in the streamlined Maserati. Maybe they were still in a position to catch Fangio.

The result of all this wishful thinking was precisely nothing: Fangio and Taruffi drove calmly and dominantly to the chequered flag. Their two cars embodied the whole range of development carried out on the W 196 in its 1$^{1}/_{2}$ years of life. Fangio was in chassis number 2, that same long-wheelbase car with streamlined bodywork driven by Hans Herrmann in the French Grand Prix at Reims on 4th July 1954. Piero Taruffi on the other hand was at the wheel of the last W 196 to be built, chassis number 15 with the short wheelbase and open-wheel bodywork.

277

The final chequered flag of the 1955 season, and the last for Mercedes: Fangio wins ahead of Taruffi.

The remainder of the race passed without drama, except that the Italians were going frantic with Taruffi edging up on Fangio. Was an Italian Mercedes driver going to win here in Italy, like the Englishman had in England? Fangio's winning margin over Taruffi was seven-tenths of a second, having driven the closing laps no faster than was absolutely necessary, and thus he won his last race for Mercedes as he had won his first – with just enough of a margin over his team mate to be comfortable. In 3rd was the young Eugenio Castellotti who had made great strides throughout the season, but on this occasion he was powerless against Fangio whom he trailed by more than 45 seconds. Using all his driving skill, Behra managed

to nurse his Maserati home after 500 km: his car had been smoking dreadfully for several laps and was running on only five cylinders. Menditeguy (Maserati) and Maglioli (Ferrari) were next across the line. The final positions in the World Championship table read: Fangio (42 points), Moss (23), Castellotti (12), Trintignant (11^1/3), Farina (10^1/3) and Taruffi who had 9 points in the bank. As far as Mercedes was concerned, along with the chequered flag at Monza dropped the curtain on the whole of its Formula 1 exploits. The firm was finally withdrawing after two seasons of success and leaving the way clear for the Italians it had so often kept in check in the past.

In 1956 a Maserati won from a Ferrari, giving the

278

Even with the trophy already in his hands Fangio looks less happy with a victory than Taruffi who came home in 2nd.

Italian spectators more than enough to shout about. Stirling Moss was the man, making it third time lucky after twice leaving Monza empty-handed. Juan Manuel Fangio came in 2nd – giving him the World Championship for a fourth time – but only after taking over the wheel of the Lancia-Ferrari selflessly offered by Peter Collins, who himself could have won the Championship, after the Argentinian had had to pull out. Thus the design that was born under Dr Gianni Lancia did eventually achieve great honour: the question of its likely performance against a more highly developed version of the W 196 must remain in the realm of speculation.

WITHDRAWAL

Tragedy

Le Mans 24 Hours, Le Mans, 11th June 1955

Right up to the present day, Mercedes' withdrawal from motor sport continues to be put down to the accident at Le Mans, the most horrific catastrophe that ever befell the sport. Judged objectively, however, this assertion does not stand up. In February, the firm's board had already voted to take no further part in Grand Prix racing from 1956 onwards. There was a public announcement of the decision, and everyone who was in the least interested in motor racing was well aware of it.

What, then, is the reason for the persistence of the contrary, false opinion? In the first place it is simpler now, 30 years after the event, to accept the apparent logic of the Le Mans withdrawal chain of events than to attempt to isolate the true causes of Mercedes' move. On the other hand the tragedy at Le Mans certainly played some part in Daimler's decision to withdraw at the end of 1955 – but it was not the prime reason, as it continues to be characterized. Far more important were other considerations: the huge success in three separate categories of international racing (see also following chapter); the utter impossibility of ever improving on the results achieved in 1955; and, above all, the fact that there were highly skilled workers tied up in the racing department who were needed for work on series production.

Perhaps the decision was accelerated by the Le Mans accident, but on the other hand the disaster and the withdrawal were separated by almost four months, four months in which Mercedes won the three remaining rounds in the World Championship, as well as three great sports car events with the 300 SLRs, one of which had been involved in the Le Mans accident, thus also securing that important championship.

Mercedes' withdrawal was well considered, just as the firm's entry into the sport had been a couple of years before. Just at Daimler-Benz remained pragmatic in all areas concerning motor racing, so the firm could certainly have decided pragmatically to withdraw from all forms of racing directly after Le Mans – if it had been deemed necessary. The "pro motor racing" decision, not easy to take in that dismal month of June, proved just what little impact the Le Mans accident had on the firm's withdrawal.

The very critical might choose to say that Daimler-Benz just wanted to snatch the prestigious Formula 1 and sports car titles before turning its back on racing. If that was the case then the two remaining 300 SLRs would certainly not have been voluntarily retired from the Le Mans race during the night, one of them from a clear leading position. Besides this, motor racing events of every type were regarded less than favourably in the wake of Le Mans by organizers, governments and public alike – and for good reason. Thus Mercedes might have reaped far greater publicity had it pulled out of racing directly after Le Mans.

So what really happened at Le Mans in 1955?

Pierre Levegh (left) with John Fitch and Neubauer during practice for Le Mans.

Anyone interested in motor racing knows that a Mercedes flew into the crowd, but when asked the name of the driver, most would hesitate a while before answering. The aim of this chapter is to bring those dreadul events back to life, not out of a desire for sensationalism, nor yet because of a "duty to inform", so often cited by the media when it comes to pictures of disasters. The Le Mans 24 Hours of 1955 appears here simply because it is all part of the story: the story of Mercedes at that time.

The roads around Le Mans were jam-packed. People had come from far and wide, just as they did every year at this time. Women in their light summer attire sat in the sun outside the cafés attended by sporty-looking gents in white trousers.

The second weekend of June 1955 saw the 23rd running of the biggest and most arduous race of them all – the Le Mans 24 Hours. The Italians with their colourful gestures were all part of the scene as were moustachioed English and cigar-chewing Americans in check trousers. Le Mans was part of the timetable for race fans the world over; the combination of race and funfair with its roundabouts and shooting galleries exerted a unique pull on hundreds and thousands of people.

For many, being there was important. See-and-be-seen was their watchword. For many of the so-called top ten thousand, attendance at Le Mans was as necessary as putting in an appearance at the Casino in Monte Carlo or spending the evening at the Lido in Paris.

For those manufacturers taking part, a win in the race would often herald surges in demand for their series production vehicles. Ferrari and Jaguar chased sports car sales in their main export territory, the USA, through advertisements in the form of success at Le Mans. Victory in the classic race is an accepted image booster.

In 1955 Ferrari turned up with a new 4.4-litre 6-cylinder. Jaguar's contender was the D-Type with that prominent vertical fin on the car's tail. The aerodynamic features were intended to improve directional stability at speeds beyond the 200 km/h mark.

It was Daimler-Benz who took the biscuit, however, with a new device. An air-brake had been developed in order to reduce the demands on the brakes which, especially at the end of the long, long Mulsanne Straight, were often on the verge of melting here at Le Mans. As the 300 SLR approached a bend the driver operated a small lever in the cockpit. Behind him, where the boot would be found on a production car, a flap emerged into the slipstream to decelerate the car before the conventional inboard brakes took over.

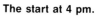

The start at 4 pm.

At this point car number 26 (the Austin-Healey of Macklin) and number 20 (Levegh) are in line astern. Their meeting a few hours later had disastrous consequences.

283

This novel "brake booster" had worked superbly in practice, keeping the Mercedes among the fastest. The three German cars were in the hands of Fangio/Moss, Kling/Simon and Levegh/Fitch.

Levegh, a Frenchman whose full name was Pierre Eugène Alfred Bouillin-Levegh, was 49 years old. Three years before, in 1952, he had acquired the status of a French national hero at Le Mans. With an hour and a half to go he was leading the pair of Mercedes 300 coupés driven by Lang/Riess and Helfrich/Niedermayer. The Germans were four and six laps behind him respectively when he came into the pits for a final fuel stop at 2.35 pm.

The Frenchman had been at the wheel since the start of the race at 4 pm the previous day: he had been driving unrelieved for 22 hours and now, on the very brink of a mighty victory, he naturally did not want to hand over. Levegh, a formal national ice hockey player, a yachtsman and an excellent golfer, returned to the fray, carried on his way by the jubilation and encouragement of his home crowd who were unable fully to grasp the situation unfolding before them. By now though, Levegh was more robot than man, with bloodshot eyes and deep wrinkles in his ashen face. The sensation was not to be. Less than a lap later, between Arnage and Maison Blanche, the Talbot coasted to a halt with engine failure. Sheer fatigue had caused Levegh to miss a gear and buzz the engine well past its limit. Hardly able to believe his ill fortune he tumbled from his car into the grass where he fell fast asleep. Victory was thus inherited by the silver cars from Stuttgart.

Mercedes manager Alfred Neubauer had naturally kept a keen eye on the heroic drive. When the crews were being picked for the 1955 race he immediately recalled Levegh's incredible performance. The Mercedes driving line-up was truly cosmopolitan, reflecting the status of the race itself: Karl Kling was the only German and he was joined by two Frenchmen (Levegh and André Simon), an Argentinian (Fangio), an Englishman (Moss), and an American (John Fitch).

Levegh would be unable to repeat his attempted flag-to-flag victory of three years before. An amendment to the regulations had been made, limiting unrelieved driving to a maximum of 80 consecutive laps or 18 hours in total. Levegh's partner, John Fitch, was down to drive a 300 SLR in the Mille Miglia at the beginning of May but when

Moss was contracted to the team, the drive fell through. The American had no idea that his Le Mans appearance would also be cut short . . .

Over 300,000 spectators had massed around the circuit in the French *département* of Sarthe to witness the start of the race at 4 pm on Saturday 11th June. A total of 40 helicopters and light aircraft circulated above the track crammed with photographers and cameramen, all wanting to get an aerial view of the opening stages of the race.

A sparkling blue sky stretched above the 13 km circuit and the sun was doing its best to keep the spectators and participants cheery. There was a bustle in the pits: the heat was putting particular emphasis on the correct choice of tyres. With track surface temperatures so high, a soft compound tyre would melt like a chocolate fireguard.

The Mercedes had dominated practice. Moss had set the time to beat on Thursday afternoon with a lap in 4:15.3. Stablemates Simon (4:16.8) and Fangio (4:17.5) were up there with him. Eugenio Castellotti was just on six seconds slower than Moss in his Ferrari, and the Jaguars of Tony Rolt and the blond Mike Hawthorn were also among the fastest with times of 4:23.3 and 4:23.4. The race promised to be an exciting one. The show could go on.

And "show" was still an apt description at that time. The opening scene involved the drivers lining up opposite their cars on the stand side of the track, then sprinting to their mounts which were lined up in the pits facing out at an angle to the track. The start came on the stroke of 4 pm. The amusement tents were quite empty for the first time that day, the roundabouts stopped dead, even the loudspeakers around the track fell silent for just a moment. Only the fluttering of flags in the wind leavened the tension in the summer air.

Go! The start was like that of a 100 metre race, the athletes being 60 white-clad drivers – relief drivers had to wear grey overalls to allow spectators to distinguish between the two – who sprinted across the track to their cars. Castellotti was first away, followed by his team mate Maglioli, and the Mercedes found themselves half way down the field; Fangio made a particularly poor start.

Mike Hawthorn was dealing with the traffic on the track as though his opponents were out for a Sunday afternoon spin. Fangio was doing likewise. The Briton and the Argentinian were going at it hammer and tongs, as though it were a Grand Prix that would run for only 120 minutes instead of 24 hours. If only that had been true.

The lap record tumbled practically every lap and after 22 laps Fangio had set a mark at 4:08.6 (the previous lap record, set by Alberto Ascari was over 4:16). Hawthorn was not dragging his feet either: on lap 24 he went round in exactly 4:08, prompting Fangio to reply with 4:07.8 until the Jaguar driver had the last word on lap 28 with a time of 4:06.6.

At this point, nearly two hours into the race, the green Jaguar and the silver Mercedes had been occupying the first two places for some considerable time, separated by the merest whisker, just 2.8 seconds. Fangio might be just ahead of Hawthorn at some points, only for the Englishman to be back in the lead after a few hundred metres. Le Mans 1955 was developing into a fantastic race between two awesome talents. It was film-script racing. The two fighting cocks, setting new standards all the while, were followed by Castellotti and Maglioli in the Ferraris who had Karl Kling and Pierre Levegh in the two 300 SLRs just behind them.

At the end of lap 35, at exactly 6.20pm, disaster struck suddenly, without warning and with devastating effect. That accident remains the very worst ever to occur at a motor race.

In the heat of battle Hawthorn, who had to visit the pits to refuel, tried to overtake his fellow Briton, Lance Macklin, in the Austin-Healey. At that time the pit lane was not separated from the track itself by the wall which these days would have forced the drivers to reduce their speed long before reaching their allotted place. After passing the red Healey, Hawthorn pulled sharply over to the right and slammed on his brakes. In spite of this he still overshot his pit by 80 metres.

For his part, Macklin, surprised by the Jaguar's risky manoeuvre, veered sharply to the left to avoid a collision. His reaction was tragic in the true, original Greek sense of the word: if he had not made that move he would have collided with Mike Hawthorn – the result was that Pierre Levegh, following, had no chance.

Levegh was hurtling along the straight at about 60 or 70 km/h faster than the Austin-Healey (the 300 SLRs were travelling at about 260 km/h at this point) and was on the left-hand side of the track, shaping up to go past the car ahead of him. The gap that had been there for him to go through just a split second before was now blocked by Macklin.

Levegh's right arm shot skyward as a reflex warning to Fangio who was following him, and then he cannoned into the Healey.

The consequences were horrific. The Mercedes flew over the embankment and Levegh was killed instantly as he was flung from the car. With a deafening crash the 300 SLR disintegrated. In the enormous impact the engine and complete front axle, suspension and brakes were ripped from the chassis and scythed through the crowd; bodywork flew like shrapnel. In front of the main grandstand there was a bloodbath.

The start-finish area was a scene of true horror after that moment. The screams of the wounded and the cries of grief from those who had lost fathers, sisters, husbands or children drowned the din of the cars screaming past on the track. Blue lights flashed, ambulancemen dashed around trying to help, priests gave the last rites in what resembled the scene of a bomb blast. The hospitals in Le Mans and the surrounding area were filled to bursting point in a trice and slowly the full extent of the catastrophe became clear: 82 were dead, including the innocent Levegh.

The agony experienced by those close to the scene of the accident did not, however, spread to affect everyone else. The roundabouts in the funfair continued to turn, the din from the shooting galleries was unabated, and the race went right on. Just a few hundred metres from that scene of death, life carried on exuberantly to the sound of music and laughter.

The elderly Charles Faroux, who had founded the 24-hour Le Mans classic in 1923 and was acting as Clerk of the Course for the 1955 event, saw no reason to call off "his" race. Panic would spread throughout the crowd, he felt sure. In reply to the many questions put to him in the weeks following that sad event, the 84-year-old said that such a situation would have jeopardized the speedy and efficient removal of the many injured spectators. Another version leaked out, however: Faroux was said to be concerned that many teams would claim compensation if the race was stopped. There were numerous articles and discussions in the weeks after the race which maintained that this kind of commercial pressure had been uppermost in Faroux's mind.

The race went ahead, then, but during the night, with Fangio and Moss running several laps clear of the field at the front, and Simon/Kling in 3rd spot, the Mercedes 300 SLRs were withdrawn. The team had no wish to win a race that stood under such a cloud. As the Mercedes transporters left the paddock at the dawn of a new day, the public stood to applaud.

No one today can say who would have won the race, and how important was it anyway after such an incident? Very important to the British, apparently. The very characteristic headline in *The Motor* read "Another British Victory at Le Mans". Winners were Mike Hawthorn and Ivor Bueb in the Jaguar D-Type, Hawthorn being at least partly to blame for the accident. Things reached an all-time low during the last hours of the race when the rain fell in sheets.

The impact of Le Mans was felt far and wide. In France all types of motor sport were forbidden to begin with – although the French Grand Prix returned to the racing calendar the following year. The Swiss did not stop at a temporary ban – all types of motor racing events on Swiss soil have been prohibited since 1955. As well as the 1955 French Grand Prix, the races in Germany, Spain and Switzerland were called off that year, and there also began an unprecedented campaign against motor racing.

It is worth remembering that twice World Champion, Alberto Ascari, had been killed just a few weeks before, as had the twice Indianapolis winner, Bill Vukovich. It was open season for the cartoonists who plumbed new depths of tastelessness. One cartoon showed the grim reaper squatting on the 13km marker opposite the main grandstand at Le Mans gripping an hourglass in his skeletal fingers. The caption: The timekeeper at Le Mans. Another depicted a car crossing the line, winning comfortably from the rest of the field. A skull leered from the cockpit. The caption: Death as the victor.

The week after the accident a press conference was held at Daimler-Benz in Unterürkheim where the firm attempted to dispel any last doubts about their innocence. There had been increasing rumblings about the magnesium bodywork having exploded, triggering the catastrophe. Countering these claims came the argument that magnesium only burns at temperatures above 600°C. Judicial investigation into the accident eventually came to a close in the autumn of 1956. On 13th October the wreckage of Levegh's 300 SLR was taken back to Stuttgart from the garage near the circuit where it had been housed. There had been calls from many quarters for proceedings to be opened against Hawthorn, but they never were. The Le Mans tragedy did bring about improvements in safety standards for spectators, drivers and pit crews at tracks all over the world. Pit complexes at most tracks were separated by a wall from the track itself and spectator accommodation was given better protection from wayward cars.

Pierre Levegh was buried at the Père Lachaise cemetery in Paris; Daimler-Benz looked after his widow most generously. A French insurance group took responsibility for the families of the other 81 killed. What remained was the memory of the most horrific accident in the history of motor racing – and any number of persistent misinterpretations.

Fangio after the Mercedes team's withdrawal during the night.

The Successes

Mercedes-Benz's list of victories, 1955

On Saturday 22nd October 1955 the curtain came down on Daimler-Benz's works participation in motor racing. In a symbolic act, team manager Alfred Neubauer and the drivers Juan Manuel Fangio, Stirling Moss and Karl Kling covered an open-wheeled W 196 with a large white sheet. It was similar to the ceremonial unveiling of a memorial, taking place after speeches of remembrance or exhortation. On this occasion, however, things were quite different outside Building 136a on the Daimler-Strasse at the factory in Untertürkheim: after the speeches the car was covered up, a car which, in the 1956 season and with a few modifications, would probably also have beaten its competitors. The symbolic veiling made the W 196 into a memorial to the firm's sporting success in the mid-1950s. When the white veil was finally removed, the car had taken its place in the works museum alongside the fabulous pre-war cars: the white French Grand Prix victor of 1914 and the super-charged silver monsters of the 1930s.

The W 196 that carried Juan Manuel Fangio to the 1954 World Championship and his dominant defence of that title the following year was not, however, the only car contributing to the firm's overwhelming success in 1955. It was simply the most famous and probably signified the most important success because then, as now, the Formula 1 World Championship was the pinnacle of the sport.

The next most important category, the World Sports Car Championship, also fell to Mercedes-Benz. The 300 SLR, the car so directly derived from the W 196 that it was given the factory designation W 196S, had shown its absolute authority over all comers in every race for which it was entered, just as its companion model had done in Formula 1. Victories had been scored in all but a single race: it won the renowned Mille Miglia, that bastion that had appeared unconquerable to foreigners for so

288

long; the International Eifelrennen at the Nürburgring; the Swedish Grand Prix at Kristianstad; the Tourist Trophy in Ireland; and, to cap them all, a victory that was just six days old, having been achieved on 16th October 1955, the classic Targa Florio in Sicily.

The only event at which the 300 SLR took the start but failed to finish as the winner was the Le Mans 24 Hours in June. Moss and Fangio had been leading, but as a result of the terrible accident that befell Pierrre Levegh in his 300 SLR, the team chiefs pulled the remaining two cars out of the race at 2 am. But the other wins underscored Untertürkheim's success in the sports car category, even if the World Championship was only decided at the final encounter in favour of Mercedes over Ferrari.

But the roll of honour does not stop there: a Mercedes also took the European Touring Car Championship. The title did not fall to a works-entered car, but if anything that says even more for the reliability and speed of the vehicles from Untertürkheim. Werner Engel from Hamburg contested the series, alternating between a 220 A and a 300 SL, and beat the opposition by steady accumulation of points in events like the Tulip Rally, the Rallye Adria and the long-distance event, the Liège-Rome-Liège. Schock and Moll were another crew to finish in good placings in a number of events in their black 220 A, for instance the Sestrière.

The American sports car champion, Paul O'Shea, took the title after 13 rounds of the SCCA (Sports Car Club of America) Championship in his gull-wing 300 SL. The significance of this success in America, the most important country from the point of view of export, lay in the series being contested by production cars, of which at least 500 examples had to be built.

The Belgian Olivier Gendebien scored some impressive wins in a number of long-distance events in his private 300 SL: he won the Coppa d'Oro delle Dolomiti near Cortina d'Ampezzo and the Stella Alpina in Italy, and also the Liège-Rome-Liège classic.

Success after success, then, for Mercedes-Benz. The Board's decision to pull out of racing thus becomes less and less surprising. What was there left to prove? Even Alfred Neubauer, who was so much in favour of motor racing and made such a contribution to Mercedes' postwar return to the international scene, realized that it was "tactically correct and intelligent once the height of success had been reached" to withdraw from the fray. The 300 SLR's career thus ended slightly prematurely (the original plan was to ignore Grand Prix racing for 1956 but continue in sports car events), but the car had taken the Championship in its début season.

There was nothing left to prove – success was complete on every front. It was so overwhelming that Mercedes-Benz can still afford to dine out on it to this very day. Nearly everyone was convinced that if the Stuttgart firm ever returned to racing, its car would be back in the winner's enclosure. Until very recently, the firm has seen no reason to attempt to prove this theory. The racing record of 1954 and 1955 is mostly to thank for that.

Plans

Ideas for 1956

It was quite early in 1955 that the Board voted to discontinue Grand Prix racing in 1956. By May the staff of the racing department knew that works involvement the following year would be restricted to the sports car field. By this time, however, Rudolf Uhlenhaut and his colleagues had, of course, already had any number of ideas for the future development of the W 196. The plans were so sweeping that any vehicle that had resulted would certainly not have carried the designation W 196, but rather some combination of figures around the 200 mark. Ideas continued to be developed during the 1955 Grand Prix season – after all, there was still the possibility that the Board would reverse its decision.

To begin with, a completely new engine would be built. In February 1986 Rudolf Uhlenhaut described it thus: "It was going to be a V8 with four valves per cylinder, probably without desmodromic operation. Four valves still gave better breathing than two, even if they were of a large diameter." Engine output of well over 300PS (and probably as high as 350 to 360PS) would have been likely, and that would guarantee a continued power superiority for Mercedes in the coming years.

The V8 would also have been much shorter than the rather long inline M 196 and ideal in the quest for a shorter and nimbler car. Besides this, the team was considering a four-wheel-drive Grand Prix car and extra room would have been needed up front to accommodate the transmission to the front wheels. The four-wheel drive would not necessarily be in permanent engagement: the idea was that drive to the front wheels would only be engaged with the car in first gear at the start, resulting in a massive increase in traction. During the race itself only the rear wheels would be driven, though a permanent four-wheel-drive system for wet races was also under consideration.

A further refinement tested at the Nürburgring in the summer of 1955 was an inlet tract length governed by engine speed. At low revs the inlet pipes would be shortened by comparison with their length at high speeds. Improved breathing at low revs was the aim to allow better acceleration out of corners. The usable rev band would also have been broadened.

Disc brakes were another avenue being explored by the racing department at Untertürkheim. Jaguar sports cars had been equipped with the new type of brake for three years and they had proved their reliability under rigorous conditions in the Le Mans 24 Hours. Drum brakes, even as generously proportioned as on the W 196, were prey to a creeping reduction in effectiveness towards the end of a race. Consistently effective brakes were at least as important for race success as a powerful engine, especially on twisty circuits.

The gearshift was another component that was due for fundamental revision. Uhlenhaut, who had himself driven the car often enough, had realized that especially in changing down before right corners at the end of long straights, for instance from 5th gear to 2nd, the driver was, firstly, hard at work and, secondly, had to take his tight hand off the wheel to change. It was a very simple observation, but Uhlenhaut's mind was at work on countering this phenomenon.

Having to take one hand off the wheel was undesirable, especially when the brakes were fading or pulling to one side. The solution was simple enough – and for that reason would certainly have become an overnight success. The new Formula 1 Mercedes would have a foot-operated gearchange, like a motorcycle. Thus the drivers would have been able to change at least as quickly as with the lever (perhaps even faster bearing in mind the relatively long throw), but they would have both hands on the wheel throughout, allowing them to corner far more accurately when changing down.

It virtually goes without saying that a completely redesigned car would certainly have had a new aerodynamic body. A wider nose (including more aerodynamically efficient wheel covering) similar to the 1955 Gordini or the Bugatti 251 would have been a possibility. Tests with a more sharply tapering nose than on the previous W 196 streamlined bodywork (allowing the driver a better line of sight during cornering) had appeared in testing at Monza in 1955.

We may rest assured that Mercedes would have come up with many more improvements to give its rivals headaches in following seasons. The racing department with the original mind of Rudolf Uhlenhaut as its guide was not likely to run short of ideas. But even today, more than 30 years after the event, a cloak of secrecy is spread over many details. Some secrets never grow old.

The Stablemate

The 300 SLR sports car

No book on the W 196 would be truly complete without a chapter on Mercedes' 1955 sports car, the 300 SLR. This was the car that brought victory for Daimler-Benz in the World Championship of Makes, the most important international racing category after Formula 1. A detailed technical description of the 300 SLR need not appear here, since the similarities between the Grand Prix contender and the sports car are so numerous. This similarity is emphasized by the factory designations given to the two cars: whereas the Formula 1 machine was known as the W 196R (for *Rennwagen,* or racing car), the 300 SLR was known as the W 196S *(Sportwagen).*

The engine of the 300 SLR was derived from the 2.5-litre Grand Prix power unit. To arrive at the desired capacity of 3 litres the Daimler-Benz engineers enlarged the bore and stroke to make the unit "square" at 78 x 78 mm (compared with a bore x stroke of 76 x 68.8 mm in the case of the Grand Prix machine). The capacity of each cylinder was increased from 312 to 374 cc, giving a total capacity of 2992 cc. The 3-litre engine was made of a different material to the 2.5-litre unit. Whereas the water jackets of the latter were welded from steel sheet, the cylinder block of the former was an alloy casting containing a sizeable percentage of magnesium. Maximum engine speed was reduced by 900 rpm to 7600 rpm to allow only a slight increase in piston speed (17 m/sec) despite the longer stroke. The compression ratio was 12:1 and the engine could run on Super pump petrol.

The chassis frame of the W 196R needed very little modification. It was just altered slightly halfway along its length to allow the provision of two seats side by side. Accommodation for the enlarged fuel tank made other slight modifications necessary. Although the track of the two vehicles remained the same at 1330 mm, the wheelbase of the 300 SLR was extended to 2380 mm. Suspension and

67171

Fangio won at the Nürburgring.

brakes were unchanged.

A new body shape had to be tailored for the two-seater, though its shape was strongly reminiscent of the streamlined version of the W 196. A hallmark of the 300 SLR's exterior was the very steeply angled windscreen which was sometimes replaced by a smaller screen.

At Le Mans the 300 SLR appeared with an air brake, which was intended to cut the demands made on the car's drum brakes in slowing the vehicle from speeds of upwards of 200 km/h. The air brake consisted of a flap behind the driver which was swung into the airstream when required. After Le Mans the brake only made one more appearance (at the Swedish Grand Prix).

Fangio with the first version of the 300 SLR at Monza in 1954.

The sheer power can be sensed in the car's very shape: the 1955 300 SLR.

The W 196's stablemate was tested for the first time after the 1954 Italian Grand Prix at Monza. Its engine was given its baptism of fire in the Grand Prix chassis at the Grand Prix of Buenos Aires, the non-formula race on 30th January 1955. The car's first race was on 1st May 1955 in the notorious Mille Miglia, where it scored a début win, thus emulating the achievement of the Grand Prix car from the Untertürkheim stable.

Once the leading crews, Hans Herrmann in one car and Karl Kling in another, had dropped out (Kling in an accident shortly after leaving Rome and Herrmann because of a lost fuel tank cap), Stirling Moss and his navigator Denis Jenkinson, the British motoring journalist and passenger to former World Sidecar Champion, Eric Oliver, stepped in to win the Mille Miglia at a new record average speed of over 157 km/h. Despite driving the last 1600 km of the race on only seven cylinders, Juan Manuel Fangio crossed the line 2nd.

The 300 SLR won the Tourist Trophy . . .

The next event, the International Eifelrennen on the North Loop of the Nürburgring, providing another tale of Mercedes domination. Fangio won ahead of Moss, with Kling coming home in 4th. For Le Mans on 11th June, three crews had been nominated: Fangio/Moss, Kling/Simon and Levegh/Fitch. The race was cut short by the terrible catastrophe which claimed the lives of over 80 spectators as well as local hero, Pierre Levegh. The two remaining cars were withdrawn from leading positions during the night.

In the Swedish Grand Prix at Kristianstad on 7th August Fangio and Moss scored another one-two, and after taking all three top placings on the Tourist Trophy at Dundrod in Northern Ireland in the order Moss/Fitch, Fangio/Kling and von Trips/Simon, Daimler-Benz went to the Targa Florio needing a victory to secure the International Championship for Makes. There was just one thing, however: the best Ferrari had to finish no higher than 3rd.

After a dramatic race the all-British crew of Stirling Moss and Peter Collins, a new signing for this race, crossed the line in front of Fangio/Kling. Fitch/Titterington were 4th. The one-two gave Daimler-Benz the title by a whisker ahead of Ferrari to add to the firm's success in the Formula 1 World Championship. The success meant there was no longer any need for the company to contest the 1956 sports car series, which had been the intention, and Daimler-Benz thus announced its withdrawal from all forms of racing.

The 300 SLR had proved so superior in its first season's racing that it was no longer necessary to send it back out on the championship trail the following year. Mercedes had achieved a clean sweep with its winning duo, the W 196R and W 196S.

. . . and secured the
1955 International
Championship of
Makes on the Targa
Florio.

The Transporter

Specially built for the W 196

A curious vehicle was turned out by the experimental department at Daimler-Benz in Untertürkheim in the spring of 1955. The cab was well forward of the front axle, it was powered by the 300 SL sports car engine and there was a flat bed at the rear equipped with wheel pans. The vehicle, clad in aluminium and steel panels, was painted the characteristic blue of the rest of the works transporters and service vehicles that accompanied the Mercedes team on all its travels.

The stylish vehicle had been built under the watchful eye of Rudolf Uhlenhaut and was nothing more or less than a transporter for the W 196 (and the 300 SLR, too). The transporter was supposed to enable rapid transfer of a car back to the factory from any circuit should a problem arise that could not be solved on the spot. That, at least, was the official version explaining the construction of the vehicle.

In fact it was no more than an effective piece of fun and proof of the free rein that was given to the experimental department. Of course it was very nice to be able to speed from Stuttgart to Hockenheim or the Nürburgring (it was capable of up to 170 km/h), but a conventional transporter would have done the job too.

Another angle quickly became apparent – probably intentionally: the blue truck was soon to be seen in papers and magazines and ensured some good publicity for Daimler-Benz AG. The low-slung vehicle carrying an even lower racing car on the back was an impressive sight, like a glimpse of things to come: there was something futuristic about the combination. It would not have been Uhlenhaut's style to leave such a vehicle bereft of interesting features.

The weight (a kerb weight of 2100 kg plug 700 – 800 kg for the car) needed a reliable braking system to decelerate from high speeds. Uhlenhaut did something special in this department. Besides drum

299

The transporter was capable of carrying both the W 196 . . .

brakes all round with Bosch brake booster there was a disc brake on the transmission between propshaft and differential. This additional disc made the vehicle's braking almost as impressive as its overall performance. To get the piggyback machine safely (and above all quickly) through the bends, there was a rear swing axle with a low split pivot point for the axle assemblies. Even the transporter was a true "racer". After the firm's withdrawal from racing there were countless inquiries about the sale of the transporter. The British were especially keen on the blue one-off. Eventually it was Rudolf Uhlenhaut himself who put an end to the story: in December 1967, all of 12 years after its creation, the transporter was scrapped.

For those who simply have to know all the facts, here are some technical details:

Engine: 300 SL power unit, 6-cylinder in-line, bore x stroke 85 x 88 mm, capacity 2996 cc, compression 8.3:1, output 192PS @ 5500 rpm, maximum torque 25.8 kgm @ 4700 rpm, ohv, fuel injection, average fuel consumption 25 litres per 100 km

Transmission: Daimler-Benz single dry-plate clutch, 4-speed all-synchro gearbox, hypoid rear axle, involute gear teeth.

Chassis: 300 S chassis frame extended forward and rearward, front suspension by coil springs and Fichtel & Sachs dampers, rear swing axle with low, split pivot point on both half shafts, coil springs with auxiliary torsion bars and Fichtel & Sachs dampers, 4-wheel hydraulic brakes with Bosch brake booster, compound brake drums, disc brake between propshaft and differential, 150 litre fuel tank, 12 v electrics.

Weights and dimensions: Wheelbase 3050 mm, track front/rear 1480/1525 mm, length 6750 mm, width 2000 mm, height 1750 mm, dry weight 1865 kg, tyres front and rear 7.60 x 15.

Bodywork in aluminium and sheet steel, paintwork Daimler-Benz blue.

. . . and the 300 SLR.

APPENDIX

The People

Race appearances

II. Gran Premio de la Republica Argentina
Buenos Aires, 17th January 1954

Distance: 3 hours (87 laps of 3.912 km circuit = 340.34 km)
Weather: overcast, dry at first, heavy rain at times later

```
                        Starting grid
J. M. Hawthorn   J. M. Fangio    J. F. Gonzalez     G. Farina
   Ferrari         Maserati         Ferrari          Ferrari

(1 min 47.0 sec) (1 min 45.7 sec) (1 min 44.9 sec)  (1 min 44.8 sec)

           L. Musso*        O. Marimon      M. Trintignant
            Maserati         Maserati          Ferrari

         (1 min 48.2 sec)  (1 min 47.7 sec) (1 min 47.7 sec)

  U. Maglioli      H. Schell        B. Bira          R. Mières
   Ferrari         Maserati        Maserati          Maserati

(1 min 50.2 sec) (1 min 50.0 sec) (1 min 49.3 sec)  (1 min 49.0 sec)

           E. Bayol         L. Rosier      E. de Graffenried
            Gordini          Ferrari          Maserati

         (1 min 52.6 sec)  (1 min 51.6 sec) (1 min 51.0 sec)

           G. Daponte        J. Behra         R. Loyer
            Maserati         Gordini          Gordini

         (1 min 56.7 sec)  (1 min 53.0 sec) (1 min 52.6 sec)

    *Non starter: L. Musso (engine failure in practice)
```

Result: 1st. Juan Manuel Fangio, Maserati, 340.34 km in 3 hr 00 min 55.8 sec = 112.86 km/h; 2nd Giuseppe Farina, Ferrari, 3:02:14.8; 3rd José Froilan Gonzalez, Ferrari, 3:02:56.8; 4th Maurice Trintignant, Ferrari, 1 lap behind; 5th Elie Bayol, Gordini, 2 laps behind; 6th Harry Schell, Maserati, 3 laps behind; 7th Prince Bira, Maserati, 4 laps behind; 8th Emmanuel de Graffenried, Maserati, 4 laps behind; 9th Umberto Maglioli, Ferrari, 5 laps behind.
Fastest Lap: Gonzalez in 1:48.2 min = 129.975 km/h
Retirements: Rosier (accident), Marimon (spin), Hawthorn (disqualified for receiving outside assistance), Behra (disqualified for receiving outside assistance), Daponte (oil pump), Loyer (oil pump), Mières (engine).

XVI. Grote Prijs van België/Grand Prix de Belgique
Spa-Francorchamps, 20th June 1954

Distance: 36 laps of 14.12 km circuit = 508.32 km
Weather: warm and sunny

```
                     Starting grid
   J. M. Fangio      J. F. Gonzalez      G. Farina
     Maserati           Ferrari          Ferrari

  (4 min 22.1 sec)   (4 min 23.6 sec)  (4 min 26.0 sec)

        O. Marimon       J. M. Hawthorn
         Maserati           Ferrari

      (4 min 27.6 sec)   (4 min 29.4 sec)

 M. Trintignant       J. Behra          A. Pilette
   Ferrari            Gordini           Gordini

 (4 min 30.0 sec)   (4 min 34.5 sec)  (4 min 40.0 sec)

          S. Moss          P. Frère
         Maserati          Gordini

      (4 min 40.8 sec)   (4 min 42.0 sec)

 S. Mantovani        R. Mières          B. Bira
   Maserati          Maserati          Maserati

 (4 min 43.2 sec)   (4 min 43.8 sec)  (4 min 46.5 sec)

                  J. Swaters
                   Ferrari

                (4 min 54.2 sec)
```

Result: 1st Juan Manuel Fangio, Maserati, 508.32 km in 2 hr 44 min 42.4 sec = 185.172 km/h; 2nd Maurice Trintignant, Ferrari, 2:45:06.6; 3rd Stirling Moss, Maserati, 1 lap behind; 4th Mike Hawthorn/José Froilan Gonzalez, Ferrari, 1 lap behind; 5th André Pilette, Gordini, 1 lap behind; 6th Prince Bira, Maserati, 1 lap behind; 7th Sergio Mantovani, Maserati, 2 laps behind.

Fastest Lap: Fangio (lap 13) in 4:25.2 min = 191.547 km/h
Retirements: Mières (fire lap 1), Swaters (lap 1 engine), Gonzalez (lap 1 engine), Marimon (lap 3 engine), Behra (lap 12 broken rear suspension), Farina (lap 15 ignition), Frère (lap 15 rear axle)

XLI. Grand Prix de l'ACF Reims, 4th July 1954

Distance: 61 laps of 8.302 km circuit = 506.42 km
Weather: cloudy, dry at first, drizzle later

Starting grid

A. Ascari Maserati (2 min 30.5 sec)	K. Kling Mercedes-Benz (2 min 30.4 sec)	J. M. Fangio Mercedes-Benz (2 min 29.4 sec)

O. Marimon Maserati (2 min 31.6 sec)	J. F. Gonzalez Ferrari (2 min 30.6 sec)

J. M. Hawthorn Ferrari (2 min 35.6 sec)	H. Herrmann Mercedes-Benz (2 min 35.3 sec)	B. Bira Maserati (2 min 35.1 sec)

R. Salvadori Maserati (2 min 36.3 sec)	M. Trintignant Ferrari (2 min 36.1 sec)

L. Rosier Ferrari (2 min 42.1 sec)	R. Manzon Ferrari (2 min 42.0 sec)	R. Mières Maserati (2 min 38.7 sec)

L. Macklin H. W. M. (2 min 52.5 sec)	L. Villoresi Maserati (2 min 42.7 sec)

J. Pollet Gordini (No time)	J. Behra Gordini (No time)	K. Wharton Maserati (3 min 09.3 sec)

G. Berger Gordini (No time)	P. Frère Gordini (No time)

H. Schell Maserati (No time)

Result: 1st. Juan Manuel Fangio, Mercedes-Benz, 506.42 km in 2 hr 42 min 47.9 sec = 186.638 km/h; 2nd Karl Kling, Mercedes-Benz, 2:42:48.0; 3rd Robert Manzon, Ferrari, 1 lap behind; 4th Prince Bira, Maserati, 1 lap behind; 5th Luigi Villoresi, Maserati, 3 laps behind; 6th Jean Behra, Gordini, 5 laps behind; 7th Paul Frère, Gordini, 11 laps behind.
Fastest Lap: Herrmann (lap 3) in 2:32.9 min = 195.463 km/h
Retirements: Ascari (lap 1 transmission), Pollet (lap 9 engine), Berger (lap 9 engine), Hawthorn (lap 10 engine), Macklin (lap 10 engine), Gonzalez (lap 13 engine), Salvadori (lap 15 transmission), Herrmann (lap 17 engine), Wharton (lap 20 gearbox), Schell (lap 20 fuel pump), Mières (lap 25 engine), Rosier (lap 28 engine), Marimon (lap 28 gearbox), Trintignant (lap 36 engine).

VIIth British Grand Prix, Silverstone, 17th July 1954

Distance: 90 laps of 4.7105 km circuit = 423.95 km
Weather: cold and wet

Starting grid

S. Moss Maserati (1 min 47 sec)	J. M. Hawthorn Ferrari (1 min 46 sec)	J. F. Gonzalez Ferrari (1 min 46 sec)	J. M. Fangio Mercedes-Benz (1 min 45 sec)

R. Salvadori Maserati (1 min 48 sec)	K. Kling Mercedes-Benz (1 min 48 sec)	J. Behra Gordini (1 min 48 sec)

P. Collins Vanwall Special (1 min 50 sec)	B. Bira Maserati (1 min 49 sec)	K. Wharton Maserati (1 min 49 sec)	M. Trintignant Ferrari (1 min 48 sec)

R. Parnell Ferrari (1 min 52 sec)	C. Bucci Gordini (1 min 52 sec)	A. Pilette Gordini (1 min 51 sec)

F. R. Gerard Cooper-Bristol (1 min 55 sec)	D. Beauman Connaught (1 min 55 sec)	H. Schell Maserati (1 min 53 sec)	R. Manzon Ferrari (1 min 52 sec)

Continued over page

Result: José Froilan Gonzalez, Ferrari, 423.95 km in 2 hr 56 min 14.0 sec = 144.34 km/h; 2nd Mike Hawthorn, Ferrari, 2:57:24.0; 3rd Onofre Marimon, 1 lap behind; 4th Juan Manuel Fangio, Mercedes-Benz, 1 lap behind; 5th Maurice Trintignant, Ferrari, 5 laps behind; 6th Roberto Mières, Maserati, 3 laps behind; 7th Karl Kling, Mercedes-Benz, 3 laps behind; 8th Ken Wharton, Maserati, 4 laps behind; 9th

Continued

J. R-Prichard	H. Gould	W. Whitehouse
Connaught	Cooper-Bristol	Connaught
(1 min 58 sec)	(1 min 56 sec)	(1 min 56 sec)

E. Brandon	P. Whitehead	L. Thorne	L. Marr
Cooper	Cooper-Alta	Connaught	Connaught
(2 min 05 sec)	(2 min 00 sec)	(1 min 59 sec)	(1 min 58 sec)

O. Marimon	L. Villoresi	A. Brown*
Maserati	Maserati	Cooper-Bristol
(No time)	(No time)	(No time)

R. Mières	A. Ascari	L. Rosier
Maserati	Maserati	Ferrari
(No time)	(No time)	(No time)

*Non starter: A Brown (Cooper-Bristol)

André Pilette, Gordini, 4 laps behind; 10th F R Gerard, Cooper-Bristol, 5 laps behind; 11th D Beauman, Connaught, 6 laps behind; 12th Harry Schell, Maserati, 7 laps behind; 13th Leslie Marr, Connaught, 8 laps behind; 14th L Thorne, Connaught, 12 laps behind.

Fastest Lap: Gonzalez, Hawthorn, Marimon, Fangio, Moss, Behra and Ascari all 1:50.0 min = 154.16 km/h

Retirements: Brandon (lap 3), Rosier (lap 3 engine), Whitehead (lap 5 oil hose), Manzon (lap 16 holed cylinder block), Collins (lap 17 cylinder head gasket), Bucci (lap 18 accident), Ascari (lap 21 damaged valve), Parnell (lap 26 engine), Villoresi (lap 41 propshaft), Riseley-Pritchard (lap 41 accident), Bira/Flockhart (lap 41 accident), Salvadori (lap 54 transmission), Behra (lap 55 broken rear suspension), Whitehouse (lap 64 engine), Moss (lap 80 rear axle).

Grosser Preis von Europa Nürburgring, 1st August 1954

Distance: 22 laps of 22.772 km circuit = 501.82 km
Weather: warm and dry

Starting grid

S. Moss	J. M. Hawthorn	J. M. Fangio
Maserati	Ferrari	Mercedes-Benz
(10 min 00.7 sec)	(9 min 53.3 sec)	(9 min 50.1 sec)

J. F. Gonzalez	H. Herrmann
Ferrari	Mercedes-Benz
(10 min 01.8 sec)	(10 min 01.5 sec)

O. Marimon	M. Trintignant	P. Frère
Maserati	Ferrari	Gordini
(*)	(10 min 07.5 sec)	(10 min 05.9 sec)

L. Villoresi	J. Behra
Maserati	Gordini
(**)	(10 min 11.9 sec)

P. Taruffi	R. Manzon	H. Lang
Ferrari	Ferrari	Mercedes-Benz
(10 min 23.0 sec)	(10 min 16.1 sec)	(10 min 13.1 sec)

S. Mantovani	H. Schell
Maserati	Maserati
(10 min 39.1 sec)	(10 min 28.7 sec)

L. Rosier	R. Mières	C. Bucci
Ferrari	Maserati	Gordini
(11 min 04.3 sec)	(10 min 47.0 sec)	(10 min 43.7 sec)

A. Pilette	B. Bira
Gordini	Maserati
(11 min 13.4 sec)	(11 min 10.3 sec)

K. Kling	T. Helfrich
Mercedes-Benz	Klenk-Meteor
(No time)	(11 min 18.3 sec)

*O. Marimon (Maserati) Fatal accident in practice
**L. Villoresi (Maserati) withdrew after Marimon's accident

Result: 1st Juan Manuel Fangio, Mercedes-Benz, 501.82 km in 3 hr 45 min 45.8 sec = 133.37 km/h; 2nd José Froilan Gonzalez, Ferrari, 3:47:22.3; 3rd Maurice Trintignant, Ferrari, 3:50:54.4; 4th Karl Kling, Mercedes-Benz, 3:51:52.3; 5th Sergio Mantovani, Maserati, 3:54:36.3; 6th Piero Taruffi, Ferrari, 1 lap behind; 7th Harry Schell, Maserati, 1 lap behind; 8th Louis Rosier, Ferrari, 1 lap behind; 9th Robert Manzon, Ferrari, 2 laps behind; 10th Jean Behra, Gordini, 2 laps behind.

Fastest Lap: Kling (lap 16) in 9:55.1 min = 137.99 km/h

Retirements: Pilette (lap 1 front suspension), Moss (lap 2 engine), Mières (lap 3 leaking fuel tank), Hawthorn (lap 4 rear axle), Frère (lap 5 broken wheel), Herrmann (lap 8 injection pump), Helfrich (lap 9 engine), Bucci (lap 9 broken wheel), Lang (lap 11 engine and spin), Bira (lap 19 steering).

XIV. Grosser Preis der Schweiz
Bremgarten, nr Berne, 22nd August 1954

Distance: 66 laps of 7.28 km circuit = 480.48 km
Weather: wet, track drying throughout race

Starting grid

S. Moss Maserati (2 min 41,4 sec)	J. M. Fangio Mercedes-Benz (2 min 39.7 sec)	J. F. Gonzalez Ferrari (2 min 39.5 sec)
	K. Kling Mercedes-Benz (2 min 41.9 sec)	M. Trintignant Ferrari (2 min 41.7 sec)
K. Wharton Maserati (2 min 46.2 sec)	H. Herrmann Mercedes-Benz (2 min 45.0 sec)	J. M. Hawthorn Ferrari (2 min 43.2 sec)
	C. Bucci Gordini (3 min 04.1 sec)	S. Mantovani Maserati (2 min 56.9 sec)
H. Schell Maserati (3 min 12.1 sec)	R. Mières Maserati (3 min 09.3 sec)	U. Maglioli Ferrari (3 min 08.2 sec)
	F. Wacker Gordini (3 min 20.3 sec)	J. Behra Gordini (3 min 16.4 sec)
	J. Swaters Ferrari (3 min 20.4 sec)	

Non starters: R. Manzon (Ferrari) practice accident; R. Salvadori (Maserati); E. de Graffenried (Maserati)

Result: 1st Juan Manuel Fangio, Mercedes-Benz, 480.48 km in 3 hr 00 min 34.5 sec = 159.65 km/h; 2nd José Froilan Gonzalez, Ferrari, 3:01:32.3; 3rd Hans Herrmann, Mercedes-Benz, 1 lap behind; 4th Roberto Mières, Maserati, 2 laps behind; 5th Sergio Mantovani, Maserati, 2 laps behind; 6th Ken Wharton, Maserati, 2 laps behind; 7th Umberto Maglioli, Ferrari, 5 laps behind; 8th Jacques Swaters, Ferrari, 8 laps behind.

Fastest Lap: Fangio (lap 34) in 2:39.7 min = 164.108 km/h
Retirements: Bucci (lap 1 oil pump), Behra (lap 8 clutch), Wacker (lap 10 transmission), Moss (lap 22 oil pressure), Schell (lap 23 oil pressure), Hawthorn (lap 31 fuel pump), Trintignant (lap 33 engine), Kling (lap 39 engine).

XXV. Gran Premio d'Italia
Monza, 5th September 1954

Distance: 80 laps of 6.3 km circuit = 504.0 km
Weather: warm and dry

Starting grid

S. Moss Maserati (1 min 59.3 sec)	A. Ascari Ferrari (1 min 59.2 sec)	J. M. Fangio Mercedes-Benz (1 min 59.0 sec)
L. Villoresi Maserati (2 min 00.2 sec)	J. F. Gonzalez Ferrari (2 min 00.0 sec)	K. Kling Mercedes-Benz (1 min 59.6 sec)
S. Mantovani Maserati (2 min 01.6 sec)	H. Herrmann Mercedes-Benz (2 min 01.4 sec)	J. M. Hawthorn Ferrari (2 min 00.2 sec)
J. Behra Gordini (2 min 02.4 sec)	M. Trintignant Ferrari (2 min 02.3 sec)	R. Mières Maserati (2 min 01.7 sec)
R. Manzon Ferrari (2 min 04.7 sec)	L. Musso Maserati (2 min 03.5 sec)	U. Maglioli Ferrari (2 min 03.5 sec)
F. Wacker Gordini (2 min 08.0 sec)	C. Bucci Gordini (2 min 05.5 sec)	P. Collins Vanwall Special (2 min 05.2 sec)
L. Rosier Maserati (2 min 11.0 sec)	G. Daponte Maserati (2 min 09.5 sec)	

Result: 1st Juan Manuel Fangio, Mercedes-Benz, 504.0 km in 2 hr 47 min 47.9 sec = 180.218 km/h; 2nd Mike Hawthorn, Ferrari, 1 lap behind; 3rd Umberto Maglioli/José Froilan Gonzalez, Ferrari, 2 laps behind; 4th Hans Herrmann, Mercedes-Benz, 3 laps behind; 5th Maurice Trintignant, Ferrari, 5 laps behind; 6th F Wacker, 5 laps behind; 7th Peter Collins, Vanwall, 5 laps behind; 8th Louis Rosier, Maserati, 6 laps behind; 9th Sergio Mantovani, Maserati, 6 laps behind; 10th Stirling Moss, Maserati, 9 laps behind (had retired but classified by virtue of distance covered); 11th G Daponte, Maserati, 10 laps behind.

Fastest Lap: Gonzalez (lap 2) in 2:00.8 min = 187.748 km/h
Retirements: Behra (lap 3 engine), Bucci (lap 14 gearbox), Gonzalez (lap 17 gearbox), Manzon (lap 17 engine), Musso (lap 33 transmission), Mières (lap 35 suspension breakage), Kling (lap 37 oil hose burst resulting in accident), Villoresi (lap 43 clutch), Ascari (lap 49 damaged valve), Moss (lap 71 engine).

Grosser Preis von Berlin
Avus, 19th September 1954

Distance: 60 laps of 8.4 km circuit = 504 km
Weather: overcast, cool, final stages of race run in gathering gloom

```
                      Starting grid

        K. Kling         H. Herrmann       J. M. Fangio
     Mercedes-Benz     Mercedes-Benz     Mercedes-Benz
     (2 min 15,1 sec)   (2 min 13,6 sec)  (2 min 12,3 sec)

              J. Swaters        J. Behra
               Ferrari          Gordini
           (2 min 26,9 sec)   (2 min 25,0 sec)

        R. Manzon        A. Pilette        L. Rosier
         Ferrari          Gordini          Maserati
      (2 min 30,3 sec)  (2 min 27,4 sec)  (2 min 27,0 sec)

           Niedermayer        F. Wacker
          Klenk-Meteor        Gordini
          (2 min 37,4 sec)   (2 min 32,9 sec)

                      H. Schell
                      Maserati
                   (2 min 52,1 sec)

   Manzon failed to come to the start on Sunday having damaged his
   engine during Saturday practice
```

Result: 1st Karl Kling, Mercedes-Benz, 504 km in 2 hr 19 min 59.8 sec = 213.5 km/h; 2nd Juan Manuel Fangio, Mercedes-Benz, 2:20:00.3; 3rd Hans Herrmann, Mercedes-Benz, 2:20:00.3; 4th André Pilette, Gordini, 3 laps behind; 5th Jacques Swaters, Ferrari, 4 laps behind; 6th Fred Wacker, Gordini, 5 laps behind; 7th Helmut Niedermayer, Klenk-Meteor, 8 laps behind; 8th Harry Schell, Maserati, 10 laps behind.
Fastest Lap: Fangio (lap 52) in 2:13.4 min = 224 km/h
Retirements: Rosier (broke propshaft at start), Behra (lap 15 engine).

XII. Gran Premio de España
Pedralbes, 24th October 1954

Distance: 80 laps of 6.316 km circuit = 505.28 km
Weather: very hot and sunny

```
                         Starting grid

     H. Schell      J. M. Hawthorn    J. M.Fangio       A. Ascari
      Maserati         Ferrari       Mercedes-Benz        Lancia
   (2 min 20.6 sec)  (2 min 20.6 sec) (2 min 19.1 sec)  (2 min 18.1 sec)

           L. Musso          S. Moss        L. Villoresi
           Maserati         Maserati          Lancia
        (2 min 21.5 sec)  (2 min 21.1 sec)  (2 min 21.0 sec)

      R. Mières     S. Mantovani     H. Herrmann     M. Trintignant
      Maserati        Maserati      Mercedes-Benz       Ferrari
   (2 min 22.3 sec) (2 min. 22.0 sec) (2 min 21.9 sec) (2 min 21.9 sec)

          K. Wharton        F. Godia          K. Kling
           Maserati         Maserati       Mercedes-Benz
        (2 min 25.7 sec)  (2 min 24.2 sec)  (2 min 23.4 sec)

      J. Behra        R. Manzon       J. Pollet        B. Bira
      Gordini          Ferrari        Gordini         Maserati
   (2 min 27.8 sec) (2 min 27.5 sec) (2 min 27.4 sec) (2 min 26.1 sec)

       E. de Graffenried    L. Rosier       J. Swaters
           Maserati         Maserati        Ferrari
        (2 min 29.8 sec)  (2 min 29.8 sec)  (2 min 28.0 sec)

   Non starter: P. Collins (Vanwall Special) following practice
   accident
```

Result: 1st Mike Hawthorn, Ferrari, 505.28 km in 3 hr 13 min 52.1 sec = 156.378 km/h; 2nd Luigi Musso, Maserati, 3:15:5.3; 3rd Juan Manuel Fangio, Mercedes-Benz, 1 lap behind; 4th Roberto Mières, Maserati, 1 lap behind; 5th Karl Kling, Mercedes-Benz, 1 lap behind; 6th Francesco Godia, Maserati, 4 laps behind; 7th Louis Rosier, Maserati, 6 laps behind; 8th Ken Wharton, Maserati, 6 laps behind; 9th Prince Bira, Maserati, 12 laps behind.
Fastest Lap: Ascari (lap 3) in 2:20.4 min = 161.947 km/h
Retirements: Manzon (lap 2 ignition), Villoresi (lap 2 brakes and engine), Ascari (lap 10 clutch and engine), Swaters (lap 16 engine), Behra (lap 17 brakes), Moss (lap 20 oil pump), Schell (lap 29 rear axle), Pollet (lap 38), Trintignant (lap 48 gearbox), Herrmann (lap 51 injection pump), de Graffenried (lap 58 engine), Mantovani (lap 59 locking brakes).

III. Gran Premio de la Republica Argentina
Buenos Aires, 16th January 1955

Distance: 96 laps of 3.912 km circuit = 375.55 km
Weather: sunny, very hot

```
┌──────────────────────────────────────────────────────────┐
│                      Starting grid                         │
│                                                            │
│   J. Behra      J. M. Fangio      A. Ascari    J. F. Gonzalez │
│   Maserati     Mercedes-Benz      Lancia          Ferrari    │
│                                                            │
│ (1 min 43.8 sec) (1 min 43.6 sec) (1 min 43.6 sec) (1 min 43.1 sec) │
│                                                            │
│       H. Schell       K. Kling        G. Farina            │
│       Maserati      Mercedes-Benz      Ferrari             │
│                                                            │
│   (1 min 44.3 sec)  (1 min 44.1 sec)  (1 min 43.8 sec)     │
│                                                            │
│   L. Villoresi   H. Herrmann      P. Birger     S. Moss    │
│     Lancia      Mercedes-Benz      Gordini    Mercedes-Benz │
│                                                            │
│ (1 min 45.2 sec) (1 min 44.8 sec) (1 min 44.8 sec) (1 min 44.4 sec) │
│                                                            │
│    M. Trintignant   C. Menditeguy   E. Castellotti         │
│       Ferrari         Maserati         Lancia              │
│                                                            │
│   (1 min 45.8 sec)  (1 min 45.4 sec)  (1 min 45.3 sec)     │
│                                                            │
│   L. Musso      J. Iglesias       R. Mières     E. Bayol   │
│   Maserati       Gordini          Maserati      Gordini    │
│                                                            │
│ (1 min 46.5 sec) (1 min 46.4 sec) (1 min 46.3 sec) (1 min 46.1 sec) │
│                                                            │
│       A. Uria         C. Bucci        S. Mantovani         │
│       Maserati        Maserati          Maserati           │
│                                                            │
│   (1 min 51.2 sec)  (1 min 48.8 sec)  (1 min 47.6 sec)     │
└──────────────────────────────────────────────────────────┘
```

Result: 1st Juan Manuel Fangio, Mercedes-Benz, 375.55 km in 3 hr 00 min 38.6 sec = 124.738km/h; 2nd Gonzalez/Farina/Trintignant 3:02:8.2; 3rd Farina/Trintignant/Maglioli, 2 laps behind; 4th Herrmann/Kling/Moss, Mercedes-Benz, 2 laps behind; 5th Roberto Mières, Maserati, 5 laps behind; 6th Harry Schell/Jean Behra, Maserati, 8 laps behind; 7th Luigi Musso/Harry Schell, Maserati, 13 laps behind.
Fastest Lap: Fangio (lap 45) in 1:48.3 min = 130.05 km/h
Retirements: Villoresi (lap 2 fuel feed), Behra, Birger, Kling and Menditeguy (lap 2 accident), Bayol (lap 8 transmission), Ascari (lap 22 accident), Uria (lap 23 fuel feed), Moss (lap 30 exhaustion), Castellotti/Villoresi (lap 36 accident), Trintignant (lap 37 broken valve), Iglesias (lap 39 transmission), Bucci/Menditeguy (lap 56 ran out of fuel), Mantovani/Behra/Musso (lap 56 ran out of fuel).

Gran Premio de Buenos Aires, Formule Libre race,
Buenos Aires, 30th January 1955

Distance: two heats, each of 30 laps of 4.7 km circuit = 282 km
Weather: sunny and hot

```
┌──────────────────────────────────────────────────────────┐
│                      Starting grid                         │
│                                                            │
│  J. M. Fangio   M. Trintignant  J. F. Gonzalez   S. Moss   │
│ Mercedes-Benz      Ferrari         Ferrari    Mercedes-Benz │
│                                                            │
│        K. Kling       G. Farina        J. Behra            │
│      Mercedes-Benz     Ferrari         Maserati            │
│                                                            │
│  C. Menditeguy    H. Schell      S. Mantovani    C. Bucci  │
│    Maserati       Maserati        Maserati       Ferrari   │
│                                                            │
│        E. Bayol       H. Herrmann       U. Maglioli        │
│        Gordini       Mercedes-Benz       Ferrari           │
└──────────────────────────────────────────────────────────┘
```

Result: 1st Giuseppe Farina, Ferrari, 141 km in 1 hr 11 min 35.8 sec = 118.33 km/h; 2nd Juan Manuel Fangio, Mercedes-Benz, 1:11:46.3; 3rd Stirling Moss, Mercedes-Benz, 1:12:01.2; 4th Karl Kling, Mercedes-Benz, 1:12:01.7
Heat 2: 1st Stirling Moss, Mercedes-Benz, 141 km in 1 hr 11 min 29.6 sec = 180.50 km/h; 2nd Juan Manuel Fangio, Mercedes-Benz, 1:11:32.6; 3rd Maurice Trintignant, Ferrari, 1:11:33.5; 4th Harry Schell, Maserati, 1:12:03.0
Result on aggregate: 1st Juan Manuel Fangio, Mercedes-Benz, 2 hr 23 min 18.9 sec; 2nd Stirling Moss, Mercedes-Benz, 2:23:30.8; 3rd Maurice Trintignant, Ferrari, 2:23:53.1; 4th Karl Kling, Mercedes-Benz, 2:24:17.5; 5th Jean Behra, Maserati, 2:24:21.2; 6th Carlos Menditeguy, Maserati, 2:25:39.6; 7th Harry Schell, Maserati, 2:25:50.9
Fastest Lap: Farina at 121.46 km/h

Grand Prix of Europe and XIII. Monaco Grand Prix, Monte Carlo, 22nd May 1955

Distance: 100 laps of 3.145 km circuit = 314.5 km
Weather: sunny and hot

<table>
<tr><td colspan="3" align="center">Starting grid</td></tr>
<tr>
<td align="center">S. Moss
Mercedes-Benz
(1 min 41.2 sec)</td>
<td align="center">A. Ascari
Lancia
(1 min 41.1 sec)</td>
<td align="center">J. M. Fangio
Mercedes-Benz
(1 min 41.1 sec)</td>
</tr>
<tr>
<td align="center" colspan="3">J. Behra   E. Castellotti
Maserati   Lancia
(1 min 42.6 sec)   (1 min 42.0 sec)</td>
</tr>
<tr>
<td align="center">L. Musso
Maserati
(1 min 44.3 sec)</td>
<td align="center">L. Villoresi
Lancia
(1 min 43.7 sec)</td>
<td align="center">R. Mières
Maserati
(1 min 43.7 sec)</td>
</tr>
<tr>
<td align="center" colspan="3">A. Simon   M. Trintignant
Mercedes-Benz   Ferrari
(1 min 45.5 sec)   (1 min 44.4 sec)</td>
</tr>
<tr>
<td align="center">R. Manzon
Gordini
(1 min 46.0 sec)</td>
<td align="center">J. M. Hawthorn
Vanwall
(1 min 45.6 sec)</td>
<td align="center">C. Perdisa
Maserati
(1 min 45.6 sec)</td>
</tr>
<tr>
<td align="center" colspan="3">P. Taruffi   G. Farina
Ferrari   Ferrari
(1 min 46.0 sec)   (1 min 46.0 sec)</td>
</tr>
<tr>
<td align="center">H. Schell
Ferrari
(1 min 46.8 sec)</td>
<td align="center">L. Rosier
Maserati
(1 min 46.7 sec)</td>
<td align="center">E. Bayol
Gordini
(1 min 46.5 sec)</td>
</tr>
<tr>
<td align="center" colspan="3">J. Pollet   L. Chiron
Gordini   Lancia
(1 min 49.4 sec)   (1 min 47.3 sec)</td>
</tr>
<tr><td colspan="3">Did not qualify: L. Macklin (Maserati) 1 min 49.4 sec; E.N. Whiteway (HWM) 1 min 57.2 secs</td></tr>
</table>

Result: 1st Maurice Trintignant, Ferrari, 314.5 km in 2 hr 58 min 9.7 sec = 105.914 km/h; 2nd Eugenio Castellotti, Lancia 2:58:30.0; 3rd Jean Behra/Cesare Perdisa, Maserati, 1 lap behind; 4th Giuseppe Farina, Ferrari, 1 lap behind; 5th Luigi Villoresi, Lancia, 1 lap behind; 6th Louis Chiron, Lancia, 5 laps behind; 7th Jean Pollet, Gordini, 9 laps behind; 8th Piero Taruffi/Paul Frère, Ferrari, 14 laps behind; 9th Stirling Moss, Mercedes-Benz, 19 laps behind (not running at finish).
Fastest Lap: Fangio (lap 27) in 1:42.4 min = 110.568 km/h
Retirements: Musso (lap 8 transmission), Rosier (lap 9 fuel tank), Hawthorn (lap 23 from effect of fumes), Simon (lap 25 valve gear), Manzon (lap 39 gearbox), Fangio (lap 50 valve gear), Bayol (lap 64 rear axle), Mières (lap 65 rear axle), Schell (lap 68 engine), Moss (lap 81 engine), Ascari (lap 81 accident).

XVII. Grote Prijs van België/Grand Prix de Belgique Spa-Francorchamps, 5th June 1955

Distance: 36 laps of 14.12 km circuit = 508.32 km
Weather: warm and dry

<table>
<tr><td colspan="3" align="center">Starting grid</td></tr>
<tr>
<td align="center">E. Castellotti
Lancia
(4 min 18.1 sec)</td>
<td align="center">J. M. Fangio
Mercedes-Benz
(4 min 18.6 sec)</td>
<td align="center">S. Moss
Mercedes-Benz
(4 min 19.2 sec)</td>
</tr>
<tr>
<td align="center" colspan="3">G. Farina   J. Behra
Ferrari   Maserati
(4 min 20.9 sec)   (4 min 23.6 sec)</td>
</tr>
<tr>
<td align="center">K. Kling
Mercedes-Benz
(4 min 24.0 sec)</td>
<td align="center">L. Musso
Maserati
(4 min 26.4 sec)</td>
<td align="center">P. Frère
Ferrari
(4 min 29.7 sec)</td>
</tr>
<tr>
<td align="center" colspan="3">J. M. Hawthorn   M. Trintignant
Vanwall   Ferrari
(4 min 33.0 sec)   (4 min 33.2 sec)</td>
</tr>
<tr>
<td align="center">C. Perdisa
Maserati
(4 min 50.9 sec)</td>
<td align="center">L. Rosier
Maserati
(4 min 55.4 sec)</td>
<td align="center">R. Mières
Maserati
(5 min 09.0 sec)</td>
</tr>
<tr><td colspan="3">Non starter: J. Claes (Maserati)</td></tr>
</table>

Result: 1st Juan Manuel Fangio, Mercedes-Benz, 508.32 km in 2 hr 39 min 29.0 sec = 191.237km/h; 2nd Stirling Moss, Mercedes-Benz, 2:39:37.1; 3rd Giuseppe Farina, Ferrari, 2:41:9.5; 4th Paul Frère, Ferrari, 2:42:54.5; 5th Roberto Mières/Jean Behra, Maserati, 1 lap behind; 6th Maurice Trintignant, Ferrari, 1 lap behind; 7th Luigi Musso, Maserati, 2 laps behind; 8th Cesare Perdisa, Maserati, 3 laps behind; 9th Louis Rosier, Maserati, 3 laps behind.
Fastest Lap: Fangio (lap 18) 4:20.6 min = 195.097 km/h
Retirements: Behra (lap 4 accident), Hawthorn (lap 9 gearbox), Castellotti (lap 17 gearbox), Kling (lap 22 oil hose).

VI. Grote Prijs van Nederland
Zandvoort, 19th June 1955

Distance: 100 laps of 4.193 km circuit = 419.3 km
Weather: cool, overcast

```
                        Starting grid

      K. Kling          S. Moss          J. M. Fangio
  Mercedes-Benz     Mercedes-Benz      Mercedes-Benz
  (1 min 41.1 sec)  (1 min 40.4 sec)   (1 min 40.0 sec)

           J. M. Hawthorn       L. Musso
              Ferrari           Maserati
           (1 min 41.5 sec)   (1 min 41.2 sec)

     M. Trintignant      R. Mières          J. Behra
         Ferrari         Maserati          Maserati
     (1 min 42.4 sec)  (1 min 42.1 sec)  (1 min 41.5 sec)

            P. Walker          E. Castellotti
            Maserati              Ferrari
         (1 min 44.9 sec)     (1 min 42.7 sec)

       L. Rosier         J. Pollet         R. Manzon
       Maserati          Gordini           Gordini
     (1 min 49.2 sec)  (1 min 48.6 sec)  (1 min 46.0 sec)

            H. Gould       H. da Silva Ramos
            Maserati           Gordini
         (1 min 50.4 sec)   (1 min 50.2 sec)

                        J. Claes
                         Ferrari
                     (1 min 53.3 sec)
```

Result: 1st Juan Manuel Fangio, Mercedes-Benz, 419.3 km in 2 hr 54 min 23.8 sec = 144.268 km/h; 2nd Stirling Moss, Mercedes-Benz, 2:54:24.1; 3rd Luigi Musso, Maserati, 2:55:20.9; 4th Roberto Mières, Maserati, 1 lap behind; 5th Eugenio Castellotti, Ferrari, 3 laps behind; 6th Jean Behra, Maserati. 3 laps behind; 7th Mike Hawthorn, Ferrari, 5 laps behind; 8th Hernando da Silva Ramos, Gordini, 8 laps behind; 9th Louis Rosier, Maserati, 8 laps behind; 10th Jacques Pollet, Gordini, 10 laps behind; 11th Jean Claes, Ferrari, 12 laps behind.
Fastest Lap: Mières (lap 3) in 1:40.9 min = 149.601 km/h
Retirements: Walker (lap 3 cylinder head gasket), Kling (lap 22 spun off into sand), Gould (lap 24 spun off into sand), Manzon (lap 44 engine), Trintignant (lap 65 gearbox).

VIIIth British Grand Prix
Aintree, 16th July 1955

Distance: 90 laps of 4.828 km circuit = 434.52 km
Weather: sunny and hot

```
                        Starting grid

      S. Moss          J. M. Fangio        J. Behra
  Mercedes-Benz      Mercedes-Benz        Maserati
  (2 min 00.4 sec)  (2 min 00.6 sec)    (2 min 01.4 sec)

           K. Kling            P. Taruffi
       Mercedes-Benz       Mercedes-Benz
       (2 min 02.0 sec)    (2 min 03.0 sec)

      R. Mières          H. Schell          A. Simon
      Maserati           Vanwall           Maserati
    (2 min 03.2 sec)  (2 min 03.8 sec)  (2 min 04.0 sec)

            L. Musso          E. Castellotti
            Maserati              Ferrari
         (2 min 04.2 sec)    (2 min 05.0 sec)

     R. Manzon       J. M. Hawthorn    M. Trintignant
      Gordini           Ferrari           Ferrari
   (2 min 05.0 sec)  (2 min 05.4 sec)  (2 min 05.4 sec)

            A. Rolt           K. Wharton
           Connaught            Vanwall
         (2 min 06.6 sec)   (2 min 08.4 sec)

     L. Macklin       K. McAlpine     H. da Silva Ramos
     Maserati         Connaught          Gordini
   (2 min 08.4 sec)  (2 min 09.6 sec)  (2 min 10.6 sec)

            L. Marr          R. Salvadori
           Connaught            Maserati
         (2 min 11.6 sec)   (2 min 11.6 sec)

     J. Fairman        H. Gould          M. Sparken
     Connaught         Maserati           Gordini
   (2 min 11.6 sec)  (2 min 11.8 sec)  (2 min 12.6 sec)

            P. Collins          J. Brabham
            Maserati          Cooper-Bristol
         (2 min 13.4 sec)    (2 min 27.4 sec)
```

Non starter: J. Fairman (Connaught)

Result: 1st Stirling Moss, Mercedes-Benz, 434.52 km in 3 hr 07 min 21.2 sec = 139.16 km/h; 2nd Juan Manuel Fangio, Mercedes-Benz, 3:07:21.4; 3rd Karl Kling, Mercedes-Benz, 3:08:33.0; 4th Piero Taruffi, Mercedes-Benz, 1 lap behind; 5th Luigi Musso, Maserati, 1 lap behind; 6th Mike Hawthorn/ Eugenio Castellotti, Ferrari, 3 laps behind; 7th Mike Sparken, Gordini, 9 laps behind; 8th Lance Macklin, Maserati, 11 laps behind; 9th Ken Wharton/Harry Schell, Vanwall, 18 laps behind.

Fastest Lap: Moss (lap 88) in 2.04.0 min = 144.36 km/h

Retirements: Manzon (lap 5 transmission), Behra (lap 10 burst oil hose), Simon (lap 10 gearbox), Castellotti (lap 17 transmission), Marr (lap 19 brakes), Rolt/Walker (lap 20 transmission), Schell (lap 21 broken throttle pedal), Gould (lap 23 brakes), Salvadori (lap 24 gearbox), da Silva Ramos (lap 27 oil pressure), Collins (lap 30 clutch), McAlpine (lap 31 oil pressure), Brabham (lap 34 bent valve), Mières (lap 48 damaged piston), Trintignant (lap 60 cylinder head gasket).

XXVI. Gran Premio d'Italia
Monza, 11th September 1955

Distance: 50 laps of 10 km circuit = 500 km

Weather: sunny and warm

Result: 1st Juan Manuel Fangio, Mercedes-Benz, 500 km in 2 hr 25 min 04.4 sec = 206.791 km/h; 2nd Piero Taruffi, Mercedes-Benz, 2:25:05.1; 3rd Eugenio Castellotti, Ferrari, 2:25:50.6; 4th Jean Behra, Maserati, 2:29:01.9; 5th Carlos Menditeguy, Maserati, 1 lap behind; 6th Umberto Maglioli, Ferrari, 1 lap behind; 7th Roberto Mières, Maserati, 2 laps behind; 8th Maurice Trintignant, Ferrari, 3 laps behind; 9th John Fitch, Maserati, 4 laps behind.

Fastest Lap: Moss (lap 21) in 2:46.9 min = 215.698 km/h

Retirements: Wharton (lap 1 broken fuel injection pump mounting), Schell (lap 8 broken de Dion strut), Lucas (lap 8 engine), Collins (lap 23 suspension), da Silva Ramos (lap 24 fuel pump), Pollet (lap 27 engine), Moss (lap 28 drive shaft), Musso (lap 32 gearbox) Gould (lap 32 suspension), Kling (lap 33 propshaft), Hawthorn (lap 39 broken gearbox mounting).

Starting grid

K. Kling	S. Moss	J. M. Fangio
Mercedes-Benz	Mercedes-Benz	Mercedes-Benz
(2 min 48.3 sec)	(2 min 46.8 sec)	(2 min 46.5 sec)

*	E. Castellotti	
	Ferrari	
	(2 min 49.6 sec)	

*	R. Mières	J. Behra
	Maserati	Maserati
	(2 min 51.1 sec)	(2 min 50.1 sec)

L. Musso	P. Taruffi
Maserati	Mercedes-Benz
(2 min 52.1 sec)	(2 min 51.8 sec)

H. Schell	U. Maglioli	P. Collins
Vanwall	Ferrari	Maserati
(2 min 55.5 sec)	(2 min 55.4 sec)	(2 min 55.3 sec)

M. Trintignant	J. M. Hawthorn
Ferrari	Ferrari
(2 min 56.3 sec)	(2 min 56.2 sec)

H. da Silva Ramos	K. Wharton	C. Menditeguy
Gordini	Vanwall	Maserati
(2 min 59.8 sec)	(2 min 59.5 sec)	(2 min 58.4 sec)

J. Fitch	J. Pollet
Maserati	Gordini
(3 min 03.1 sec)	(2 min 59.9 sec)

J. Lucas	H. Gould
Gordini	Maserati
(3 min 15.9 sec)	(3 min 05.2 sec)

*Non starters: G. Farina (Lancia-Ferrari); L. Villoresi (Lancia-Ferrari)

Individual Racing History

Mercedes-Benz W 196 2.5 litre Formula One Racing Cars 1954 and 1955

Race	Car No.	Start No.	Wheelbase mm	Front brakes	Driver	Bodywork	Remarks
French Grand Prix Reims 4 July 1954	3	18	2350	inboard	Fangio	Streamlined	1st
	5	20	2350	inboard	Kling	Streamlined	2nd
	2	22	2350	inboard	Herrmann	Streamlined	Retired, engine
	4	T	2350	inboard	Training	—	
British Grand Prix Silverstone 17 July 1954	3	1	2350	inboard	Fangio	Streamlined	4th
	4	2	2350	inboard	Kling	Streamlined	7th
German Grand Prix Nürburgring 1 Aug 1954	6	18	2350	inboard	Fangio	Monoposto	1st
	3	19	2350	inboard	Kling	Monoposto	4th
	5	21	2350	inboard	Lang	Monoposto	Retired, engine, went off track
European Grand Prix	2	20	2350	inboard	Herrmann	Streamlined	Retired, damaged fuel tank and pipe
	4	T	2350	inboard	Training	Monoposto	not used
Swiss Grand Prix Bern 22 Aug 1954	6	4	2350	inboard	Fangio	Monoposto	1st
	4	6	2350	inboard	Herrmann	Monoposto	3rd
	5	8	2350	inboard	Kling	Monoposto	Retired, engine
Italian Grand Prix Monza 5 Sept 1954	4	10	2350	inboard	Fangio	Streamlined	1st
	6	12	2350	inboard	Herrmann	Monoposto	4th
	7	14	2350	inboard	Kling	Streamlined	Retired, went off track
	3	T	2350	inboard	Training	Monoposto	—
Avus Berlin 19 Sept 1954 Grand Prix of Berlin	5	4	2350	inboard	Kling	Streamlined	1st
	4	2	2350	inboard	Fangio	Streamlined	2nd
	2	6	2350	inboard	Herrmann	Streamlined	3rd
Spanish Grand Prix Barcelona 24 Oct 1954	8	2	2350	inboard	Fangio	Monoposto	3rd
	5	4	2350	inboard	Kling	Monoposto	5th
	4	T	2350	inboard	Training	Streamlined	—
	6	6	2350	inboard	Herrman	Monoposto	Retired, engine

Race	Car No.	Start No.	Wheelbase mm	Front brakes	Driver	Bodywork	Remarks
Argentinian Grand Prix Buenos Aires 16 Jan 1954	4	2	2210	inboard	Fangio	Monoposto	1st
	10	8	2350	inboard	Herrmann	Monoposto	4th, Herrmann/ Kling/Moss
	3	4	2210	inboard	Kling	Monoposto	Retired, went off track
	5	6	2350	inboard	Moss	Monoposto	Retired due to heat
	8	T	2350	inboard	Training	Monoposto	–
Grand Prix of Buenos Aires unrestricted 3-litre race 20 Jan 1955	9	2	2350	inboard	Fangio	Monoposto	1st, unrestricted 3-litre engine
	7	6	2350	inboard	Moss	Monoposto	2nd, unrestricted 3-litre engine
	8	4	2350	inboard	Kling	Monoposto	4th, unrestricted 3-litre engine
	4	8	2210	inboard	Herrmann	Monoposto	Retired with gear linkage fault 2.5-litre engine
	3	T	2210	inboard	Training	Monoposto	2.5-litre engine
	5	T	2350	inboard	Training	Monoposto	2.5-litre engine
	10	T	2350	inboard	Training	Monoposto	2.5-litre engine
European Grand Prix Monte Carlo 22 May 1955	12	6	2150	outboard	Moss	Monoposto	Engine mounted 60mm further back, retired
	13	2	2150	outboard	Fangio	Monoposto	Retired, engine safety bolt
	3	4	2210	inboard	Simon	Monoposto	Engine in normal position, retired, engine safety bolt
	4	(4)	2210	inboard	Herrmann	Monoposto	Did not start, practice accident
Belgian Grand Prix Spa 5 June 1955	8	10	2350	inboard	Fangio	Monoposto	1st
	10	14	2210	inboard	Moss	Monoposto	2nd
	5	12	2350	inboard	Kling	Monoposto	Retired, broken oil pipe
	10	T	2210	outboard	Training	Monoposto	Intended for Fangio, used as spare
Dutch Grand Prix Zandvoort 19 June 1955	13	12	2150	outboard	Fangio	Monoposto	1st
	10	10	2210	inboard	Moss	Monoposto	2nd
	14	12	2210	outboard	Kling	Monoposto	Retired, went off track
	3	T	2210	inboard	Training	Monoposto	Intended for Fangio, used as spare
British Grand Prix Aintree 16 July 1955	12	12	2150	outboard	Moss	Monoposto	1st, engine in normal position
	13	10	2150	outboard	Fangio	Monoposto	2nd, engine in normal position
	14	14	2150	outboard	Kling	Monoposto	3rd, engine in normal position
	15	50	2150	outboard	Taruffi	Monoposto	4th, engine in normal position
	3	T	2210	inboard	Training	Monoposto	Engine in normal position

314

Race	Car No.	Start No.	Wheelbase mm	Front brakes	Driver	Bodywork	Remarks
Italian Grand Prix	2	18	2350	inboard	Fangio	Streamlined	1st
Monza 11 Sept 1955	15	14	2150	outboard	Taruffi	Monoposto	2nd
	9	16	2350	inboard	Moss	Streamlined	Retired, piston failure
	6	20	2350	inboard	Kling	Monoposto	Retired, gearbox failure
	14	T	2210	outboard	Training	Monoposto	–
	10	–	2210	outboard	Training	Streamlined	Were cars 10, 12
	12	–	2210	outboard	Training	Streamlined	and 1, short-wheelbase/streamline
	13	–	2210	outboard	Training	Streamlined	Intended as spare car but not used because of poor handling
In the 1954-5 seasons, 8 different cars were used		a)	2350	inboard		Streamlined	
		b)	2350	inboard		Monoposto	
		c)	2210	inboard		Monoposto	
		d)	2150	outboard		Monoposto	Engine mounted 60 mm further back
		e)	2150	outboard		Monoposto	Engine in normal position
		f)	2210	outboard		Monoposto	
		g)	2210	outboard		Streamlined	
		h)	2350	inboard		Monoposto	3-litre unrestricted sports car engine

1

2 a) 2350, inboard, streamlined

3 a) 2350, inboard, streamlined; b) 2350, inboard, monoposto; c) 2210, inboard, monoposto

4 a) 2350, inboard, streamlined; b) 2350, inboard, monoposto; a) 2350, inboard, streamlined; c) 2350, inboard, monoposto

5 a) 2350, inboard, streamlined; b) 2350, inboard, monoposto; a) 2350, inboard, streamlined; b) 2350, inboard, monoposto

6 b) 2350, inboard, monoposto

7 a) 2350, inboard, streamlined; h) 2350, inboard, monoposto, 3-litre engine

8 b) 2350, monoposto; h) 2350, inboard, monoposto, 3-litre engine; b) 2350, inboard, monoposto

9 h) 2350, inboard, monoposto, 3-litre engine; a) 2350, inboard, streamlined

10 b) 2350, inboard, monoposto; c) 2210, inboard, monoposto; f) 2210, outboard, monoposto; g) 2210, outboard, streamlined

11

12 d) 2150, outboard, monoposto, engine 60 mm; c) 2150, outboard, monoposto; g) 2210, outboard, streamlined

13 e) 2150, outboard, monoposto; g) 2210, outboard, streamlined

14 f) 2210, outboard, monoposto; c) 2150, outboard, monoposto; f) 2210, outboard, monoposto, 3-litre engine

15 e) 2150, outboard, monoposto

Engine of chassis number 00013/55 was constantly changed as was bodywork (monoposto or streamlined)

Car was only used during 1955

22 May 1955	16 July 1955	19 June 1955	11 Sept 1955
Monte Carlo (1st appearance)	Aintree (British Grand Prix)	Zandvoort (Holland)	Monza (Italy)
Start no. 2	Start no. 10	Start no. 8	Bodywork: Streamlined
Driver: Fangio	Driver: Fangio	Driver: Fangio	
Bodywork: Monoposto	Bodywork: Monoposto	Bodywork: Monoposto	
(retired with engine failure)	2nd	1st	Practice car only

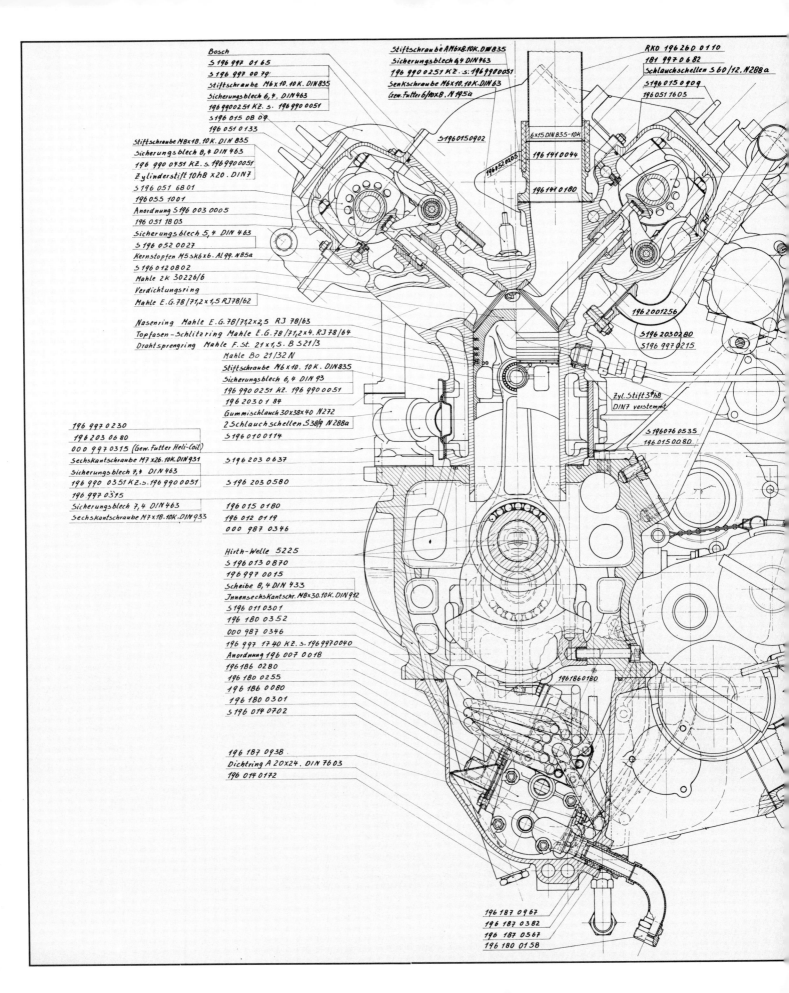

Bosch
S 196 997 01 65
S 196 997 00 79
Stiftschraube M6x10.10K. DIN835
Sicherungsblech 6,4. DIN463
196 9900 251 KZ. s. 196 990 0051
S 196 015 08 09
196 051 0133
Stiftschraube M8x18.10K. DIN 835
Sicherungsblech 8,4 DIN 463
196 990 0451 KZ. s. 1969900051
Zylinderstift 10h8 x20. DIN7
S 196 051 68 01
196 055 1001
Anordnung S 196 003 0005
196 051 18 03
Sicherungsblech 5,4 DIN 463
S 196 052 0027
Kernstopfen M5 sk6x6. Al 99. N85a
S 196 012 0802
Mahle 2K 30226/6
Verdichtungsring
Mahle E.G. 78/71,2 x 1,5 RJ78/62

Nasenring Mahle E.G. 78/71,2 x 2,5 RJ 78/63
Topfasen-Schlitzring Mahle E.G. 78/71,2x4. RJ78/64
Drahtsprengring Mahle F.St. 21x1,5. B S21/3
Mahle Bo 21/32 N
Stiftschraube M6x10. 10K. DIN835
Sicherungsblech 6,4 DIN 93
196 990 0251 kz. 196 990 0051
196 2030 1 84
Gummischlauch 30x38x40 N272
2 Schlauchschellen S 38/9 N 288a
S 196 010 0114

196 997 0230
196 203 0680
000 997 0315 (Gew. Futter Heli-Coil)
Sechskantschraube M7 x26.10K.DIN 931
Sicherungsblech 7,4 DIN 463
196 990 0351 KZ.s.196 990 0051
196 997 0315
Sicherungsblech 7,4 DIN 463
Sechskantschraube M7x18.10K.DIN933

S 196 203 0637

S 196 203 0580

196 015 0180
196 012 0119
000 987 0346

Hirth-Welle 5225
S 196 013 0870
196 997 0015
Scheibe 8,4 DIN 433
Innensechskantschr. M8x30.10K. DIN 912
S 196 011 0301
196 180 0352
000 987 0346
196 997 17 40 KZ. s. 196 997 0040
Anordnung 196 007 0018
196 186 0280
196 180 0255
196 186 0080
196 180 0301
S 196 014 0702

196 187 0938
Dichtring A 20x24. DIN 7603
196 014 0172

Stiftschraube A M6x8.10K. DIN835
Sicherungsblech 6,4 DIN463
196 990 0251 KZ. s. 196 990 0051
SenKschraube M6x10.10K.DIN 63
Gew. Futter 6/10x8. N 195a

S 196 015 0902

196 152 0205

RKO 196 260 0110
181 997 0 6 82
Schlauchschellen S 60/12. N288a
S 196 0150909
196 051 1603

6x15 DIN B35-10K
196 141 0044
196 141 0180

196 200 1256
S 196 2030 280
S 196 997 0215

Zyl. Stift 3*h8
DIN7 verstemmt

S 196 076 0535
196 015 00 80

196 186 0180

196 187 0967
196 187 0382
196 187 0567
196 180 0158

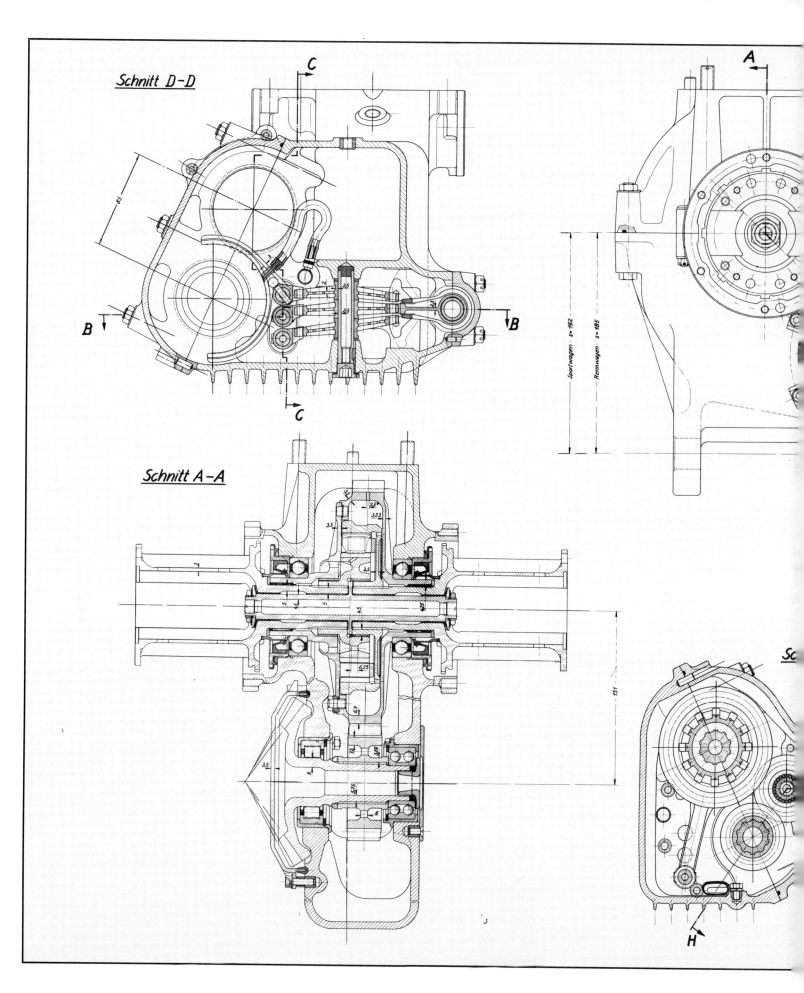

Schnitt D-D

Schnitt A-A

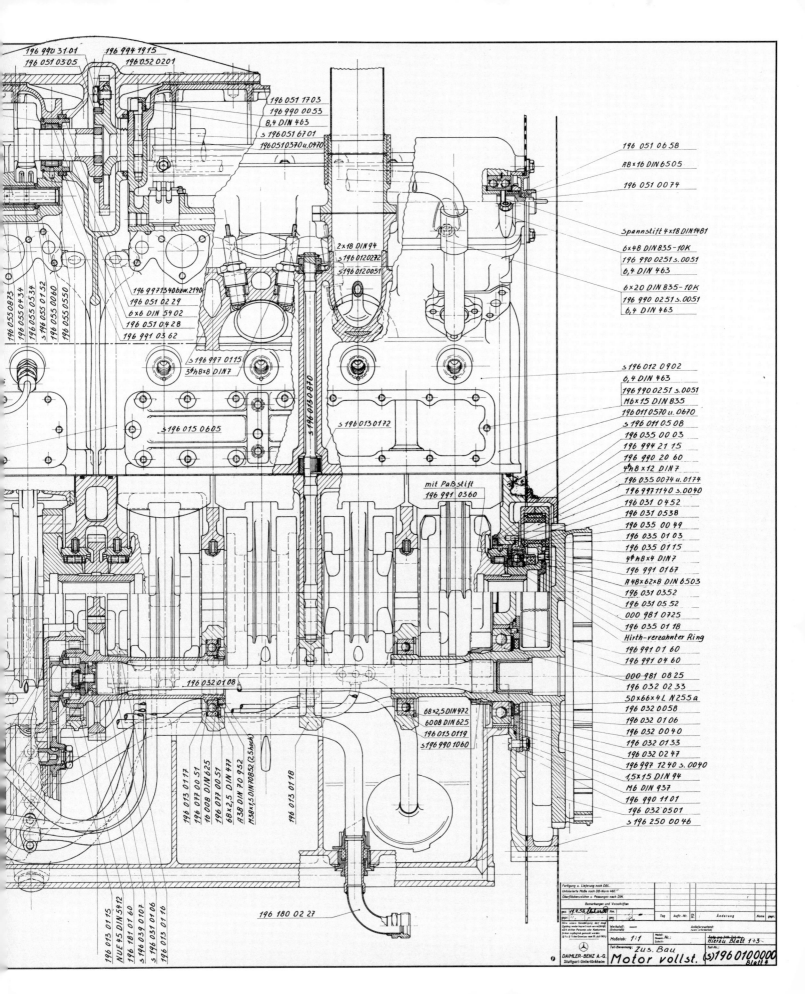

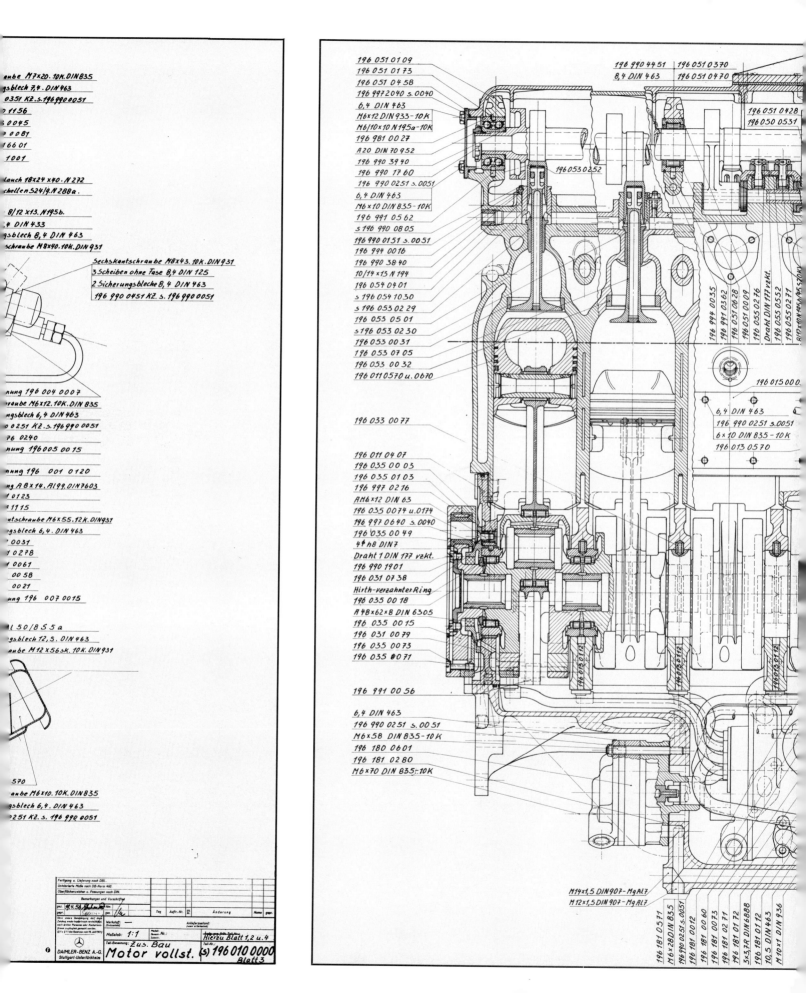

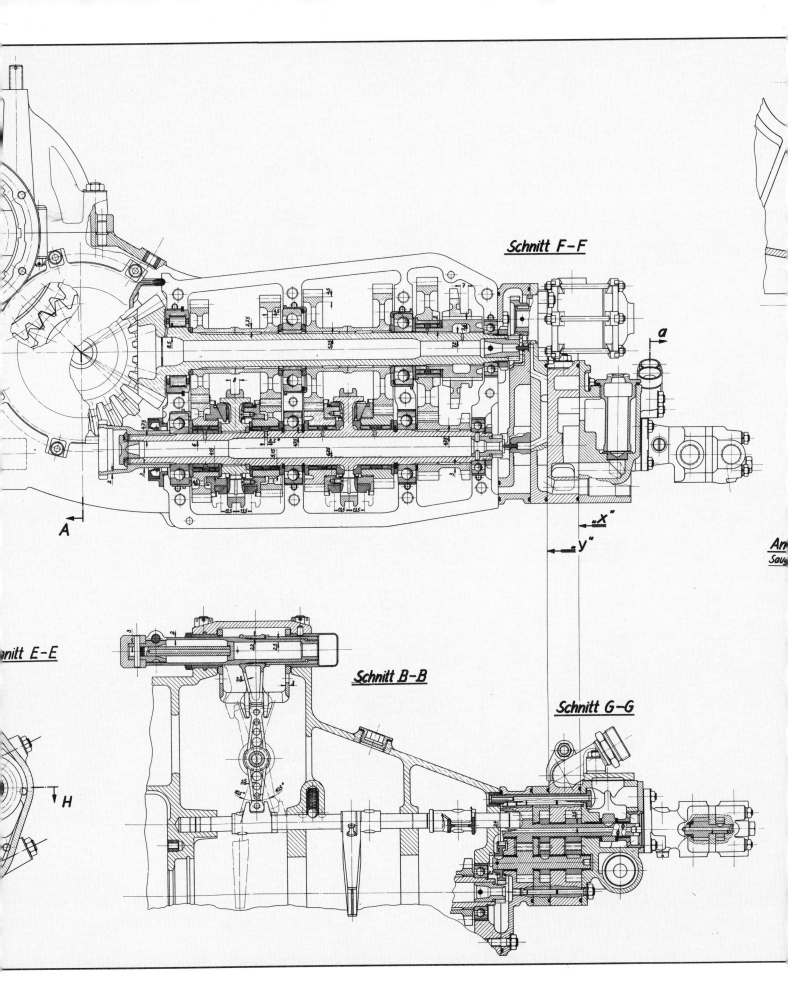

Schnitt F–F

a

"x"

"y"

Schnitt E–E

Schnitt B–B

Schnitt G–G

A

H

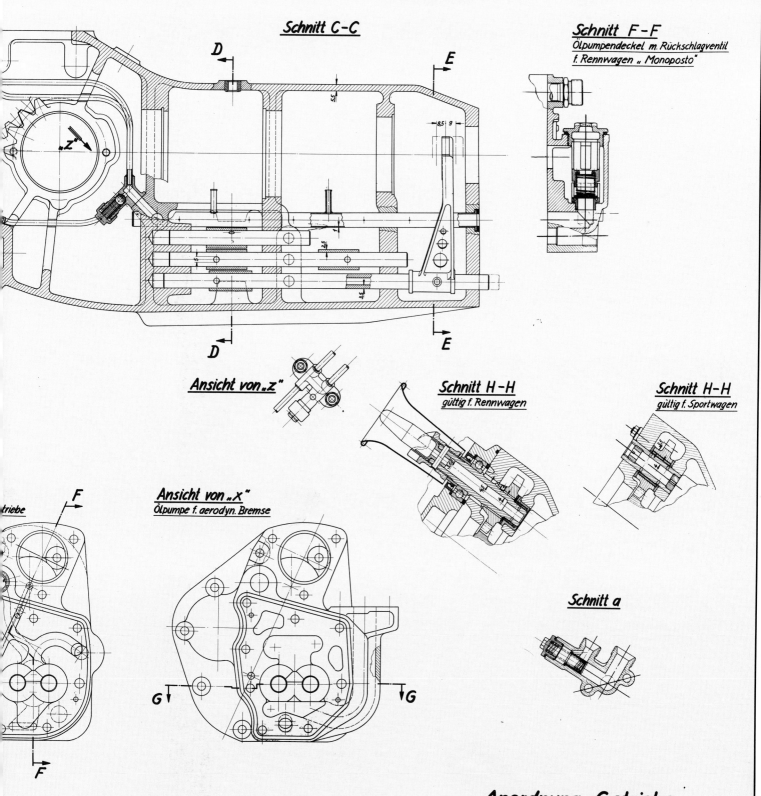

Schnitt C-C

D *E*

5,5

8,5 9

D *E*

Schnitt F-F
Ölpumpendeckel m. Rückschlagventil
f. Rennwagen „Monoposto"

Ansicht von „z"

Ansicht von „x"
Ölpumpe f. aerodyn. Bremse

F *F*

G *G*

F

Schnitt H-H
gültig f. Rennwagen

Schnitt H-H
gültig f. Sportwagen

Schnitt a

Anordnung Getriebe
Porsche Synchronisierung Schaltweg 13,5 mm

16.4.1956   Wolf   Blatt: 1   196 000 00 26

W 196: Technical Data

Engine: Straight-eight with central power take-off, welded steel cylinders, bore x stroke = 76 x 68.8 mm, capacity 2496 cc, power output 257 PS @ 8250 rpm (French GP 1954), later up to 280 PS @ 8700 rpm (summer of 1955), maximum torque 25.2 kgm @ 6300 rpm, roller bearing crankshaft (Hirth system), roller bearing rocker shaft, four operating shafts, desmodromic valve system, two valves per cylinder, inlet valve ø 50 mm, 13 mm travel, exhaust valve ø 43 mm, 12 mm travel, Bosch dual ignition, firing order 1-4-7-6-8-5-2-3, Bosch mechanical fuel injection, engine weight 204 kg (French GP 1954), later 195 kg, oil supply from central tank.

Transmission: 240 mm ø single dry plate clutch (ten springs), 5-speed gearbox (reverse engaged via inhibitor gate), locking differential with nine different ratios available between 2.167:1 and 3.154:1, 2nd–5th gears fitted with Porsche synchromesh, wide range of interchangeable ratios for the various gears.

Chassis: Space frame of 20 mm and 25 mm ø steel tubes, wall thickness 0.8 mm and 1.0 mm. Weight of frame 36 kg, independent front suspension with twin radius arms ball-jointed to wheel hubs), inboard drum brakes (from Monaco 1955 onwards, also outboard), drums made of Alfin ribbed and fitted with sheet aluminium shroud for better ventilation, ø at front 350 mm, ø at rear 275 mm, lining width front and rear 90 mm, lining thickness 7 mm (lining width on outboard brakes 68 mm), lining type Textar PV 65, later compound lining 1/3 Energit, 2/3 Textar (front) and 1/3 Energit, 2/3 Ferodo (rear), dual circuit brake system, hydraulic brake servo by Alfred Teves (Ate), Frankfurt, from 1955 giving 2.6 times pedal pressure, hydraulic steering damper, telescopic hydraulic dampers, rear axle with low pivot point (Scherenberg patent), H-section swing axles, wheel location by welded tubular struts, rear wheel camber 3° negative (with compensation for decreasing fuel load by auxiliary spring system after British Grand Prix 1955), 16 inch wire spoke wheels, steering ratio 12.65:1.

Weights and dimensions: Track front/rear 1330/1358 mm, wheelbase 2350 mm, (from Argentina 1955 also 2210 mm, from Monaco 1955 also 2150 mm), maximum overall length (with streamlined bodywork) 4160 mm, width (not including exhaust) 1625 mm, height (including windscreen) 1040 mm, tyres (Continental) front 6.0 x 16, rear 7.00 x 16, weight 650 kg (dry, with wheels) for monoposto version, 700 kg for streamlined version.

Bodywork: Aluminium bodywork for both streamlined and monoposto versions, numerous modifications often from race to race (for full details see the chapter entitled 'The external shape'), panels originally beaten over wooden blocks, small-scale production was later carried out using machined metal formers.

Location of the cars

Mercedes-Benz W 196 R, 2.5-litre Formula 1 cars

When racing activities ceased in October 1955 there was a total of 10 2.5-litre Formula 1 cars in running order:

Vehicle and chassis no.	Engine no.	Body type	Location (1978)
000 02/54	000 15/54	Streamlined	Daimler-Benz Museum
000 03/54	000 23/55	Monoposto	*Donated to* Turin Motor Museum (1957)
000 06/54	000 06/54	Monoposto	*Donated to* Beaulieu Motor Museum (1973)
000 08/54	000 64/55 3-litre engine	Monoposto	Daimler-Benz Museum
000 09/54	000 26/55	Streamlined	*Donated to* Indianapolis Speedway Museum (1965)
000 10/55	000 22/55	Streamlined	Daimler-Benz Museum
000 12/55	000 21/55	Streamlined	*Donated to* Vienna Museum of Technology (1958)
000 13/55	000 14/54	Monoposto	Daimler-Benz Museum
000 14/55	000 17/54	Monoposto short	Daimler-Benz Museum
000 15/55	000 11/54	Monoposto	Written off in accident at test circuit (1959)

Four vehicles are accounted for in donations and one as a write-off; the rest are in the collection at the company museum.

Mercedes-Benz 300 SLR (W 196 S) Sports Racing Cars

10 cars were built in 1955

Vehicle no.	Engine no. today	Registration no.	Remarks
0001/55	00059/55	AW-83-6261	*Donated to:* Ford Museum, Dearborn, USA (1959)
0002/55	00060/55	AW-84-7984	Daimler-Benz Museum
0003/55	00062/55	W-21-6169	*Donated to:* Deutsches Museum, Munich (1957)
0004/55	00065/55	W-21-6170	Daimler-Benz Museum
0005/55	00069/55	W-21-6171	*Exchanged with:* Schlumpff Museum Malmerspach (1966)
0006/55		W-21-6172	Destroyed in accident at Le Mans (1955)
0007/55	00066/55	W-21-6962	*Coupé:* Daimler-Benz Museum (Friedrichshafen)
0008/55	00056/55		*Coupé:* Daimler-Benz Museum (Langenburg)
0009/55			Car not completed
00010/55	00070/55		Daimler-Benz Museum (lightweight)

Race appearances by Mercedes-Benz 300 SLR W196S (1955)

Car no.	Start no.	Driver	Remarks
Mille Miglia (Brescia, Italy) 1st May 1955			
0004/55	722	Stirling Moss	1st Co-driver: Denis Jenkinson
0003/55	658	J M Fangio	2nd
0006/55	704	Hans Herrmann	Retired Co-driver: Hermann Eger
0005/55	701	Karl Kling	Retired

Car no.	Start no.	Driver	Remarks
International Eifelrennen (Nürburgring, West Germany) 29th May 1955			
0003/55	1	J M Fangio	1st
0004/55	3	Stirling Moss	2nd
0006/55	2	Karl Kling	4th
	T	Uhlenhaut	Practice car

Le Mans (France) 11th June 1955			
0003/55	19	Fangio/Moss	Withdrawn, air brake
0004/55	21	Kling/Simon	Withdrawn, air brake
0006/55	20	Levegh/Fitch	Accident, air brake, car destroyed

Swedish Grand Prix (Kristianstad) 1st August 1955			
0003/55	1	J M Fangio	1st, air brake
0004/55	2	Stirling Moss	2nd, air brake

Tourist Trophy (Dundrod, N. Ireland) 17th September 1955			
0004/55	10	Moss/Fitch	1st
0003/55	9	Fangio/Kling	2nd
0003/55	11	von Trips/Simon	3rd

Targa Florio (Sicily) 16th October 1955			
0004/55	104	Moss/Collins	1st
0005/55	106	Fangio/Kling	2nd
0003/55	112	Fitch/Titterington	4th

When racing activities ceased in October 1955 there were a total of 8 300 SLRs in running order

Car and chassis no.	Engine no.	Body type	Location (1978)
000 01/54	000 59/55	open/air brake	Donated to: Ford Museum, Dearborn, USA (1959)
000 02/55	000 60/55	open/air brake	Daimler-Benz Museum
000 03/55	000 62/55	open	Donated to: Deutsches Museum, Munich (1957)
000 04/55	000 65/55	open	Daimler-Benz Museum
000 05/55	000 69/55	open	Exchanged with: Schlumpff Museum, Malmerspach (1966)
000 07/55	000 66/55	closed coupé	Daimler-Benz Museum
000 08/55	000 56/55	closed coupé	Daimler-Benz Museum
000 10/55	000 70/55	open/ lightweight	Daimler-Benz Museum

Donations and exchanges have reduced the number of cars by three; the rest were given to the Daimler-Benz Museum

Bibliography

1. ALFIERI, Bruna (ed.): *Lancia, Catalogue raisonné 1907–1983,* Automobilia, Milan, 1983

2. *Auto-Jahr,* vols 3 & 4, 1954/55 and 1955/56: World Championship races

3. *AUTO, MOTOR und SPORT,* vols 1953, 1954 and 1955

4. *The Car,* various edns, London

5. DESCHENAUX, Jacques: *Marlboro Grand Prix Guide, 1954–1980*

6. FRANCK, Dieter (ed.): *Die fünfziger Jahre, als das Leben wieder anfing,* Piper Verlag, Munich, 1981

7. KRAUS, Ludwig: "Konstruktionsprobleme und Erfahrungen am Mercedes-Rennwagen", in *ATZ, Automobiltechnische Zeitschrift,* vol. 59, no. 5, May 1957

8. LANG, Hermann: *Vom Rennmonteur zum Europameister,* Verlag Knorr & Hirth, Munich, 1943

9. LEWANDOWSKI, Jürgen: *Maserati, Geschichte – Technik – Typen – Sport,* Motorbuch Verlag, Stuttgart, 1981

10. LUDVIGSEN, Karl: *Mercedes-Benz Renn- und Sportwagen,* Bleicher Verlag, Gerlingen, 1981

11. LUDVIGSEN, Karl: "The Grand Prix Cars of the Fifties" *Automobile Quarterly",* New York, USA

12. MOLTER, Günther: *Juan Manuel Fangio und seine Gegner,* Motorbuch Verlag, Stuttgart, 1967

13. MONKHOUSE George: *Racing with Mercedes-Benz*

14. NALLINGER, Dr Ing Fritz: "Die Entstehung des Mercedes-Benz-Rennwagens" in *Motor Revue,* no. 11, Autumn 1954

15. SCHERENBERG, Dr Ing Hans: "Aus der Konstruktion and Berechnung des 2.5 1-Lercedes-Benz-Formel-Rennwagens", in *ATZ, Automobiltechnische Zeitschrift,* vol. 57, no. 6, June 1955

16. SOHRE, Helmut, and HERRMANN, Hans: *Hans Herrmann – Ich habe überlebt,* Motorbuch Verlag, Stuttgart, 1971

17. *Der Spiegel,* title story, "Wer tankt verliert", 28th July 1954 on Alfred Neubauer

18. TANNER, Hans, with Doug Nye: *Ferrari,* Haynes Publishing Group, Yeovil, UK

19. TARUFFI, Piero: *Stil und Technik des Rennfahrers,* Motorbuch Verlag, Stuttgart, 1964

Other sources:

Radio report by BBC, London, on British Grand Prix, 17th July 1954. Commentators Raymond Baxter, John Bolster and Eric Tobitt

Radio report by Südwestdeutscher Rundfunk, Baden-Baden, on French Grand Prix, 4th July 1954. Commentators Rainer Günzler and Günther Jendrich

Documents from the archives of Daimler-Benz AG, Stuttgart, Untertürkheim